WHAT IS PROTEIN COMPLEMENTARITY?

The combination, in the proper proportions, of non-meat foods, that produces high-grade protein nutrition equivalent to—or better than—meat proteins.

This book is about protein—how we as a nation are caught in a pattern that squanders it: and how you can choose the opposite—a way of eating that makes the most of the earth's capacity to supply this vital nutrient.
—Frances Moore Lappé

The world has come a long way toward recognizing some of its problems in the last few years. No final solutions have been found, but a trend that has been realized and acknowledged—at least on the part of young people—is the movement away from waste, away from heavily polluted foods.

The concepts in this book are no final solution either. But they represent a giant step in the right direction. For the first time it is possible to implement an end to the gross waste of literally millions of tons of high-grade protein, to release men from the confines of a largely meat diet, to enjoy nutritionally sound protein from the richer and far more abundant sources that the earth provides. Here, step by step, is how you, the individual, can improve your own style-of-life —and at the same time help your very small planet.

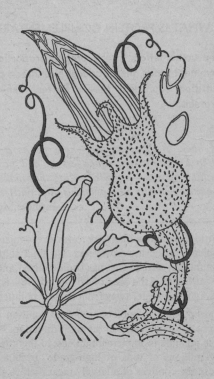

DIET
FOR A SMALL
PLANET

Frances Moore Lappé

REVISED EDITION

Illustrated
by
Kathleen Zimmerman
and
Ralph Iwamoto

BALLANTINE BOOKS • NEW YORK

ISBN 0-345-27429-6

Manufactured in the United States of America

First Edition: September 1971
Fourteenth Printing: January 1975

Revised Edition:
First Printing: April 1975
Seventh Printing: August 1977

Cover art by Charles Fracé

For Marc

Oats

Contents

List of Charts, Tables and Protein Tables

CHARTS

TABLES

PROTEIN TABLES

Acknowledgments

As I look back now on the six years since the germination of this idea, I see one person who must be recognized above all—my husband, Marc, for his absolute support, the loving presence that alone can give one the strength to proceed along a new and uncharted path.

In the first edition of the book I expressed my gratitude to Lloyd Linford, my initial "volunteer editor," and to Marian Ferguson and Walter Meagher, for believing that a national publisher would be interested even when I doubted it. They found just the right publisher in the person of Betty Ballantine, then, with her husband, head of Ballantine Books. Mrs. Ballantine turned my stereotypes about New York publishers completely upside down! At every point in putting the book together, she followed my wishes. Literally, she made a dream come true.

That was in 1971, and now it is 1975 and two children later. Having two small children has meant that I have many more people to thank this time for help in the tedious work of putting a revised edition together. My parents, John and Ina Moore, and my sister-in-law, Joanna Moore, offered both moral support and concrete assistance: in updating the protein cost comparison, in improving the chapter on protein need, and in testing and rewriting endless recipes. All that in addition to typing and baby-sitting! My husband's parents, Paul and Jeanette Lappé, also contributed by caring for Anna and Anthony so that I might work, confident that they were being lovingly cared for. And the assistance of Linda Kravitz in digging up data for me in Washington was invaluable.

For the first edition there was one person whose kitchen-touch made the recipe section fun to work on: that was Ellen Ewald. And since then, she has gone on to write her own book, *Recipes for a Small Planet*. Because Ellen is not nearby, I wondered how I could do the book again without her—until I made a miraculous discovery right in my own "back yard." The discovery was Susan Kanor, who has thrown herself into the project as if she were writing her own cookbook—as well she should. Sue has a way with food that combines an appreciation of good taste with an artist's touch. She has been testing recipes around the clock, offering suggestions and improvements.

I was fortunate also to have complementary protein recipes submitted by two professional home economists: Barbara Peter of Lake Forest, Illinois, and Carol Ackerman Albiani of Highland Park, Illinois. Both have worked with and taught complementary protein cooking for several years. They may soon be working on their own book on soybean preparation; to give you an idea of how good it will be, for the Buttermilk Oatmeal Pancakes, Carrot Corn Bread, Johnnycakes, Sweet Rice Delight, and Sweet and Sour Tempura in my book you have Mrs. Albiani to thank, and for the Soybean Pie you can thank Mrs. Peter. Out of their experience in using the earlier edition and by talking to nutritionists about it, both Mrs. Peter and Mrs. Albiani offered many points of valuable critique of that edition. I thank them both.

Also, I appreciate now more than ever those who worked on recipes for the first edition, for many of these have become family favorites and are again included here. Many came from: Sandye Carroll, Diane Coleman, Marian Coleman, Nancy Posselt, Jackie Potts, Paul Prensky, and Joyce Gardner. Some new recipes for this revised edition came from Susan Dart, foods columnist, Pioneer Press; from my dear friend Nancy Meister; and from a long-lost friend, Robin

MacFarlane; as well as from my youngest assistant, Jamie Seymour.

For typing help beyond the call of duty, to meet a short deadline, I want to thank Ellen McAvoy and Lorraine Jordan.

Peanuts grow underground

Preface to the Revised Edition

In 1970 I wrote *Diet for a Small Planet*. I had just discovered the incredible level of protein waste built into the American meat-centered diet. This discovery turned my world view upside down. Along with many others in the late 60's, I had started out asking the question, "How close are we to the limit of the earth's capacity to provide food for all humanity?" only to be overwhelmed by the realization that I was part of a system actively *reducing* that capacity. I began with the assumption that our food problems were agricultural ones that only the food experts could solve, but came to the conclusion that feeding the earth's people is more profoundly a political and economic problem which you and I must help to solve.

Since 1971, when the book was published, I have received letters from practically every state in the union, from young people living in collectives in the Northwest to an elderly woman living on social security in a trailer home in upstate New York. They said the book changed their lives; it has changed my life too. When the book was first released I had several fears: in the first place my ideas all seem so obvious that I felt they must be wrong; I felt like the boy in the fairy tale who cries "But the emperor wears no clothes!" Why did we go on *wasting* our agricultural resources when a diet that would use the earth efficiently could be as healthful and satisfying, if not more so? It just didn't make sense, I didn't understand it, so I had the lurking doubt that *I* must be wrong—somewhere.

But the emperor in fact was naked! The more I read

and the more I talked to experts, the more convinced I became of the facts.

However, I had a more profound doubt than merely about those basic facts: what of the impact, what of the direction that I was suggesting for people's lives. Would the readers of my book become so interested in, even fixated on, the nutritional nuances as to forget or neglect the real message after all? In the question-and-answer period following my first speech as the "author" Frances Lappé, a student at the University of Michigan raised his hand to ask, "What is the nutritional difference between long-grain and short-grain brown rice?" I wilted. I had wanted to convey the felt-sense of how our diet relates each of us to the broadest questions of food supply for all of humanity. I had wanted to convey the way in which economic factors rather than natural, agricultural ones have determined land and food use. Was I doing just the opposite? Was I helping people to close in on themselves, on their own bodies' needs instead of using the information to help them relate to global needs?

Well, three years have passed since that first question, and I feel more hopeful about focusing on food as a way to help us see our place in the world more accurately, as a way of relating to the world as world citizens with a sense of responsibility for how our actions and our government's policies affect all the world's peoples.

Because our food habits are so personal and yet food needs are universal, food has the unique capacity to capture our interest and also to teach us. I have become more confident of the value of "seeing the world through food," for when we do, it suddenly becomes clear that any economic system must be judged above all else upon how it produces and uses its food resources. How does our present system stand up under such scrutiny? That is the question that must be confronted.

When economic mechanisms so break down that food is actually destroyed while people are starving (as happened this past year), we all ask, shocked and dismayed, how did this terrible waste ever happen? Yet on a global scale we have evolved a *system* of food destruction that shocks very few—because it is largely invisible and everywhere taken for granted. As long as the poor and hungry world cannot pay, grain and soybean growers will find it more profitable to sell to the rich countries, where this food will be called "feed" and reduced to a tiny fraction of its real potential. It will not be burned or buried—but is there really a difference?

I knew I wanted this new edition to make food a more forceful vehicle, for a larger message, but I knew also that it was equally important to make its strictly personal, kitchen-level information more accessible. Initially, having no idea that my book would ever be published nationwide, I wrote for a tiny audience that was already familiar with many of the foods and kitchen techniques I was just then becoming comfortable with myself. Now, after four years of actually practicing what I preach, I have many more ideas on how to communicate a basic change in dietary pattern —a change that can be simple, satisfying and fun. So this is what I am hoping for in presenting this new edition: that the cooking will be simpler, the eating better, and that the political and social significance of our choices will be made ever clearer.

Pumpkin and Squash

Part I

Earth's Labor
Lost

Two kinds of Millet
Hungarian Grass and Broomcorn (common) Millet

A. Diet for a Small Planet Revisited

In 1971 my book began:

"When your mother told you to eat everything on your plate because people were starving in India, you thought it was pretty silly. You knew that the family dog would be the only one affected by what you did or didn't waste. Since then you've probably continued to think that making any sort of *ethical* issue about eating is absurd. You eat what your family always ate, altered only perhaps by proddings from the food industry. It's probably a pretty unconscious affair, and you like it that way. But eating habits can have a meaning, a meaning that not only feels closer to you than an abstract ethic but brings you pleasure too. What I am about to describe to you may sound at first like just another ethical rule for eating, but to me it feels like common sense far removed from the abstract."

That common-sense ethic that I went on to tell you about sprung from my discovery that in 1968 the amount of humanly edible protein fed to American livestock and not returned for human consumption approached the whole world's protein deficit! "Is this necessary?" I asked. There had to be an alternative. Indeed, the practical information which made up, and still makes up, the bulk of this book demonstrates that alternative: by relying more on non-meat protein sources we can eat in a way that both maximizes the earth's potential to meet our nutritional needs and, at the same time, minimizes the disruption of the earth necessary to sustain us.

Now, while I claimed that my "ethic" was not abstract, it was, I'll admit, highly theoretical. As late as 1972 we were holding over 50 million metric tons of grain in reserve and one acre was being held out of production for every four and one-half acres we harvested.[1] When we were paying farmers $3.6 billion to hold land out of production,[2] was it really our grain-wasting, meat-centered diet that most limited our ability to provide food in a hungry world? In 1971 the answer had to be: only in part.

In 1975 we live in a different world.

Today there is virtually no American farmland being held out of production. In the last two years we have discovered that much of our 60-million-acre reserve may have been an illusion. When it was released from controls, not much more than half turned out to be profitably cultivatable.[3]

The year after I wrote the original book, world agricultural production dropped for the first time since World War II.[4] The world is now 134 million tons below a safe carryover of cereals;[5] our reserves are down to less than 10 percent of the grain consumed.[6] And in 1974 world production of grain was estimated to be down again, even more sharply. To supply grain for import needs, only two areas are left as grain exporters: North America and Australia.

Up to 1970, world fish catches had been rising 4 to 5 percent a year—or more rapidly than the rate of world population growth. Now total catches are falling, and so are catches per person.[7] According to Lester Brown, ". . . many marine biologists now feel that the global catch of table-grade fish is very close to the maximum sustainable level."[8]

While world production dipped, world demand increased, both because of the additional 70 million people added each year and because of the increased appetite of the richer countries for more grain-consuming livestock products. Most dramatic was the Russian purchase of one-quarter of the American wheat crop in 1973, in large part to help satisfy that appetite. The result has been that the price of world grain has jumped several fold—up beyond the reach of those with real food needs. Compared to the early 1970's the hungry world is paying $5 billion *more* to us for food annually,[9] a staggering burden that largely preceded and compounded that of the major oil price rise. The question is not whether the grain *exists*—but who can pay for it? The unmet need of the hungry world for grain, 7–11 million tons in late 1974, remains in early 1975 at least 3 million tons. This reduction in the hunger gap has been largely due not to aid, but to purchases by the poor countries in the costly commercial market—expenditures that have displaced funds for long-term development.

In 1971 my book's message was more illustrative than practical. Today, four years later, it is both. Then, the practical effect of our diet was conditioned by many other factors. Today, with no cushion in the form of land held out of production and with little reserve stock, the amount that each of us consumes helps determine directly the ultimate price of grain in the world market and, as well, our capacity to provide food assistance.

In the face of all of these harsh reminders of the limits of the earth's agricultural capacity, these four years have brought forth two solutions that I see offered again and again. First is the notion that the world food problem has been caused by rapid population growth and that, therefore, the answer to the food crisis must lie in slowing that population growth. To me it seems clear that a secure food supply is a necessary precondition *before* a society, or a couple, would be motivated to limit its reproduction. For without the most basic security need—food—can there be any other? Then children must and do fill—for a society or a couple—all the needs: for laborers (when we are too poor to hire labor), for support in old age (when no social security exists), and for all the psychological satisfactions of child rearing (when life may offer virtually no other rewards). With only about one acre of arable land per person in the world,* and the world's population predicted to double in 30–40 years, no one can belittle the magnitude of the problem of rapid population growth; such growth makes it imperative that we confront the food problem now. A solution to the food problem is a prerequisite to solving the population problem in my view—not the other way around.

The second "answer" to the deepening hunger crisis is often couched in the wartime image of triage, a system of deciding rationally *who* is to be saved when it is clear that not everyone can be. But since there is, for now, *more* than enough to go around—enough grain alone to give each of us two loaves of bread a day—and since we are all part of a system that reduces many fold the earth's food potential, how can we claim that the only solution is to cut off part of humanity? Triage carries with it the notion that we have done everything we could on the basis of simple compassion and that it is even too late for that; that it is time for hard, rational choices in order to save anyone.

The first question to ask is whether we have done all we could on the basis of simple compassion? We have concentrated our small and shrinking aid budget overwhelmingly on military and political rather than humanitarian purposes, on industrial development over and above agricultural and social development; and we have been blind as to how our trade and monetary policies help determine the inability of the poor world to feed its people. It is not only simple compassion that has failed us; our diagnosis of the problem has been wrong.

Certainly, simple compassion is not adequate now, but what we do need is not the detached "rationality" that would allow us to condemn millions as hopeless. Rather, we need the enlightened rationality that would allow us for the *first* time to correctly diagnosis the

---

* Several recent studies have estimated that there are, in fact, two arable or potentially arable acres per person worldwide. But to bring the second into production would in most cases require large capital inputs or entail destruction of valuable forests or other probably unacceptable costs.

complex and often invisible causes of world hunger and the courage to face the monumental changes in the world economic system that will be necessary to overcome that hunger.

To understand how an economic system can reduce the capacity of the earth to provide, let us start right here in America.

B. A Protein Factory in Reverse

Think for a moment of a steer grazing. We see the steer as one link in a food chain in which we are the last link: it eats the grass and we get the steak. What could be a better arrangement! But wait; is turning grass into meat the primary function of American livestock today? Or do they serve us in another way, determined more by economics than by the natural talents of the animal?

1. How to Get Rid of It

During the last three decades the United States has experienced a "Green Revolution" in its own right, totally unrecognized by a generation of young Americans born since 1940, who have learned to take agricultural abundance for granted. Due primarily to genetic seed improvements and the widespread use of both fertilizer and pesticides, the productivity of American farm land increased 50 percent between 1950 and 1971.[1] Corn yields jumped three times per acre. But just as in the latest "Green Revolution" in Asia, the American economic environment was not ready to receive the "good news" delivered by the breakthrough in the exploitation of our natural environment. Given the sharp inequalities in wealth here and abroad, it was impossible to sell profitably all of our newly enlarged food resources. Thus, the challenge confronting American

CHART 1
OUR "GREEN REVOLUTION"

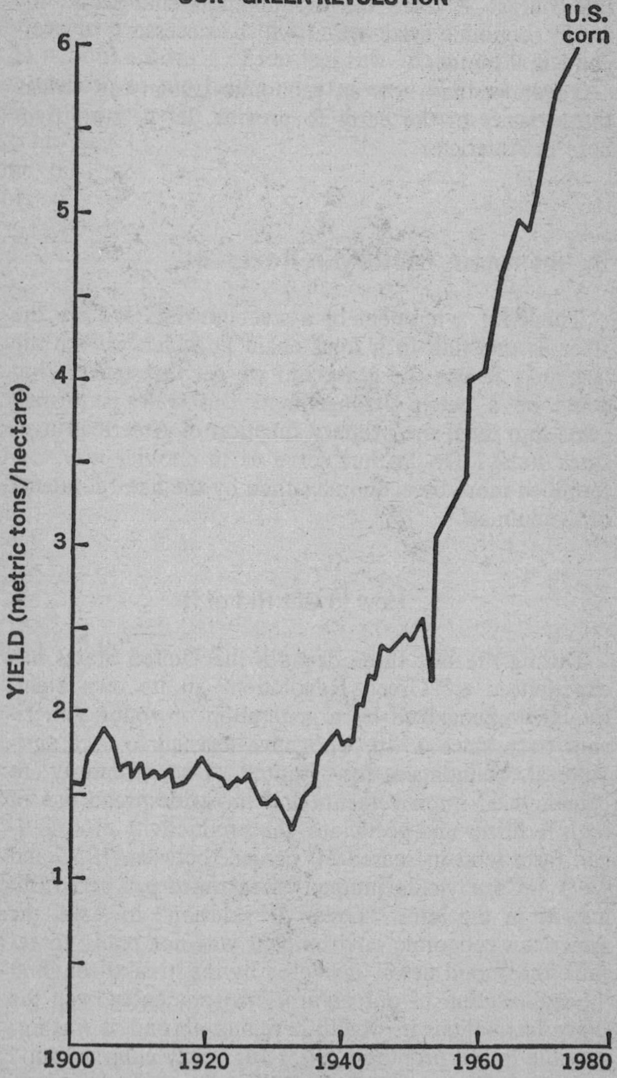
U.S. corn
6
5
4
3
2
1
YIELD (metric tons/hectare)
1900
1920
1940
1960
1980

Source: U.S. Department of Agriculture.

agriculture soon became one of disposal, of how to get rid of it all.

By far the easiest way to get rid of the problem of having "too much" was just not to grow the food at all. As late as 1972, one acre was held out of production for every four and one-half acres we harvested. (In that year farmers were paid $3.6 billion to hold land out of production, enough to pay our current food aid bill three times over.[2]) But, even so, crops reached record highs.[3] The government helped in another way by sponsoring concessionary sales under the Food for Peace legislation, literally a "surplus disposal" program, according to agriculture textbook terminology.[4]

College professors were also assigned to tackle our food "problem." An agricultural scientist at Purdue University recalled recently that during the 1940's he had received a state grant "to figure out someway to use up all that food in a nonfood manner."[5] The professor claimed not to be too successful at creating "nonfood." But then, he did not need to be. The perfect solution had been found elsewhere: in the American steer.

Being the *least* efficient among his fellow ruminants as a converter of plant protein to animal protein, yet able to put something on the table that had high demand, the steer was ideally suited to our needs. Today an average steer is able to reduce 16 pounds of grain and soy to one pound of meat on our plates.[6] The other 15 pounds? It becomes inaccessible to us, for it is either used by the animal to produce energy or to make some part of its own body that we do not eat (like hair), or it is lost entirely in manure.

An interesting and (I've discovered) heated debate now rages over these conversion figures. One of the country's biggest feedlot operators has estimated the grain-to-meat ratio at 20 to 1,[7] but most defenders of our current practices put it at about 7 to 1. Why the big difference? I was confused completely until I realized that those defending the 7 to 1 figure were telling me, in effect, that the grain the animal ate put on *all* the edible meat. But when you look at the lifetime of a steer, it is clear that the grain is responsible for less than half the table-ready meat. (If you want to see the sample figures I used, and my method, look at note 6 for this chapter at the end of the book.)

Livestock other than the steer are considerably more efficient, as you can see on the accompanying chart: hogs consume six, turkeys four, and chickens three pounds of grain and soy to produce one pound of meat.[8] Milk production by cows is much more efficient. In fact, less than one pound of grain is fed for every pint of milk produced.

Another way of assessing the relative inefficiency of livestock as protein converters is by comparison with plants. An acre of cereals can produce *five times* more protein than an acre devoted to meat production; legumes (beans, peas, lentils) can produce *ten times* more; and leafy vegetables *fifteen times* more. These figures are averages; some plants in each category actually produce even more. Spinach, for example, can produce *up to twenty-six times* more protein per acre than can beef.[9]

Granted that the steer is an inefficient converter of grain. The U.S. Department of Agriculture has pointed

Cows

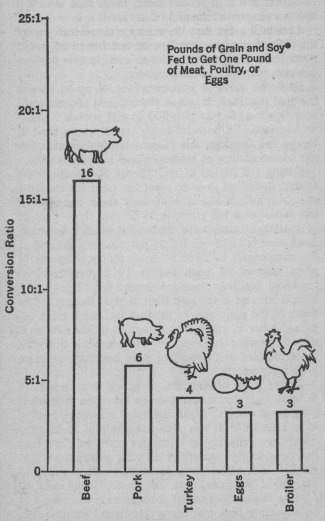

CHART 2
·A PROTEIN FACTORY IN REVERSE

Pounds of Grain and Soy* Fed to Get One Pound of Meat, Poultry, or Eggs

Conversion Ratio

25:1

20:1

15:1

10:1

5:1

0

16 — Beef

6 — Pork

4 — Turkey

3 — Eggs

3 — Broiler

Source: USDA, Economic Research Service, Beltsville, Maryland. See also notes 6 and 8 for Part I, section 8 at the back of the book.
*Soy constitutes only 12% of steer feed and 20-25% of poultry.

out that grain makes up only 25 percent of feed units that cattle consume—the rest is inedible forage that they transform into high-protein meat. That's true. And this makes even *more* incredible that fact that into that 25 percent of the diet represented by grain we can funnel the bulk of our agricultural resources! But to make this possible we first had to devise an entirely new production concept: the feedlot operation.

Here the steer, in concentrations of up to several hundred thousand, is taught the business of getting rid of over a ton of grain plus 300 to 400 pounds of high-protein feed.[10] Unnatural to an animal accustomed to forage and freedom, this "forced feeding" is aided by the administration of hormones and antibiotics.[11]

During this period of our "Green Revolution," the feedlot operation grew to meet the need for reducing our "surplus." While in 1940 only about one-third of our cattle were fed grain, in 1972 over three-quarters of marketed cattle were feedlot-fed grain consumers. Each steer in 1972 was fed 55 percent more grain than his counterpart in 1960.[12] Interestingly, however, a given amount of grain fed in 1972 produced less marketed beef than the same amount fed 12 years ago. This is because at the high level of grain feeding today, much of the grain goes to produce fat, and it takes the animal twice as much food energy to produce fat as it does to produce lean meat.[13] (Therefore it is likely the more marbled and expensive your beef cut, the more grain it represents.)

The capacity of American livestock thus turned out to be so great that we can now get rid of the production from about one-half of our harvested acreage by feeding it to animals.[14] It has also been helpful to label as "feed" not only highly nutritious grain and soybeans but considerable quantities of milk products,[15] fish-meal,[16] and wheat germ as well. We feed about 90 percent of our corn, oats, and barley[17] and over 90 percent of our unexported soybean crop to animals.[18] In any other time and place this "beef" would represent valuable human protein resources. For the grand scheme of protein loss through livestock conversion, look at the table entitled "The Fate of U.S. Protein Resources." We have been so effective in shrinking our protein supply that, by 1973, American livestock consumed the protein equivalent of *six times* the recommended protein allowance of our human population.[19]

TABLE I.

THE FATE OF U.S. PROTEIN RESOURCES

Resource	Average Protein Content	Proportion Fed to Livestock
1. Corn, barley, oats	8–14%	90%
2. Soybeans	35–40%	90+%
3. Wheat	11–14%	24%
4. Milk—liquid	3–4%	2%*
—solids	30–33%	
5. Total harvested acreage		50%

Based on domestic use; see note 28 at the back of the book.

* Two percent of U.S. milk production is comprised of the equivalent of 1.7 billion pounds of milk; 1.4 billion pounds of non-fat milk solids; and 63 million pounds of milk fat.

Now let us put these two factors together: the large quantities of humanly edible plants being fed to animals and the plants' inefficient conversion into food for human consumption. Some very startling statistics result. If we exclude dairy cows, the average conversion ratio for U.S. livestock is 7 pounds of grain and soy fed to produce one pound of edible meat.* According to this estimate, of the 140 million tons of grain and soy we fed to our beef cattle, poultry, and hogs in 1971, *one-seventh*, or only 20 million tons, was returned to us in meat.[20] *The rest, almost 118 million tons of grain and soy, became inaccessible for human consumption.* Although we lead the world in exports of grain and soy, this incredible volume "lost" through livestock was twice the level of our current exports. It is enough to

---

* Note that this figure is an *average* of relatively high- (chicken) and low- (steer) efficiency converters.

provide every single human being on earth with more than a cup of cooked grain each day of the year![21]

To imagine what this means in practical, everyday terms simply set yourself at a restaurant in front of an eight-ounce steak and then imagine the room filled with 45 to 50 people with empty bowls in front of them. For the "feed cost" of your steak, each of their bowls could be filled with a full cup of cooked cereal grains![22]

According to Department of Agriculture official Lyle P. Schertz, we in the developed countries use practically as much grain as *feed* as those in the poor countries eat directly as *food*.[23] Clearly the earth cannot support this level of waste. To feed everyone in the world, the way we in America do it, would take three times the current world grain production.[24] If this is true now, what would be necessary 30 years from now, when the population of the world has doubled? Clearly our present dietary pattern is unthinkable for the future.

In the late eighteenth century, when Malthus hypothesized the inevitability of an ultimate man-versus-land squeeze, he neglected to appreciate that economic imbalance, not simply numbers of people, would come to place the greatest burden on the earth's productive capacity. He failed to foresee the enormous gap between the rich minority and the poor majority—a condition in which any agricultural abundance that the world could produce could just as readily be consumed by the rich minority. But then, how could Malthus have foreseen that the world would become so economically imbalanced that it would eventually be to the advantage of the rich to concentrate the world's agricultural resources on feeding animals, not people?

Edwin Martin, State Department leader of our delegation to the World Food Conference in Rome in 1974, stated that one of the main themes of the conference was "improving the efficiency of the food systems in developing countries." Certainly this is needed, but has Ambassador Martin looked at the efficiency of our *own* system?[25]

2. How the Poor "Pay" for Our Steaks

The agricultural abundance of the United States is unparalleled by any other country in the world. So great is our natural endowment that in the words of one observer, "the problem of crop surpluses has beleaguered both the agricultural sector and government policy since the late 1890's."[26] Our fortuitous geography gave us a very special opportunity. With this great resource we might have chosen to ensure every American the basic staples of life—all the grain and legume products—regardless of his income. Instead, we have created a national consumption pattern in which the majority, who can pay, overconsume the most inefficient livestock products well beyond their biological needs (even to the point of jeopardizing their health), while the minority, who can not pay, are inadequately fed, even to the point of malnutrition. According to Ernest Hollings, in his book *The Case Against Hunger*, ". . . million of Americans are hungry, and early scientific indications are that general nutrition in this country is worse than it was at the close of World War II."

In his book Senator Hollings reports results from the National Nutrition Survey, whose director, Dr. Arnold Schaefer, has stated that the nutrition problems among the poor in the United States "seem to be similar to those we have encountered in the developing countries." The two most serious nutritional diseases are kwashiorkor, caused by severe, long-term protein deficiency, and marasmus, which results primarily from prolonged lack of food calories. (You may recall seeing pictures of starving Sahelian children whose bodies were misshapen from starvation; they were suffering from a combination of these diseases.) "Both," Senator Hollings points out, "are rare exceptions except in famine conditions. But both were found by doctors of the nutrition survey, here in our great and bounteous land."

Early samplings of the National Nutrition Survey (undertaken by the Departments of Health, Education and Welfare) in which half the families earned less than $3 thousand a year showed that more than 16 percent had serious protein deficiencies—some well below the levels normally associated with malnutrition in underdeveloped countries. Bone underdevelopment and swollen bellies due to protein or calorie malnutrition were observed in 4–5 percent. This data was gathered in Texas and Louisiana. Cases of marasmus were found in Nashville, Tennessee, and both kwashiorkor and marasmus were identified in the U.S. Public Health Hospital on an Indian reservation in Arizona. As Dr. Schaefer quietly put it, "We did not expect to find such cases in the United States."

The reason I am able to give you only preliminary data is that the National Nutrition Survey, originally intended to be nationwide, was curtailed in 1970 before an analysis of even the first ten-state study could be completed. Senator Hollings reasons that the early results of the survey were "politically embarrassing" to the Nixon Administration.

Since the time of this survey, the poor have been set back even further in their ability to buy a minimally nutritious diet. The cost of the cheapest adequate diet recommended by the Department of Agriculture for the poor rose well over twice as much as did welfare benefits and salaries of poor workers between December 1970 and December 1973. Although a Senate effort led by George McGovern blocked President Ford's recent attempt to raise the price of food stamps, the cost of the recommended diet for adequate nutrition already exceeds food stamp benefits.[27]

It is the poor that pay most for an agricultural system geared to the production of steaks for profit instead of cheap food for us all.

C. The Fatted Calf

It is astonishing that, although protein is a precious commodity in most of the world, in our livestock production we actually place a higher value on fat. The purpose of grain and high-protein feeding is *not* primarily to produce a high-protein carcass, as one would assume. On the contrary, when cattle are fed in the 120 to 150 days before slaughter, the purpose is to fatten up, or "finish" (as cattlemen say), the animal because USDA quality grading is largely based on the proportion of marbled fat in the meat. A choice-grade beef carcass, for example, has about 63 percent more fat, and therefore substantially more calories and cholesterol but *less* protein, than standard grade.

The result of this feeding for fat is incredible waste: much of it is simply trimmed away and discarded. About 20 percent of the prime, or choice, beef carcass is unwanted fat.[1] In 1973 some 2.5 billion pounds of excess fat were trimmed from beef carcasses at the retail level. (Most of these trimmings represented wasted grain.[2]) The cost to produce, ship, and then trim this excess fat is estimated by the Department of Agriculture at more than $2 billion yearly.[3]

In 1974, however, the department decided to rethink this policy of placing a premium on fat. In a calorie- and cholesterol-conscious country with greater demands being made on our grain supply, didn't it make sense to change our grading standards? The department proposed several changes; the most discussed would effect primarily the choice grade, broadening it to include more young beef, although they have less marbling than the present choice grade. The reasoning is that cattle under 30 months are tender enough without much marbling anyway.[4] And, according to the Department of Agriculture, there is no perceptible taste difference.

The significance of such a change is that it would reduce the feedlot time to produce this grade by about two weeks, saving about 140 bushels of grain annually. The price savings for the consumer would be about 8¢ a pound.[5]

Even though there would theoretically be a savings to the consumer, these proposals met with great resistance. The department received more mail than it had received on any other issue—and most of it negative. Meat packers, cattle feeders, and wholesalers all opposed the change. Consumer groups were afraid of being "ripped-off"—by distributors' charging "choice" price for "good" grade.[6]

A proposed change which would have potentially the most far-reaching effect, however, was to begin grading *all* carcasses by yield that are presently graded for quality. With a yield-grade system, the less trimmable fat a carcass has, the higher it is graded. Thus the leaner carcass is, therefore, worth more. More yield-grading could provide a powerful incentive for producing cattle with high-quality lean carcasses.[7]

The verdict as to whether the government will go ahead with the changes has not yet come down; most probably it will not, at least for the time being. This is unfortunate, for even if the change is minimal it is a step toward common sense applied to our meat production. And for all that their spokespersons have stood against the change, the American people have shown their approval of less fatty beef by readily buying up all that advertised as grain fed. What was lacking obviously was the government's commitment to really convey to the American public the value to them of the change and thereby overcome resistance by the vested interests as well consumer suspicion born of ignorance. Alas.

D. The Hidden Talent of Livestock

Nothing inherent in livestock production requires such enormous waste of protein. Historically, livestock have served us as "protein factories," but currently in the United States they just are not given the chance to show what they can really do! It is true that livestock convert land into meat for us, land that is of marginal fertility and unsuited for crops. In fact, between one-third and one-half of the continental land surface is used for grazing.[1] But the biology of ruminants is more remarkable than this figure would indicate. Animals like cattle, sheep, and goats don't need to *eat* protein to *produce* protein—neither the protein in grain nor the protein in alfalfa.

The ruminant has the most simple nutritional requirements of any animal because of a unique fermentation "vat" that lies ahead of the ruminant's true stomach. This vat, the rumen, as it is called, is a protein factory (literally). With the help of billions of bacteria and protozoa the rumen produces microbial protein which then passes on to the true stomach, where it is treated just like any other protein. Not only does the rumen enable the ruminant (and now you know where this name comes from) to grow with the aid of neither dietary protein, B vitamins, nor essential fatty acids, it also enables the animal to digest large quantities of fibrous feedstuffs.[2]

Ruminants, however, do need a source of nitrogen: urea, uric acid, biuret—all will work. Dairy cows fed a diet of urea, ammonium salts, potato starch, cellulose, and sucrose—without any other source of protein—have produced milk in quantities only 25 percent less than those on a standard American forage-and-feed diet. The vitamin and mineral content of the "deprived cow's" milk was normal.[3]

The head beef expert of the Animal Husbandry Research Division of the USDA states that cattle can be weaned on to a protein-free diet and the meat produced will be no different from that of cattle fed a natural diet. The amino acid content is not changed. A taste panel concluded that the flavor, juiciness, tenderness, and overall desirability was no different either. The only difference in those fed no protein was a slower rate of growth and a later puberty age. Considering the great advantage of grain-free feedings, this slower growth rate did not seem to dim the enthusiasm of the researchers.[4]

Because of the special virtues of the ruminant, it can recycle a wide variety of waste products into high-protein food. Successful animal feeds have come from orange juice squeeze remainders in Florida, cocoa residue in Ghana,[5] residue from coffee processing in Britain,[6] and bananas (too ripe to export) in the Caribbean.[7] Ruminants will thrive on bacteria that have been killed and processed,[8] and they can utilize some of the cellulose in waste products such as wood pulp, newsprint, and bark.[9]

But the research on these possibilities, much less the use of them, is slight. Not only have we ignored the capacity of ruminants to convert waste into protein, we have not even begun to explore the real potential of traditional forages. Why bother, when we have been preoccupied with the need to get rid of all that grain? But with the demand for our grain by a hungry world beginning to be felt, there is increased attention to livestock forages such as grass, alfalfa, and clover. In 1975, cattle fed solely on the range will represent 30 percent of all those marketed—an increase of 18 percent over recent years.[10]

More cattle are being fed for longer periods on forage—on the more than 750 million acres we devote to grazing and range (at least 40 percent of the continental land surface). Much or most of this acreage is unsuited to tillage because it is too steep, poorly drained, or of the wrong soil type.[11] But we are not ready to take advantage of the real potential of forage because, according to the experts, there is a technological gap resulting from cutbacks in forage and range research in the past decade. Dr. Harlow Hodgson, an agronomist with the Department of Agriculture, has estimated that forage and range research decreased by 120 science-man years between 1966 and 1970. He states that there is "virtually no basic genetic research on forages, compared with many other crops," and predicts that if our forage crops and grazing land were used optimally, we could reduce the grain we feed our livestock by 50 percent without reducing our meat output at all![12] Another recent study estimates that currently enough rough forage (corn and sorghum *stalks*) is *unused* to feed 12–30 million head of beef annually.[13]

While some agronomists would have us concentrate on maximizing the neglected potential of forages, others have concentrated on trying to improve the already remarkable ruminant itself—and have succeeded. After 15 years of work, D. C. Basolo, Jr., came up with a cross between buffalo and domestic cattle: the "beefalo." He claims his creation can reach the desirable market weight of 1,000 pounds six to eight months faster than the standard steer, and on grass *alone*. And be leaner, tastier, and have more protein to boot![14]

Obviously there would be many possible courses open to us if we were truly interested in maximizing our food resources' potential.

E. Wasting the Waste

Some people believe that although we do feed enormous quantities of high-grade protein nutrients to livestock with relatively little return as food for humans, there is really no loss. After all, we live in a closed system. Animal waste returns to the soil, providing nutrients for the crops that the animals themselves will eventually eat—thus completing a natural ecological cycle. If this were only true!

Animal waste in the U.S. amounts to 2.0 billion tons annually, equivalent to the waste of 2.0 billion people, or more than half of the world's population.[1] What a Herculean task it would be to collect and distribute this quantity of animal waste in order to complete our idealized ecological cycle! In contrast to the agricultural practices of other countries, conditions of livestock production in the U.S. completely militate against any such possibility. Concentration of from 10,000 to several hundred thousand animals in a single feedlot results in a surfeit of potential fertilizer far exceeding the capacity of the surrounding farmland. And, since it is not economical to transport the waste to where it might be used, most of the waste finds its way into our water systems. Georg Borgstrom, an authority on the geography of food, has estimated that the contribution of livestock to water pollution is more than ten times that of people and more than three times that of industry.[2] In a feedlot much of the nitrogen-containing waste is converted into ammonia and into nitrate that leaches into the ground water beneath the soil or runs directly into surface water; it then contributes to the high nitrate levels in some rural wells that tap the ground water. In streams and lakes, high levels of waste runoff contribute to oxygen depletion and algae overgrowth.[3]

In the last five years, however, new interest has developed in livestock waste as a potential resource, both for recycling as feed and as an energy source. The USDA has estimated that the potential protein present in the manure of American livestock is equivalent to our entire highly prized soybean crop![4]

When fed to steers, treated droppings from caged poultry have proved to be nutritionally equal to soybean meal rations.[5] Other experimenters have used unicellular organisms, and even the housefly and earthworm, to successfully "harvest" the nitrogen in the manure. These organisms in turn are then treated to become feed.[6]

In addition to retrievable protein, livestock waste contains valuable quantities of retrievable methane gas. It has been estimated that the waste from a feedlot producing 100,000 cattle annually could be converted into 3 billion cubic feet of methane worth 510–990 thousand dollars—enough to supply the natural gas needs of 30,000 people at present rates of use.[7] One of the largest feedlot operations in the country, Monfort of

Greeley, Colorado, will soon be getting all of its gas needs met by the methane to be produced from its cattle manure. The by-product will be a dry concentrate.[8]

All of these projects are apparently being pursued with the assumption that feedlots are here to stay. Actually they are a quite recent phenomenon, of the last 30 years. Should we accept them as a given? Before we become captivated by the notion of "recycling," is there not a question of priorities to be posed? Producing methane from feedlot waste is really producing fuel from grain. The methane produced in the example cited above could provide for the fuel needs of 30,000 people. That sounds great. But if the grain that the livestock ate to produce that gas had been eaten by people instead, it could have sustained a population of half a million people.[9]

F. The Protein Sink

We in the Western World think of ourselves as bounteous providers for the hungry world; food shipments from the rich to the poor are what we hear about. But there is another side to food trade of which we are little aware. To quote Georg Borgstrom:

> Through oilseeds [peanuts, palm kernels, copra, etc.], oilseed products, and fish meal, the Western World is currently acquiring from the hungry world one million metric tons more protein than is delivered to the hungry world through grains. In other words, the Western World is exchanging approximately 3 million metric tons of cereal protein for 4 million metric tons of other proteins which are all superior in nutritive aspect.[1]

And, once imported, this protein-rich plant food goes primarily to livestock. Dr. Borgstrom has estimated that one-third of Africa's peanut crop (containing the same percent protein as does meat) ends up in the stomachs of dairy cattle and poultry in Western Europe.[2] In the late 1960's it was estimated that, if eaten by human beings, oilseeds could provide as much protein as all the animal protein produced in the world.[3]

TABLE II.
THE FATE OF THE WORLD'S PROTEIN RESOURCES

Commodity	Average Protein Content	Proportion Fed to Livestock
1. Grain	8–14%	33–35%
2. Oilseeds (peanuts, palm kernels, etc.)	26–40%	60–70%
3. Fish	15–25%	40–50%
4. Milk products	3–33%	25–40%

For sources, see note 15 at the back of the book.

Although we think of the poor world as dependent on imports of food, it is actually the rich that place the greatest burden on exportable world food supplies. According to the *Fact Book of U.S. Agriculture,* in the early 1970's West Germany and the United States were the world's leading agricultural importers. Japan and Western Europe together have about one-sixth the population of the poor world; yet they import 20 percent more grain than all the underdeveloped nations taken together![4] Per capita, the world's leading importers of plant protein are Denmark, Israel, The Netherlands, and Belgium—not Chad, Senegal, or Bangladesh.[5]

Sometimes our food-related images of a country are terribly misleading. This is particularly true of The Netherlands, which evokes for me the picture of a pig-tailed dairy maiden, milk pail in hand—filled to overflowing. Yet The Netherlands is a leading *importer* of milk protein. During the mid-1960's The Netherlands annually took in more non-fat milk solids (mainly for raising veal) than did the entire poor world![6]

The United States, known worldwide for its Texas

roundups, is in reality the world's leading importer of beef.[7] We import about five pounds of meat per capita,[8] or enough every year to give every one of us a hamburger a day for most of a month. Although this amounts to only about 7 percent of our consumption, it is equivalent to the *total* yearly meat intake in much of the poor world.

Almost half of this imported meat comes from the poorest, most protein-deficient sections of Central America: Costa Rica, Nicaragua, Honduras, and Guatemala.[9] And what is the impact of this export pattern, which is really only a drop in our meat larder? According to Alan Berg, nutrition expert on the staff of the World Bank, the production of beef in Central America increased dramatically during the 1960's while the per capita consumption of meat in those countries either increased only slightly or actually declined. The most extreme example he notes is Costa Rica, where meat production increased 92 percent but per capita consumption of meat went down 26 percent. The meat, Berg says, is "ending up not in Latin American stomachs but in franchised restaurant hamburgers in the United States."[10]

In the first edition of this book, I reported the vast quantities of fishmeal that the United States imported from Latin America as well. Since then, our fishmeal imports have declined to the lowest point in over 25 years. (The Peruvian anchovy crop on which we depended for much of our high-protein feed dropped drastically several years ago for reasons not yet totally understood.) But certainly this resource loss was in part due to heavy fishing of the waters for the profitable business of satisfying the rich world's seemingly insatiable demand for cheap livestock feed. Now the Peruvian government has introduced a quota of one million metric tons on its anchovy catch in order to try to restore this invaluable protein source.[11]) But the United States still leads the world in the importation of certain other seafood products. We import about one-quarter of world imports of fresh and frozen fish and about one-third of the shellfish in world trade[12]—with most of our shrimp coming from Mexico and India.[13] All told, we and the other rich countries who are only one-third of the world's people consume about 75 percent of the world's fish supply.[14]

G. Land That Grows Money Can't Grow Food

So far I have concentrated on how livestock can reduce instead of increase the potential of the earth to support us. But the world's agricultural potential depends not only on what we do with what we grow but —even more basically—what we choose to grow in the first place.

Sitting in a coffeehouse with friends several years ago, it suddenly occurred to me that that tasty cup of capuccino I was drinking symbolized millions of acres of agricultural land in the hungry world. How is it that some country unable to feed its own people is supplying *me* with coffee? Incredibly, I had never even thought of this before.

Beginning over 300 years ago, the wealthy Western powers established the plantation system in their subject lands. The plantation's sole purpose was to produce wealth for the colonizers, not food for men. Thus most of the crops selected by the colonizers—tobacco, rubber, tea, coffee, cocoa, cotton and other fibers— had little or no nutritional value. The name subsequently given to them, "cash crops," is quite an appropriate label.

Cash crops became established in world trade, so that even after their emancipation from formal colonial control Third World countries were "economically hooked" on these crops as their only means of survival. Coffee, for example, the second most valuable commodity in world trade, is the economic lifeblood of fourteen developing countries.

Obviously, cash crops usurp land—often the best

agricultural land—that could be growing food for an undernourished local population. Roger Revelle, director of the Center for Population Studies at Harvard, estimates that one out of every ten cropped acres in the world is planted with non-nutritious cash crops such as cotton, tobacco, rubber, coffee, tea, jute, etc.[1] This non-food acreage is comparable to all the tilled land in Europe![2] During the mid-1960's the Food and Agriculture Organization of the United Nations reported that in the poor world this non-edible agricultural production was growing at a far greater rate than the production of edible food[3]—not surprising, in light of the fact that until the recent "Green Revolution," irrigation and fertilizers were reserved almost exclusively for the soils of these export crops.[4]

As a result of the fixation on non-food crops for export, the position of subsistence farmers and of local markets worsened in much of the poor world. More and more imported food was necessary. The irony is that a poor country has to give up much of what it has earned from its cash crop in order to pay for imported food! And, the imported food is so costly that it goes primarily to the rich minority there. Georg Borgstrom estimates, for example, that in the Ivory Coast "the imported protein in the shape of canned meat, milk and fish costs about 11 times more than the exported protein in the shape of peanuts and oilseed cakes."[5]

When I used the expression "economically hooked" I meant by this that getting away from cash crops can be a painful process. Even if a poor country would like to shift to food crops, many obstacles remain. One is that any change takes capital: for research to determine best soil use, for reconditioning the soil, for different agricultural equipment, and for building a domestic distribution system to replace the export system. And how do you get that foreign exchange? By selling more cash crops? The poor world has tried that, increasing the volume of its agricultural exportation by more than one-third since 1952. For their effort, they have received a gain in cash income of only 4 percent![6]

A second obstacle is that if a country shifts from relying on agricultural crops for its source of foreign exchange, it must have another export to take its place. The alternative is manufactured goods, or, to begin with, processing its own raw agricultural products (as there is more profit to make in the processed product than the raw commodity). However, the rich countries place higher tariffs on processed imports than on raw products (e.g., there is no tariff on hides, 5 percent on leather, 10 percent on shoes[7]). In addition, there are significant non-tariff barriers to poor-world manufacturers. It has, therefore, been hard for the poor world to secure markets in the rich world; its share of world trade has declined markedly in the last 20 years.[8]

But beyond the problem of international trade constraints that limit the options open to poor-world governments are the antinutrition influences of multinational agribusiness. In a recently published study explaining how global corporations have compounded the world hunger problem, Richard Barnet and Ronald Müller state, "It is good business to grow high-profit crops for export rather than to raise corn, wheat, and rice to support an indigent local population." They cite the example of Colombia, where "a hectare devoted to carnations brings a million pesos a year, while wheat or corn brings only twelve thousand, five hundred

Barley, Rye, Millet, Oats, Wheat

pesos. As a result, Colombia, like most other poor countries in Latin America, must use scarce foreign exchange to import basic foodstuffs." Barnet and Müller conclude that, "The policies of the global corporations feature increased production of luxury items such as strawberries and asparagus. But the money does not flow to the hungry majority, and those who used to subsist on local fruits and vegetables now find them priced beyond their reach."[9]

Even in the face of these obstacles, some poor countries are attempting to shift their productivity into food for their own people. For example, some West African countries report that their national goals include crop diversification. Sierra Leone, exporter of cocoa and coffee, is attempting to increase its rice production (and the United States has helped this effort with a $5.6 million loan[10]). Gambia, where 90 percent of the export earnings come from peanuts, is attempting both to process its own peanuts as well as diversify its crops.[11]

But given the many constraints, just where *will* the foreign exchange come from to make this shift possible on a large scale? The answer for some countries has been to form a commodity group that can cooperate to maintain a stable price for their products—a price that is more in line with what they must pay for imports from the rich world. Take coffee, for example. In 1960, El Salvador could buy a tractor with earnings from 165 bags of its coffee.[12] By the early 1970's, El Salvador needed 316 bags of coffee to buy one tractor. The last straw for the coffee producers came when the rich countries, particularly the United States, refused to allow an increase in coffee prices to compensate the producers for losses due to our dollar devaluations. The coffee countries responded by forming their own organization to make sure that the price of coffee reflected these higher prices they have to pay for all our products.[13]

What we inherited from our colonizing forebears in the form of cheap agricultural and mineral products from the poor world was the illusion of the limitless capacity of the earth to support us—and our indulgences: coffee and cocoa, for example. As the poor world gains economic strength we will have to give up this maladaptive illusion—to everyone's benefit. A world agricultural system that reflects this new and correct sense of the earth's finitude will require nothing less than a complete restructuring of the world economic system. Nutritive values, not profit, must become our guide to the use of the earth's limited agricultural resources.

H. Mining the Soil

But let us for a moment accept the rules of the economic game. Since the United States can "afford" this waste of protein, why not indulge ourselves? Why not continue our inefficient livestock production and heavy importation of protein until such time as the pressure of our own population, or political changes abroad, forces us to use our resources more wisely?

This reasoning assumes that the only cost of our present indulgence is wasted protein, which at any moment could be retrieved. But in reality our productive capacity hinges on the quality of our soil, which, if lost, cannot so readily be regained. Our heavy use of agricultural land depletes the soil and results in lower-quality agricultural output. For example, in 1940 it was quite common for Kansas wheat to be as much as 17 percent protein. By 1951, only *eleven* years later, no Kansas wheat had over 14 percent protein, most having between 11 and 12 percent.[1]

By the early 1970's, American farmers began to discover that they had just about reached the limit of the capacity of heavy fertilization to increase yields and had perhaps gone beyond the capacity of the earth to handle fertilizers. (Along with livestock waste, heavy use of nitrogen fertilizer was contributing to dangerous levels of nitrate compounds in Midwest groundwater.) In order to meet the new demands for American crops, farmers once again began to expand the acreage under cultivation. According to Boyce Rensberger, in a special to *The New York Times,* during 1974 alone nearly nine million acres of unfarmed land was put to the plow, including "vast sections of semi-arid prairie in the West and newly drained coastal wetlands in the Southeast." But the Soil Conservation Service warns that less than half of this acreage is being farmed with adequate erosion control. In 1974 alone, Rensberger related, "60 million tons of topsoil was lost from the added area." In fact, the SCS estimates that 60 percent of *all* American farmland "lacks proper erosion control and sustains topsoil losses of more than five tons per acre each year. This means that, at a minimum, more than a billion tons of soil erodes away annually. Much of the 'lost' soil enters rivers as sediment."[2]

Do we accept this virtually irretrievable loss to our greatest natural resources as a necessary trade-off in the battle against starvation? No—not when almost half of that harvested acreage goes to feeding livestock. The great pressure on our agricultural land, leading to over-use of fertilizers and under-use of sound conservation techniques, comes not from hungry people but from the demands of our inefficiently produced meat-centered diet, a diet that bears no relation to our real biological needs.

One factor that has allowed us to push the limits of the soil's productive capacity is the use of pesticides. Let us see how they get into our diet and pertain to the main thesis of this book.

I. Eating Low on the Food Chain

By now most of us are familiar with the facts of environmental damage wrought by chlorinated pesticides like DDT. In predatory birds like pelicans and falcons, DDT and related pesticides like Dieldrin can disrupt reproductive processes; and in ocean-going fish like salmon, DDT can cause damage to the nervous system. What may be less familiar to you, and of greater importance to us here, is just why these particular species are being affected. A major reason is that these animals are at the top of long food chains in which pesticides have accumulated as one organism was eaten by another. Organochlorine pesticides like DDT and Dieldrin are retained in animal and fish fat and are difficult to break down. Thus, as big fish eat smaller fish, or as cows eat grass (or feed), whatever pesticides are therein are largely retained, and are passed on. So if people are eating at the very top of such food chains, they becomes the final consumers, and thus the recipients, of the highest concentration of pesticide residues.

Unlike most other predators (or carnivores, if you like), human beings have a choice, however, of what and how much they eat. We have already explored one of the reasons for choosing to be an herbivore, which eats low on the food chain: it is simply less wasteful. Another consideration, the one we are going to evaluate here, is that herbivores are less likely to accumulate potentially harmful environmental contaminants than are carnivores.

Now, the Food and Drug Administration of this nation knows its ecology as well or better than we do, and they have taken pains to keep pesticides out of the diets of the animals and animal products that we consume. Indeed, there are exceedingly few feed products for which the FDA has authorized pesticide spraying. In particular, through the 1960's the FDA scrupulously prevented the spraying of alfalfa with chlorinated pesticides like DDT. Does this mean that our concern about food-chain concentration of contaminants is unfounded?

Dr. Marc Lappé, my husband, as a former experimental pathologist interested in the problem of environmental contamination, pulled together the information necessary to answer that query. He turned to an important new scientific journal devoted exclusively to monitoring the levels of pesticides in the American environment, *Pesticides Monitoring Journal*. Yearly, since 1968, this journal has reported extensive studies of pesticide residues in the American diet. Between 1964 and 1968 the principal types of pesticide residues found (about 85 percent) were chlorinated pesticides like DDT.* In a summary report given in 1969, two principal investigators of pesticide contamination in the U.S. diet reached the following conclusion: "Foods of animal origin continue to be the major source of chlorinated organic pesticidal residues in the diet."[1] Subsequent reports have shown that this trend has continued into the 1970's.

This has occurred in spite of the fact that food categories such as dairy products, meat, fish, and poultry received little if any direct application of pesticides during the period when monitoring was done. Thus the "precautions" taken in the 1960's to avoid beef contamination by pesticide residues will likely continue to prove to be ecologically unsound, as long as other pesticide residues are available from indirect sources in the environment.

The accompanying bar graph, Chart 3, shows you in summary form the kind of data on which these researchers relied. The bars indicate parts of chlorinated pesticides per million parts of food (parts per million, or ppm). Note that between 1964 and 1970 meat, fish, and poultry contained two to two and a half times more chlorinated pesticides than the second-place dairy products, but about thirteen times more than the average level of the remaining seven groups. In quantitative terms, the amount of organochlorine residues decreased 22 percent between 1964–68 and 1968–70. But the

---

* DDT and its breakdown products DDE and TDE accounted for over two-thirds of the total organochlorine residues in the late 1960's. Their contribution will undoubtedly diminish as organophosphorous compounds or, hopefully, biological controls replace them in the 1970's and 1980's.

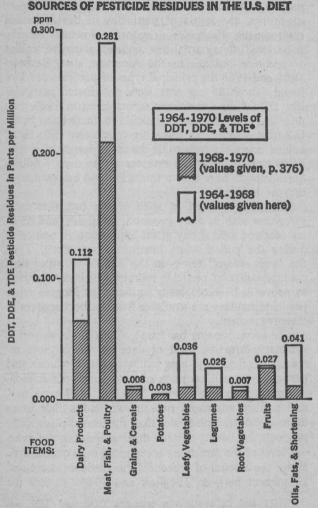

CHART 3
SOURCES OF PESTICIDE RESIDUES IN THE U.S. DIET

1964-1970 Levels of
DDT, DDE, & TDE*

1968-1970
(values given, p. 376)

1964-1968
(values given here)

FOOD
ITEMS:

Source: calculated from data presented in P. E. Corneliussen, "Pesticide Residues in Total Diet Samples (IV)," *Pesticides Monitoring Journal* (2:140-52, 1969; and *ibid.*, (VI), (5:313-30, 1972).

*Averages of combined data from five American cities: Boston, Kansas City, Los Angeles, Baltimore, and Minneapolis.

relative reduction in levels in meats (23 percent) was substantially less than that in vegetables (33–86 percent). (See Appendix E.) In practical terms this means that, had you eliminated meat, fish, and poultry entirely from your diet in 1970 and replaced them with plant sources of protein, you could have substantially reduced your intake of pesticides.

Parts per million also take on practical significance when we consider the *amount* of food we eat in each food group. (Look at Appendix E.) In the diet of a typical sixteen- to nineteen-year-old, meat, fish, and poultry are assumed to contribute 10 percent of the diet on a weight basis. (Note that this is much below the estimate given by the USDA for the consumption pattern of the average adult.) But even at this low level of consumption, meat, fish, and poultry will contribute 27 percent of the total ingested chlorinated pesticides —or more than three times their proportion by weight in the diet!

In the original report (1969), the composition of the diet was such that the weight of dairy products, grains, cereals, potatoes, leafy vegetables, legumes, and root vegetables was about six times that of meat, fish, and poultry. Nevertheless, the total amount of pesticides contributed by dairy products *plus* these plant sources was less than that contributed by meat, fish, and poultry! I have included the complete statistics from this and related studies in Appendix E for your convenience.

You may wish to note also that the types of dairy products considered in this study, which as a group showed the second-highest level of pesticide contamination, were those with an average fat content of 8–13 percent. Since virtually all of the pesticide residues considered here (chlorinated hydrocarbons) are found in the fat, you could reduce your intake of pesticide residues by a judicious choice of low-fat dairy products like cottage cheese, low-fat milk, and yogurt.

In general, we have seen that plant foods contain less pesticide residues than foods of animal origin. It is probably fair to conclude that the principal explanation for this phenomenon is an ecological one: animals consuming large quantities of plant food accumulate biologically stable molecules like pesticides. But a key question still remains unanswered: aren't these patterns of pesticide contamination likely to change now that pesticides like DDT are being phased out? The answer is: probably not to any great extent in the near future. Remember that the pesticide residues now in livestock are largely the result of *indirect* pesticide contamination coming from the general environment. As long as pesticides are in use on other agricultural products or in general use elsewhere, they seem to find their way into the body fat of higher organisms. Estimates of the life span of organochlorine pesticides already introduced into the environment range from seven to over 40 years. In the case of extremely long food chains, recent calculations indicate that the maximum concentrations of pesticide residues derived from the *original* use of DDT in the 1940's may still not have been reached in the "highest" carnivores (e.g., eagles). Indeed, the pesticides currently in our ecosystem are not likely to reach equilibrium for another 100 to 200 years, *even if pesticide usage were to stop immediately!*[2]

You may also like to know whether or not the other potentially hazardous environmental contaminants you have been hearing about might actually be an unforeseen danger in eating vegetable foods.* According to Dr. Lappé, the few reported studies on mercury and arsenic show that these substances are present to about the same extent in foods of animal and vegetable origin. Grains and cereals come under close inspection because their seeds may be dressed with mercury to retard fungal growth and decay. However, in a study conducted in December 1967 meat, fish, and poultry were found to contain about the same amounts of mercury

---

* For example, trace or small amounts (0.0001–0.002 ppm) of organophosphorous compounds have been reported in leafy vegetables and shortenings.

(0.036 ppm) as did grains and cereals (0.034 ppm).[3] It is perhaps noteworthy that dairy products and legumes had about one-fifth of this amount.

Lest you be deceived by the seemingly modest levels of mercury contamination cited for fish above, note that this does not apply to *all* species. Some species are so heavily contaminated with heavy metals like mercury as to pose a real threat to human life. Almost all of the heavily contaminated fish discovered to date have been large oceanic species which are at the ends of long food chains. Even game fish may be contaminated with mercury in states where both agricultural and industrial effluents carry mercury into watersheds. In a 1972 *Pesticides Monitoring Journal* article by C. Henderson, A. Inglis, and W. L. Johnson, it was affirmed that predatory fish like trout, bass, perch, or squawfish, and large oceanic fish like blue-fin tuna and swordfish, may contain more than 0.5 milligrams of biologically active methyl mercury for every kilogram (2.2 pounds) of body weight.[4] This concentration, equivalent to 0.5 ppm, is currently set as the "safety limit" for fish in this country. (Remember that this high limit assumes Americans eat very little fish.) Since only 70 milligrams of mercury are enough to kill you and mercury is one of those elements which can accumulate in the body, this is a real menace indeed—if you ate these species of fish in the same quantity that the average American eats meat, you could easily accumulate 10 to 20 milligrams of mercury in one year!

A fact not mentioned in the cited article is that tolerance limits in the United States for mercury through December 30, 1970, were set a *zero* because of its known toxic effects. Keeping mercury pollution down makes good health sense, but in a country that uses over 400 *tons* of costly mercury a year in its agriculture and industry, the Departments of Health, Education and Welfare and Agriculture *jointly* agreed that after December 31 zero tolerance would have to be dropped—such a level was considered "administratively impractical."[5]

But let's return to the more widespread problem of chlorinated pesticides, where the potential health hazard is less clear. All of this discussion presupposes, of course, that you wish to reduce pesticide intake or that such reduction is desirable, and here is where there are likely to be differences of opinion. While everyone agrees that pesticide residues are an unfortunate concomitant to virtually all foods, experts seem to differ radically as to what constitutes a "health hazard." Thus the authors of the article just cited in the *Pesticide Monitoring Journal* felt obliged to point out that none of the levels of pesticide residues that they measured were likely to represent a health hazard. Indeed, less than 1 percent of the samples of foods in the meat, dairy, or fish category actually exceeded the current toxicity standards established by the government.

A word to the wise: these toxicity standards are established on the basis of short-term toxicity tests on small animals. They say nothing about the possible *long-term* damage that pesticides may produce in humans, such as chronic liver damage and possible cancer. There is evidence, for example, that DDT (as well as a number of currently less prevalent pesticides) produces liver cancer in mice when they are fed large amounts over protracted periods of time. Furthermore, the governmental agencies responsible for setting so-called "safety limits" or "tolerances" have proven themselves notoriously unreliable. Tolerance levels such as those set for the organophosphorous pesticides malathion and parathion were adjusted upward as the residue levels began to increase in milk samples in one state (Montana). Thus "safety" will always be a matter of degree when it comes to biologically toxic pesticides, and safety limits will continue to be adjusted to meet public outcry or agricultural exigency.

My purpose is to show you a way to minimize the amount of ecologically concentrated pesticide and heavy metal you ingest: by eating low on the food chain, you are simply reducing the quantity of most if not all pesticide residues in your diet. If we are wrong and there are no real health hazards that accrue from this period of environmental saturation with pesticides, then no harm has been done. If time shows that accumulated pesticide residues do produce damage to humans (and we may not know this for another ten or twenty years), then you may be grateful you heeded this cautionary note.

But even to have introduced the pesticide issue may seem to some of you a bit unfair. It may be an effective tactic in trying to convince the reader to eat less meat, but does it relate directly to the theme of the book? A discussion of pesticides *is* particularly apposite here because our theme concerns the rational use of agricultural land.

In the last twenty years, American crop yields have increased sharply. The average yield per acre of corn, for example, jumped three times.[6] A major result of these greater yields, if not part of the impetus for them, has been to increase the amount of our agricultural yield available to livestock as feed. Currently, one-half of the yield of our harvested acreage is fed to animals, in part making possible our increase in meat consumption. (Beef and veal consumption has doubled in the United States in the last 35 years.)

Here is where pesticides enter in. These increased crop yields are almost entirely due to the introduction of genetic stocks of seed and fertilizer in the 1940's and, perhaps most importantly, to the organochlorine insecticides which were introduced on a wide scale in the mid-1950's. We might well ask whether it has been worth the cost of the subsequent contamination of our environment. Like the waste of protein and the overtaxing of our agricultural land, the presence of pesticide residues in our diet can be seen as yet another price we are paying for our unquestioning acceptance of increased meat production and consumption as an unassailable good.

Curtailment of pesticide use might mean that we could no longer afford this extravagance and that our population would be eating less meat. But, as I hope the information in this book will make clear, eating well does not necessarily mean eating meat. So far, however, we have just been taking for granted that Americans eat an inordinate amount of meat. You would probably like to know whether this is really true. So let's look at our protein consumption pattern.

J. The Great American Steak Religion

I have concentrated on protein waste as it is involved in our production of livestock. What about in people? I used to think that since I am not fat and don't (God forbid!) leave food on my plate, I, of course, could not be wasting food. That was before I learned about protein. Since the body cannot store protein, what we eat above what we can use is either burned as an energy source (when carbohydrate would have sufficed just as well) or excreted. Since the average American currently consumes almost twice what his body can use, we "waste" much of the protein we eat.[1] To compound this waste, most of the unnecessary increase in meat consumption in the last ten years has been in the form of increased beef consumption—the least efficient protein source.[2]

Prior to 1950 our beef consumption had been fairly stable, hovering around 60 pounds annually per person. But paralleling the increase in corn crop yields, American beef consumption doubled after 1950, even though it was sufficient then to meet our protein needs. With our current beef consumption of about 122 pounds, added to our intake of other meat products, each American now consumes about 250 pounds of meat and poultry a year.[3]

Americans eat so much unnecessary protein that we could reduce our livestock population by one-quarter and still feed every one of us half a pound of meat or poultry[4] a day—enough to meet our entire protein allowance from meat alone, not to mention the protein

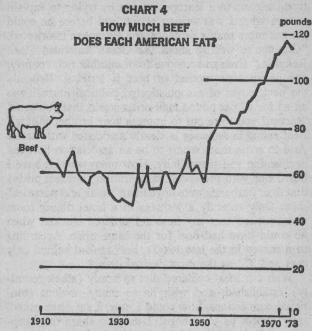

CHART 4

HOW MUCH BEEF DOES EACH AMERICAN EAT?

Beef

pounds
—120
—100
—80
—60
—40
—20
—0

1910   1930   1950   1970 '73

Source: adapted from *The New York Times*, October 25, 1974, p. 20.

we also get from dairy and grain products, beans, nuts, and vegetables. In fact, we get so much protein from these *other* sources that we could, on the average, completely eliminate meat, fish, and poultry and still get 58 grams—all most of us need.[5]

Whereas a "carbohydrate," such as rice or potato, has historically served as the center of the diet in most cultures, with animal protein in a supplementary role, we have turned that relationship on its head. Meat has become the heart of our diet, with plant food relegated to overcooked side dishes and overprocessed baked goods. Steak on a weekday night is part of the "American Dream." The 12-ounce steakhouse feature is virtually an American invention.

At a party several years ago, my husband was introducing me to a European guest by trying to explain to him what I was writing about, and before he could get out more than a sentence, the European interjected, "Oh, you're writing about the Great American Steak Religion." Even to someone from another rich country, our heavy consumption of beef is striking. Recently the back cover of a sophisticated political journal was an ad for $7 per pound mail-order steaks that you could "serve if you were out to impress your brother-in-law." Beef eating in America is clearly associated with status. And to some there seems to be an association between beef eating and masculinity. How many women have I heard sigh with pretended exasperation (but real pride) that their husbands were unyielding "steak and potatoes" men. Only recently a waitress in a hotel dining room was shocked that my husband ordered chicken when he could have had beef for the same price. According to a survey in the late 1960's, beef ranked behind only cars and TV as the most desired item. [6]

With our meat-centered diet so firmly (albeit recently) established, and with its so many obvious emotional connections, how could I ever, I am often asked, truly expect us to change? I used to share this skepticism. In fact, when I first wrote the book I did not even plan to show it to a publisher. I was going to publish it myself, so sure I was that its appeal was strictly limited. (Luckily, Ballantine Books had more foresight than I did!) The country has changed a lot since 1971.

The natural foods movement focused new interest on the possibilities of plant foods; heart disease became linked in the public mind with heavy intake of animal fat; economic conditions forced us to look for less costly protein sources. But most important, the reality of starvation in the rest of the world has made it hard to avoid recognizing that our food production and consumption is the very institutionalization of waste. Since waste is a concept only in relation to unmet need, and our economic system does not recognize need but only "effective demand" (a euphemism for ability to pay), we have been totally unable to recognize waste. But perhaps this is changing too. Our economic system may still be unable to respond on the basis of need, but it is hard for us as individual human beings not to. Can we go on consuming a meat diet that uses up the food that could have fed five people when we have just seen a child starve before our eyes on television?

But the basic question remains: can we rely more on plants and less on meat for protein without jeopardizing our nutritional well-being? (Since plant sources already contribute 70 percent of the world's protein supplies, it is a vital question.) The heart of this book, Parts II and III, are devoted to a positive answer to this question. But before we begin them, let us probe more deeply *the significance of altering our diet.*

K. Meatless, Guiltless?

An article appeared recently in the *New York Times Magazine* about one family's application of the ideas in my book. It was entitled "Meatless, Guiltless." If only it were so simple.

A change in our eating habits can only be a first step in the direction of a rational use of our world's agricultural resources. And even that first step carries with it the danger of being misused, if we do not take responsibility for determining the practical effects of our dietary change.

As food prices have risen steeply in recent years, friends have asked, "Aren't you pleased that the economic conditions are forcing people to turn to your book to learn how to feed their families?" No, frankly, I am not. The negative pressure of a general rise in food prices is an immoral method for getting people to change their diet, even if that change is in a rational direction. The poor will continue to bear the real brunt of the price increases, and certain corporate interests will continue to be beneficiaries. I am concerned that, by showing a way Americans can adapt to higher food prices, my book may inadvertently serve to take the heat off those who are actually responsible. For example, the five corporations that control 90 percent of our grain exports[1] would undoubtedly like to see an increase in our agricultural exports to other rich countries at the expense of our ability to provide food aid to famine-stricken areas—and at the cost of higher food prices at home. By showing Americans how to thrive while consuming less grain, might I be making it easier for these corporate interests to achieve these policies and greater profits? That is the last thing I would want to accomplish.

On the other hand, you might well ask what good would be gained even if the majority of Americans decided, for the *positive* reasons outlined in this book, to reduce their consumption of livestock products to the level consistent with range and waste-produce feeding? This *could* release as much as one-half of all harvested farmland[2] for the production of food that would be feeding people directly. But what would happen to this staggering abundance? Whose interests would actually be served? Your need for reasonable prices? The hungry world's need for both low international grain prices and additional food aid? Would we, through our agricultural adjustment programs, ensure that farmers would be rewarded at least as well for feeding people as they have been for feeding animals? Would our government return to a policy of paying farmers to take land out of production or design a *new* policy to guarantee for the first time that the farmers' return stays ahead of rising costs of farm inputs? Or would our government deal with this sudden surplus by increasing our exports of feed grain to Europe, Japan, or the Middle East so that they might increase *their* intake of meat? Would we use this food bonanza to continue a policy of food assistance based to a large degree on narrowly defined security interests instead of on need?

If we are to take responsibility for what we eat—and by that I mean just how our diet affects the global food supply—then we must also take responsibility for determining the answers to these political questions. Just as we cannot truly be concerned about the problem of world hunger without reducing our individual level of protein waste, neither can we take that first, purely personal step without facing the larger questions of national policy that ultimately determine whether or not our individual action is more than a righteous gesture.

We must begin, therefore, to move our country toward the following kinds of policies in regard to food, agriculture, and development assistance:

1. *Direct government support to make it profitable for farmers to convert from feed to food crops.*

This kind of action would not be new; only the intent would be new. Since the Agricultural Adjustment Act of 1933, the government has been actively involved in deciding *how much* and *what* is to be grown on American farmland.[3] As we have seen, our "problem" historically has been how to get rid of burdensome surpluses. Today we live in a smaller, hungrier world and our policies must, therefore, make an about-face.

In a world where most of the people are hungry, it should become unthinkable to feed humanly nutritious food to animals. To begin with, a nation that can export more than one-quarter of its grain production[4] and feed most of its grain to livestock[5] should be able to develop a food policy that would ensure the basic staples—grain and bean products—at practically no cost to our own people.

2. *Economic incentives for processors and consumers to encourage the direct consumption of plant food, reinforced by a broad educational campaign about the many advantages of a plant-centered diet.*

Obviously the question is not merely one of converting from feed to food crops; most crops could be either, depending upon demand.

Once, in New York's Washington Square Park, my husband overheard two new fathers comparing baby formulas. When one explained with pride that his daughter was getting a mix of soy milk, ground sesame, and brewer's yeast, the other remarked, "What's that glop? Fertilizer?" Strange world, where one man's health potion is another man's fertilizer! But tastes are not inborn. In fact, they are changing all the time, being influenced primarily by the advertising media. In the last 50 years in the United States, these changes have been mostly maladaptive: less fresh fruits and vegetables, much more sugar and meat. We do not need to ask whether or not profound dietary changes are possible. That has been proved a thousand times over by the hundreds of millions of dollars the food giants have invested in advertising; we need only ask how to design social policy to encourage *positive* change.

"But," you still ask, "is this possible?"

Norway is one country that has already instituted a system of economic incentives to encourage greater consumption of plant food and less consumption of grain-fed livestock. The reasons are manifold, not the least of which is the fact that a contemporary Norwegian man who reaches the age of 40 has less chance of becoming 70 than he did at the turn of the century. Norway's health experts believe that a great increase in animal-food consumption is the culprit.[6] So an entire country *is* changing its eating habits.

3. *The promotion of research to improve animal forages and to develop the apparently simple techniques for using waste products as feed for livestock, coupled with economic incentives to livestock producers to use such products.*

There is no reason why livestock should compete with humans for food when they can thrive on humanly inedible substances and convert them into high-quality protein. Livestock—now a major source of pollution—can actually serve to reduce waste.

4. *Control of grain exports so that the United States will be able to resume its share of responsibility for food assistance to those countries in the grip of famine,*

while participating in the rebuilding of depleted world grain reserves.

In 1974 we exported a total of over 60 million tons of grain, several times more than any other nation in the world, while our food aid was down to 3.3 million tons of grain,[7] one-sixth the level of ten years ago.[8] At the 1974 World Food Conference in Rome, it was estimated that a mere 7–11 million tons of grain would meet the starvation gap in Asia and Africa. Yet American officials refused to increase our food aid by even one million tons.

According to an internal Department of Agriculture memorandum dated only one month after the conference, the United States alone had enough grain to supply all of the deficit. The "biggest factor" in the easing of our supply, according to the *New York Times* report, was *"the reduced use of livestock feed lots in the U.S."* (Emphasis mine.)

Think of it: seven million tons of grain—only about 10 percent of our total grain exports! Couldn't we have afforded this tithe for the sake of those people most hard hit by changes in the world economy and by climatic disasters outside their control? I was in Rome, and was embarrassed by the official American view that the hungry world was asking too much of us. Do you know that the amount the United States spent on food aid in 1974 was less than half what we *profited* that year in higher-priced grain sales to the poor world? As this revision goes to press, five months after the desperate need was made explicit at the World Food Conference, President Ford has announced a 2-million ton increase in our food aid,* bringing its value to $1.6

---

* According to Leslie Gelb, in a special to *The New York Times* on February 19, 1975, this long delay means that "the increase will be bigger on paper than in fact, except for some nations, including Chile, South Korea, and Egypt, that are not officially classified as needy." This is true, because there is no longer enough time to ship to the neediest countries, like India and Bangladesh, much of their share of the increase before this fiscal year ends. (Shipments made after July 1 will be charged against next year's, smaller food-aid budget.)

billion—which *sounds* like a lot of money. But is it, in light of the fact that we are now earning $5 billion more in *food sales* to the poor countries than we did two years ago?[9]

Doesn't this fact highlight a distortion in our national image? Although we have long thought of ourselves as the world's "breadbasket," a more appropriate image was suggested to me recently by Paul McIsaacs of New York's station WBAI: America is, instead, the world's "supermarket." Many Americans (including myself at one time) have a mistaken assumption about what we do with our capacity to feed the world. Our food trade, or at least a great share of it, has been a significant source of our *wealth*, not a source of *sacrifice*. We currently export enough food to feed one-fourth of humanity a hearty meal every day.[10] But this food goes overwhelmingly to those who can pay and to those in whom we perceive national security interests. In 1971 we were exporting three times more food to Europe than to Africa and Asia combined.[11] A staggering disproportion of our agricultural productivity has gone to fatten livestock in Europe and Japan, not to feed hungry people.

Perhaps it is because of our own economic problems that many of us are tempted to adopt the attitude that since the United States has done more than its share in the past, now it is time for other rich nations to pitch in and for the poor nations to become self-sufficient. But wait a minute. Have we really done "more than our share"? This implies that the $24 billion worth of grain that we shipped abroad under Food for Peace since 1954 was really a sacrifice on our part. Although the motives of many behind this policy were humanitarian, the act was an economic plus for us. It was a way to rid ourselves of surpluses for which there was no profitable market; it was cheaper than paying farmers not to plant, *and we got paid for much of it!* Much of this food "aid" was not a giveaway but sales on concessional (meaning "easy") terms. (At present *most* of it is sales.[12]) An agricultural textbook I read recently referred to these

"P.L.480" grain shipments as a "surplus disposal" program; above all else, that is what it was.

Proof of the dearth of humanitarian intent is the hard fact that now that the surpluses are depleted, our food aid has dwindled. Food available for relief agencies has all but dried up. And most food aid we are now giving is not going to relieve famine. Seventy percent of our concessional food sales last year went to a few countries where we have "security interests," as that phrase is narrowly defined. To give but one example, in 1974 we were shipping more than four times as much food to Cambodia and South Vietnam as to starving Bangladesh and Sahelian Africa.*[13]

Because the need for food aid has been so critical in the last few years, Americans often seem to think that whole countries in the poor world are living off food imports, and there is a great deal of talk about the need for poor-world self-sufficiency. But two facts are often overlooked. First, the poor world is already largely "self-sufficient" in the sense that net imports for food represent only 7 percent of domestic grain consumption.[14] It is the rich nations of the world who are the major food importers. Japan and Europe import 20 percent more grain than all the underdeveloped countries combined.[15] For example, in the late 1960's the United Kingdom imported, per person, almost 15 times more grain than India.[16]

Obviously, in the real world, self-sufficiency has nothing to do with the level of food imports. Self-sufficiency is conditioned by one thing only: the ability to pay. And it is this question that brings us back to the central issue of this book: the irrational pattern of feeding the majority of our agricultural production to livestock. At present, farmers favor livestock production because it increases consumption of grain and keeps prices up. But in a world where most of the people are

---

* An amendment to the Foreign Aid bill passed in late 1974 restricts non-humanitarian, or political, food aid to 30 percent of the Food for Peace program. However, the interpretation of this amendment is still being debated.

hungry, do we really have to rely on *livestock* to create demand? What about people? The problem, on an international scale, is that the people who *could* make a demand directly on the grain just cannot; they simply do not have the money to buy it. Those who do may buy beef at almost any price. (Consider the Japanese firms who in 1973 were able to sell steak at $14 a pound!) The result is that livestock production remains exceedingly lucrative, and so it will as long as beef eaters can outbid the grain eaters for a given amount of food.

To begin to remove this obstacle to a rational and humane use of the earth's resources means not only supporting our own farmers' conversion to crops for direct human consumption, but also making a real contribution to genuine bottom-up development in the poor world. Only in such development lies the promise for real self-sufficiency: the ability of those with real food needs to pay for it.

Therefore, the fifth and final change in our government's policy that I would propose is:

5. *A recognition that the World Food Problem is in large part only a reflection of the World Wealth Problem and that, therefore, a recasting of all our monetary, trade, and military ties to the poor world is necessary to redress the growing maldistribution of world wealth. (This would include a commitment to development assistance comparable to that which we undertook in order to reconstruct Europe after World War II.)*

In the 1940's we saw clearly the interdependence of our own fate with the economic fate of Europe. We knew that a healthy European economy was in our own best interest. But we have been unable to perceive that this reality of interdependence is also true now of us and the poor world. The 1960's brought a trillion-dollar increase in the level of the world wealth; but 80 percent of that increase went to those who were already wealthy and only 6 percent went to the poorest countries. Such incredible inequity is injurious to us all.[17]

In 1949 we contributed 2.78 percent of our Gross

National Product to help European nations under the Marshall Plan.[18] Today we are contributing only one-tenth as much.[19] And the poor world's need is greater than ever before. Increases in the price they paid for importing food (about $5 billion of which went to us), plus oil and fertilizer, in 1974 completely wiped out any gain from the foreign assistance they received from all the industrial countries.[20]

In regard to development assistance, many Americans believe as they do about food aid: that we have always done more than our share and that it is now time to unload the burden.

But throughout the 1960's the United States never gave disproportionately more than its share in aid as a percent of our GNP. Today, far from being the world's example of generosity, we have set an example of rapid *decline* in assistance. The United States now ranks thirteenth among 17 industrialized countries as a donor of aid in relation to GNP. As a percent of GNP, our aid is half what it was in 1962, so that in real aid we are currently giving about one-quarter of 1 percent of our GNP. (The 1974 figure was down to .24 percent of our GNP.[21]) This is hardly an amount that any of us could personally miss.

How *could* we miss it? Of all aid dollars, 85–90 percent returns to purchase U.S. goods and services. In addition, loan repayments to us from the poor world averaged about $800 million in the last two years, or roughly 20 percent of the annual development assistance that most of us thought we were *giving* them. It has been estimated that, because of the aid-money purchases within the United States and because of these loan repayments, our development assistance has an overall *positive* effect on our balance of payments![22]

Many of us would conclude, seeing poverty increase around the globe, that our development efforts have failed. So why continue? But I would say that development assistance has not failed; it has just never been tried! *Bottom-up, people-oriented development aid directed at the agricultural sector, touching the lowest rungs of society, has never been attempted on the scale necessary to effect meaningful changes in people's lives in the poor countries.*

Economist Barbara Ward has suggested that we have forgotten to look to our own development for a model of the possible: according to her, early development in virtually all the now-industrialized states was based on agricultural expansion, the downward extension of economic activity away from single big centers.[23] Supposedly development planners are beginning to take heed—but the will is missing. The total Agency for International Development (AID) budget for the rural development, food, and nutrition program equals about 10 percent of what we spend for maintaining our military forces overseas.[24] The World Bank, a major source of funds for the poor world, recently reported that less than 20 percent of their loan money was going to rural development projects.[25] Liberal senators have argued against foreign aid because not enough of it has been directed toward Ward's type of "people-to-people" development but is instead distributed according to military and political considerations and used for projects that *further* the internal social inequities. But to so end our foreign aid program would be to "throw the baby out with the bath water"! The senators' position reflects an unfortunate sense of impotency on the part of congressional leaders, a feeling that they are helpless to change the direction and intent of our aid.*

In 1973 the United States spent $9.5 billion on military aid and police training for 64 countries, 25 of which were ruled by the military or permitted no opposition to the government.[26] Most Americans would be shocked to know that they were supporting the very regimes that are most suppressing the social changes necessary to real development. If we diverted half of this amount going for military assistance and added it to our current aid bill of about $4 billion, the total would

---

* The recent move by Congress to limit our "political" food aid to 30 percent of the total is a very encouraging exception.

still amount to only about one-half of 1 percent of our GNP, a level already attained by other developed countries, including France, Belgium, The Netherlands, and Australia. This would at least be a beginning.

"But," you might ask, "isn't this increased level of aid an insignificant drop in the poverty bucket?" It would not have to be *if* it were well placed. One could buy quite a few plows, and build a lot of wells, storage facilities, and access roads, or even an agricultural research center, for the price of a sophisticated fighter plane! In his valuable book *In the Human Interest,* Lester R. Brown reports that it would take only $1.6 billion for five years to wipe out illiteracy in the entire poor world (based on a UNESCO estimate), and $2.0 billion a year would provide basic maternal-health and family planning services for all the poor world (excluding China, which is already well on its way to achieving this goal).[27] The cost necessary to increase the world's irrigated land by 25 percent (57 million acres) has been estimated to be in the neighborhood of $3.5 billion for 11 years.[28] None of the figures are definitive, but they are illustrative: they show that the sums involved are not beyond the capacity of the world economy to absorb.

But if liberal congressional leaders are throwing up their hands in defeat over the misdirection of our aid, and if conservative congressional persons long ago faulted our aid because of a mistaken idea about the actual burden on our economy, then where is the leadership that will help us take the first step along this path of sanity and reason? For all that I have talked about the negative feelings of many Americans toward foreign aid, the truth is that, when questioned, over two-thirds of the American people still support it—this in spite of all the mistaken ideas about the level of our aid and its impact.[29]

Who knows what would happen if national leadership emerged that could make a thoughtful and reasoned case for the necessity of vastly increasing our commitment to world development—if leadership would emerge that could help Americans see our true role in the world economic system—so that we might see how trade and monetary policies of the rich nations operate to inhibit poor nations' development?

Experts have estimated that the recent monetary upheavals of the early 1970's (including not only the price of oil but the increased price of food and the dollar devaluations which preceded it) have cost the poor world at least ten years in development progress. The official United States position at both the World Population Conference and the World Food Conference in 1974 was to downplay the link between trade and monetary issues on the one hand and the issues of rapid population growth and food production on the other. But no. They *are* all interrelated and they are not beyond our comprehension.

How can the poor nations of the world emerge when their wealth comes primarily in the form of exports, yet their share of world trade has dropped 40 percent in the past two decades[30] and the rich nations place limitation on the import of the poor nations' processed goods (in which the most profit is to be made)?[31] How can the poor nations be expected to rise in a monetary system that overnight can unilaterally shrink the value of their reserves by over a billion dollars through a currency devaluation over which they have no control?[32]

By now you must be saying, "Who is she kidding? Who in Washington is going to make such a case?"

If it is useless to call for such leadership in Washington, then we must ourselves become the leaders—you and I. We must ensure that these decisions concerning development aid, military assistance, trade and monetary policies are not made behind closed doors by a handful of "authorities." These issues must emerge in their true importance in the public mind—not remain distant and unintelligible or (even worse) dull and uninteresting—for these are the *life and death* matters on which the story of this century will turn. Will we or will we not tolerate a world in which most of the people live trapped in unimaginable poverty?

If you feel the questions I am now asking are too enormous, and would just like to feel good about giving up hamburgers, let me share these words by Colman McCarthy, a Washington *Post* writer who questions the "seductive simplicity" of the notion that giving up meat will help feed the world: "It is the shame of political Washington that no one in power—not in Gerald Ford's White House, or in the Department of Agriculture—thinks enough of the American people to create the structure for individuals to make sacrifices that make a difference."*[33] He is right; *we* must create that structure.

The notion of "meatless, guiltless" *is* a seductively simple escape. But I am not concerned with "guilt"; the word does not apply. I cannot be guilty for the iniquitous economic system that has been created over many centuries, that has been built on a history of colonialism which determined that the best land in the now poor world would supply cheap exports to the rich world. I am not guilty for the sins of my fathers. I am not guilty for the past.

But I am responsible for the future—the direction that the human community now takes. I am responsible now for the policies of my government that directly affect the world's food supply and the world's maldistribution of wealth.

A change in diet is not an *answer*. A change in diet is a way of experiencing more of the *real* world, instead of living in the illusory world created by our current economic system, where our food resources are actively reduced and where food is treated as just another commodity on which to make profit—a profit on life itself. A change in diet is a way of saying simply: I have a choice. That is the first step. For how can we take responsibility for the future unless we can make choices now that take us, personally, off the destructive path that has been set for us by our forebears?

* The only quarrel I might have with Mr. McCarthy is that many of the changes that we as individuals can make are not sacrifices at all, as you will discover in following chapters.

Taking the Next Step

To link up with the food network, why not write to any of these active groups for more information or sample copies of their publications:

1. Agribusiness Accountability Project, 1000 Wisconsin Avenue, N.W., Washington, DC 20007. Publications: *The Fields Have Turned Brown* on U.S. food policy and others. For West Coast office see *AgBiz Tiller* in following list under publications.

2. Bread for the World, 207 East 16th Street. New York, NY 10003. Publication: newsletter.

3. Center for Rural Affairs, P.O. Box 405, Walthill, NE 68087. Publications: newsletter, *New Land Review* and research studies.

4. Center for Science in the Public Interest, 1757 S Street, N.W., Washington, DC 20009. Publication: *Nutrition Action*. Sponsors of Food Day.

5. Community Nutrition Institute, 1910 K Street, N.W., Washington, DC 20006. Publication: *Community Nutrition Institute Weekly Report*.

6. Corporate Data Exchange, 198 Broadway, Room 707, New York, NY 10038. Initiating study of ownership of agribusiness corporations.

7. Earthwork—Center for Rural Studies, 1499 Potrero Avenue, San Francisco, CA 94110. Bibliography available of educational material they distribute.

8. Economic Development Bureau, 234 Colony Road, New Haven, CN 06511. An alternative consulting service putting people with technical skills in touch with progressive Third World groups.

9. Food Action Center, 1028 Connecticut Avenue, N.W., Washington, DC 20036. Publication: *Food Action Exchange*.

10. Institute for Food and Development Policy, Box 57, Hastings-on-Hudson, NY 10706. Publication: *Food Monitor* (see coupon at end of book).

11. Institute for Local Self-Reliance, 1717 18th Street, N.W., Washington, DC 20009. Publication: *Self-Reliance*.

12. Interfaith Center for Corporate Responsibility, 475 Riverside Drive, Room 566, New York, NY 10027. Film: *Bottle Babies* (See Chapter VIII, Question 5).

13. National Catholic Rural Life Conference, 3801 Grand Avenue, Des Moines, IO 50312. Publication: *Catholic Rural Life*.

14. National Land for People, 1759 Fulton, Fresno, CA 93701. Publications: *People, Land, Food* (monthly); *Who Owns the Land* (monograph).

15. North American Congress on Latin America (NACLA), Box 57, Cathedral Station, New York, NY 10025 or P.O. Box 226, Berkeley, CA 94701. Publication: *Latin America and Empire Report*.

16. Oxfam America, P.O. Box 288, Boston, MA 02116. Sponsors self-help projects domestically and in the Third World.

17. World Hunger Year (WHY), P.O. Box 1975, Garden City, Long Island, NY 11530. Publication (with the Institute for Food and Development Policy): *Food Monitor*.

Other Important Publications

1. *Action for Development,* FAO, 00100 Rome, Italy.

2. *AgBiz Tiller,* c/o Al Krebs, San Francisco Study Center, P.O. Box 5646, San Francisco, CA 94101.

3. *Asian Action,* Newsletter of the Asican Cultural Forum on Development, Room 201; 399/1 Soi Siri, off Silom Road, Bangkok-5, Thailand.

4. *Ceres,* FAO Review on Development, UNIPUB, 650 First Avenue, P.O. Box 433, Murray Hill Station, New York, NY 10016.

5. *Food Monitor.* (That's us—see coupon at end of book.)

6. *International Bulletin,* P.O. Box 4400, Berkeley, CA 94704.

7. *Latin America* and *Latin America Economic Report,* Latin American Newsletters Ltd., 90-93 Cowcross Street, London EC1M 6BL, England.

8. *The New Internationalist,* published in England but subscribe through the New World Coalition, Room 209, 409 Boylston Street, Boston, MA 02116.

Part II

Bringing Protein
Theory Down to Earth

Brazil nuts, Pistachios, Pine nuts

Having read of the enormous food resources we will willingly squander in the production of meat, you might easily conclude that meat—and meat in large quantities—must be indispensable to human well-being and endowed with qualities unmatched by other foods. This isn't the case, as I hope to demonstrate in this chapter. Hopefully this discussion will be useful to anyone wishing to rely more on plant protein and less on meat protein for *any* reason—be it ecological, ethical, financial, medical, or political.

A. Protein Mythology

Many popular misconceptions have evolved about the body's need for protein and where to get it. Here I have contrasted what in fact are myths about protein with real nutritional fact. These eight myths-versus-facts capsulize the information in this section, Part II. Those of you who want to understand fully the fundamentals of protein nutrition will want to read all of Part II. But if you prefer to get right down to the application, go directly from "Protein Mythology" to Parts III and IV, which tell you where to get protein and then lead you right into the kitchen!

PROTEIN MYTHOLOGY*

Myths	*Facts†*
1. Meat contains more protein than any other food.	1. Containing about 25 percent protein, meat ranks about in the middle of the protein quantity scale, along with some nuts, cheese, beans, and fish. (Check the "Quantity" side of Chart 8, "The Food/Protein Continuum.")
2. Eating lots of meat is the only way to get enough protein.	2. The "average" American actually eats almost twice the protein that one's body can use. Thus most Americans could *completely eliminate* meat, fish, and poultry from their diets and still get (53–58 grams) their recommended daily allowance of protein from all the other protein-rich foods in our national diet.
3. Meat is the sole source for certain essential vitamins and minerals.	3. Except for Vitamin B_{12} non-meat sources provide more than half of our intake of each of the 11 vitamins and minerals most commonly cited. And meat is not the sole source of Vitamin B_{12}—it is found in all dairy products.
4. Meat has the highest quality protein of any food.	4. The word "quality" is an unscientific term. What it really means is usability: how much of the protein eaten is actually used by the body. The usability of egg and milk protein is

* Originally appeared in Harper's Magazine, February, 1975.
† Sources for the "Facts" are made clear in footnotes throughout the remainder of Part II.

greater than that of meat. (Check the "Usability" side of "The Food/Protein Continuum.")

5. Because plant protein is missing certain essential amino acids it can never equal the quality of meat protein.

5. All plant foods commonly eaten as sources of protein contain *all* eight essential amino acids. Plant proteins do have deficiencies in their amino acid patterns that make them generally less usable by the body than animal protein (see the "Usability" side of "The Food/Protein Continuum"). However, these deficiencies can be matched with amino acid strengths in other foods to produce protein usability equivalent or superior to meat protein. This effect is called "protein complementarity."

6. Plant-centered diets are dull.

6. Just compare! There are basically five different kinds of meat and poultry, but 40–50 different kinds of commonly eaten vegetables, 24 different kinds of peas, beans, and lentils, 20 different fruits, 12 different nuts, and nine grains. The variety of flavor, of texture and of color lies obviously in the plant world . . . though your average American restaurant would give you no clue to this fact.

7. Plant foods contain a lot of carbohydrates and are, therefore,

7. Plant foods do contain carbohydrates but they generally don't have the fat that meat does. So, ounce to ounce, most plant food

more fattening than meat.	has either about the same calories (bread is an example) or considerably fewer calories than most meat. Many fruits have one-third the calories, cooked beans have one-half, and many green vegetables have one-eighth the calories that meat contains.
8. Our meat-centered cuisine provides us with a more nutritious diet overall than that eaten in the poor world.	8. In fact, the dramatic contrast between our diet and that of the "average" Indian is not in our higher protein consumption but in our intake of sugar and fat. While we take in only 50 percent more protein, we consume eight times the fat and four times the sugar. Far from being undermined by a higher consumption of plant food, our diet might actually be improved!

B. Who Needs Protein Anyway?

Why can't people get by on a diet consisting solely of fats and carbohydrates? In the first place, while carbohydrates, fats, and protein all provide carbon, hydrogen, and oxygen, *only protein* contains nitrogen, sulfur, and phosphorus—substances which are essential to life. Even in purely quantitative terms protein's presence is quite impressive. We are 18–20 percent protein by weight! Just as cellulose provides the structural framework of a tree, protein provides the framework for animals. Skin, hair, nails, cartilage, tendons, muscles, and even the organic framework of bones are made up largely of fibrous proteins. Obviously, then, protein is needed for growth in children. But it is also needed by adults to replace tissues that are continually breaking down and to build tissues, like hair and nails, that are continually growing.

Furthermore, the body depends on protein for the myriad reactions that we group under the heading "metabolism." As regulators of metabolic processes, we call certain proteins like insulin "hormones," and as catalysts of important metabolic reactions we call other proteins "enzymes." In addition, hemoglobin, the critical oxygen-carrying molecule of the blood, is built from protein.

Not only is protein necessary to the basic chemical reactions of life, it is also necessary to maintain the body environment so that these reactions can take place. Protein in the blood helps to prevent the accumulation of either too much base or too much acid. In this way it helps maintain "body neutrality," essential to normal cellular metabolism. Similarly, protein in blood serum participates in regulating the body's water balance: the distribution of fluids on either side of the cell membrane. (The distended stomachs of starving children are the result of protein deficiency, a state which allows fluid to accumulate in the interstitial spaces between the cells.)

Lastly, and of great importance, new protein synthesis is needed for antibody formation to fight bacterial and viral infections.

Not only do we need protein for all of these vital body processes but we need to renew our body's supply every day. Whereas it takes from a few days to seven years to deplete the body's reserves of other required nutrients, amino acid reserves are depleted in a few hours.

So we need protein, but two basic questions still face us: how much and what kind? Since the answer to the question "How much?" depends, in part, on "What kind?" I'll first explore the criteria by which we can distinguish among dietary proteins.

C. Quality Makes the Product

If all proteins were the same, there would be no controversy about preferable protein sources for humans—only quantity would matter. But proteins are not identical. The proteins our bodies use are made up of 22 amino acids, in varying combinations. Eight of these amino acids cannot be synthesized by our bodies; they must be obtained from outside sources. These eight essential amino acids (which I will refer to as "EAAs") are *tryptophan, leucine, isoleucine, lysine, valine, threonine,* the *sulfur-containing amino acids,* and the *aromatic amino acids.*

To make matters more difficult, our bodies need each of the EAAs *simultaneously* in order to carry out protein synthesis. If one EAA is missing, even temporarily, protein synthesis will fall to a very low level or stop altogether. And to complicate things further, we need the EAAs in differing amounts. Basically, the body can use only *one* pattern of the EAAs; that is, each EAA must be present in a *given proportion.* In most food proteins all of the EAAs are present, but unfortunately one or more of the EAAs is usually present in a disproportionately small amount, thus deviating from the one utilizable pattern.* These EAAs are quite rightfully called the "limiting amino acids" in a food protein.

Let us put together these three critical factors about protein:

Of the 22 necessary amino acids, there are eight that our bodies cannot make but must get from outside sources.

All of these eight must be present simultaneously.

---

* We are probably better able to utilize deficient amino acids than previously thought, since mechanisms may operate in the gut to redress the natural imbalance of amino acids in foodstuffs. (Cf. E. S. Nassett, "Amino Acid Homeostasis in the Gut Lumen and Its Nutritional Significance," *World Review of Nutrition and Dietetics,* Vol. 14, 1972, pp. 134–53.)

All of these eight must be present in the right proportions.

What does this mean to the body? A great deal. If you eat protein containing enough tryptophan to satisfy 100 percent of the utilizable pattern's requirement, 100 percent of the leucine level, and so forth, but only 50 percent of the necessary lysine, then as far as your body is concerned you might as well have eaten only 50 percent of *all* the EAAs. Only 50 percent of the protein you ate is used *as* protein and the rest is literally wasted. The protein "assembling center" in the body cells uses the EAAs at the level of the "limiting amino acid" and releases the leftover amino acids to be used by the body as fuel as if they were lowly carbohydrates.[1] Chart 5 gives you a graphic illustration of what this means.

One reflection of how closely the amino acid pattern

CHART 5
THE PROBLEM OF A "LIMITING AMINO ACID"

If even *one* essential
amino acid is partially missing . . .

the result is that *all* amino acids
are reduced in the same proportion.

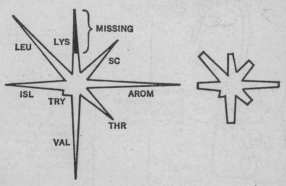

This amount of protein
in the food . . . . becomes . . . this amount of protein for
your body to use.

of a given food matches that which the body can use is what nutritionists term the biological value of a food protein. Roughly, the "biological value" is the proportion of the protein absorbed by the digestive tract that is retained by the body. In other words, the biological value is the percentage of absorbed protein that your body actually uses. But there's another question: how much gets absorbed *to begin with* by the digestive tract? That's what we call "digestibility." So the protein available to our bodies depends on its biological value *and* its digestibility. The term covering both of these factors is Net Protein Utilization or NPU.[2] Quite simply, NPU tells us how much of the protein we eat is actually available to our body (see Chart 6).

NPU is a key concept used throughout the remainder of the book, so it is important to become completely comfortable with the term. Let's take another look at

CHART 6
WHAT IS "N P U"?

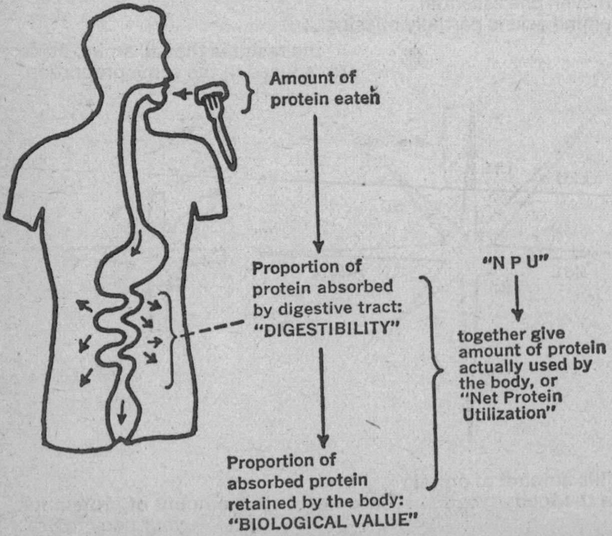

Amount of protein eaten

Proportion of protein absorbed by digestive tract: "DIGESTIBILITY"

Proportion of absorbed protein retained by the body: "BIOLOGICAL VALUE"

"N P U"

together give amount of protein actually used by the body, or "Net Protein Utilization" what determines the NPU of a given food protein. The NPU of a food is largely determined by how closely the essential amino acids in its protein match the body's one utilizable pattern. Because the protein of egg most nearly matches this ideal pattern, egg protein is used as a model for measuring the amino acid patterns in other food. Let's take an example. A glance at Chart 7 will tell you that the amino acid pattern of cheese nearly matches egg's pattern while that of peanut fails utterly. You can guess then that the NPU of cheese is significantly higher than that of peanuts. The difference is great—70 as compared to about 40.

Prepared with an understanding of the important differences among food proteins, let's now turn to the second basic question:

D. How Much Is Enough?

Some Americans brought up on the notion that one can never get too much protein decided, as young adults in the late 1960's and early 1970's, that they did not need even a minimum daily protein intake. The danger of such an overreaction was illustrated by an article in the *Berkeley Tribe* in 1970:

> Several cases of *kwashiorkor* (severe protein malnutrition), a disease native to North Africa [*sic*], have been found in Berkeley.
> An unpublished UC [University of California] hospital report blames certain fasting, vegetarian, and especially macrobiotic diets for this. Those diets often result in clinically protein-deficient people.
> Other ailments caused by protein-deficient diets are wound infections and poor healing ability.

This report, coming as I was preparing to write this book, spurred me to complete it, underscoring as it does the necessity of knowing the facts of protein nutrition before experimenting with a new diet.

CHART 7

Amino Acid Pattern of Egg Protein (Solid Lines) as Compared to Patterns of:

PEANUT (dotted lines)

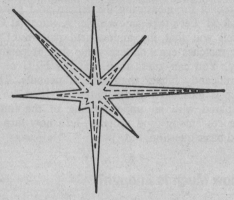

CHEESE (dotted lines)

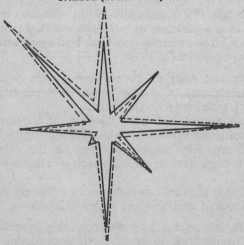

Source: *Amino Acid Content of Foods and Biological Data on Proteins,* Food and Agricultural Organization of the U.N., Rome, 1970.

So far we have talked about the two extremes: over-consumption and protein deficiency. But just how much protein is *enough?* We can arrive at a satisfactory answer, although not an absolutely definitive one, since the experts disagree somewhat. Determination of the proper protein allowance for a population involves three separate considerations: (1) minimum need; (2) an allowance for individual differences; and (3) an adjustment for protein quality. Fortunately, disagreement among nutritionists is limited to only the first consideration, the body's *minimum* need for protein. And even here the range of differences is small enough to make an average meaningful.

1. Minimum Need

Since nitrogen is a characteristic and relatively constant component of protein, scientists can measure protein by measuring nitrogen. To determine how much protein the body needs, experimenters first put subjects on a protein-free diet. They then measure how much nitrogen is lost in urine and feces. They add to this an amount to cover the small losses through the skin, sweat, and internal body structure. And, for children, additional nitrogen for growth is added. *The total of*

Mung bean sprouts, Rice, Fish, Shrimp, Snow peas

these nitrogen losses is the amount you have to replace by eating protein, and is, therefore, the basis of the minimum protein requirement for body maintenance.

Since the major expert bodies arrive at somewhat different conclusions using this "factorial" method, no established minimum now exists to guide us. Consequently, in 1971, I chose as a base line the average of the values proposed by three major expert groups: the Food and Nutrition Board of the [U.S.] National Academy of Sciences,[1] the Canadian Board of Nutrition,[2] and the Food and Agriculture Organization of the U.N..[3] (I selected these particular groups because they are representative of the range of opinion among the many national bodies with protein standards.) The resulting recommended level of minimum intake was .47 gram per kilogram of body weight per day, or .213 gram per pound. Recently I was pleased to learn that in the 1974 revision of its recommended allowance the Food and Nutrition Board had lowered its requirement to .47 gram/kilogram[4]—the same level I had recommended in 1971.

2. Allowance for Individual Differences and the Effects of Stress

An allowance must also be made for individual differences and nitrogen losses due to the ordinary stresses of daily life, such as minor infections, trauma, pain, anxiety, and loss of sleep. Fortunately most experts agree that a 30 percent allowance will cover these factors for 98 percent of a population. Adding an allowance of 30 percent to our minimum requirement of .213 gram gives us an allowance of .277 gram or *.28 gram per pound of body weight per day*. Remember that .28 applies to a healthy adult. It does not apply to pregnant women, nursing mothers, or growing children or adolescents. Allowances for them will be presented later.

Although the allowance of .28 gram per pound of

body weight is supposed to cover the healthy adult for the "ordinary stresses of daily life," Dr. Nevin Scrimshaw, leading protein nutritionist at the Massachusetts Institute of Technology, believes that we should pay added attention to our increased protein need under conditions of more severe body stress.[5] The following stress conditions are those mentioned in a recent World Health Organization report:[6] (1) *heat:* the unacclimatized individual can lose additional nitrogen in heavy sweating; (2) *heavy work:* athletes and others who are increasing their muscle mass need some additional protein, although the amount needed is not likely to be large (some studies, though not widely substantiated, recommend an additional 25 percent intake over the totals recommended here, if one is doing very heavy physical work); (3) *inadequate energy intake:* all protein requirements are valid only when energy need is being met—when energy intake is inadequate, some dietary protein is used for energy and thus not available to meet protein needs; (4) *infection:* infections, especially acute ones, cause some depletion of body nitrogen related to increased urinary excretion and poor intestinal absorption, as with diarrhea, and these losses need to be replaced with additional protein during recovery.

3. Adjustment for Protein Quality

Finally, we must take into consideration the *kind* of protein eaten. Here is where we can apply our understanding of protein quality. Recall that the basic distinction among food proteins is how completely your body can use them. Because your body cannot use low-quality protein as completely, it stands to reason that you must eat *more* of a low-quality protein than a high-quality protein to fill a daily protein allowance.

a. Allowance Based on Total Protein: But the protein allowance we have discussed so far holds only for the highest-quality protein, one that would be used *completely* by the body. Since the total grams of protein eaten are *never* fully usable by the body, the task for nutritionists is to set appropriate protein allowances for different population groups, depending on the average usability of the protein (NPU) characteristics of that national diet. That is, the grams of *total* protein recommended must be increased to take into account the fact that not all the protein consumed can be used by the body. The formula for arriving at this allowance for grams of total protein is quite simple:

Protein allowance if eating fully usable protein (.28 gram per pound of body weight)	×	$\dfrac{100}{\text{Net Protein Utilization characteristic of the national diet}}$	=	Grams of total protein recomended for that population (per person/per pound body weight/per day)

Using this formula, it is easy to determine allowance for total protein suitable for different types of national diets—diets of high-quality protein needing fewer grams of total protein and diets of lower-quality protein needing more grams. For example, 75 is an accepted average value of protein quality (NPU) of a diet based largely on animal protein (meat, eggs, milk), so we insert 75 into our formula: .28 gram × 100/75 = .37 gram. The result is an allowance of .37 gram of total protein per pound of body weight per day. For example, since the average American woman weighs 128 pounds and the average American male weighs 154 pounds—and consume largely animal protein—their daily allowance is .37 × 128 and .37 × 154, or approximately 47 grams and 57 grams of protein respectively. Other estimates, such as that of the National Academy of Science, are essentially the same (e.g., 46 grams for women).

Consider now a diet based largely on plant protein. Since a typical NPU for the quality of plant protein is

55, a higher total protein allowance is called for. Inserting 55 into our formula, the result is .51 gram of total protein per pound of body weight per day: .28 gram × 100/55 = .51 gram. Thus the recommended allowance for a 128-pound person in a population on a largely plant protein diet is 65 grams of total protein, or .51 × 128 pounds. (Notice that .51 is close to one-half the body weight; thus you can quickly estimate the grams of total protein needed for a person on a largely plant-protein diet by dividing the body weight in half and expressing the answer in grams.)

b. Allowance Based on Usable Protein: But in this book, where each food is listed individually, we can go one step further than generalizations about the protein quality in the diet of a whole population or an individual. In fact, there is no need to generalize and to obscure the wide differences in protein usability of a mixed animal- and plant-protein diet. In such a diet only one-third of the protein from some sources is usable by your body, while practically *all* the protein from other sources is usable. In the protein tables contained in Part III, I have accounted for these differences by simply *adjusting the protein in each food to the level that is fully usable by the body.* Since *each food* is adjusted for protein usability, there is no need to apply the earlier formula based on an *average* level of protein usability. So, instead of talking about grams of total protein (only part of which the body can use), I will be talking about grams of *usable protein.* Recall that the recommended daily protein allowance based on usable protein is .28 gram per pound of body weight, or 35.8 grams of usable protein a day for a person weighing 128 pounds and 43.1 grams for a person weighing 154 pounds.

This makes much more sense, and will become even clearer to you in Part III, where I explain how to use the protein food tables. But before reading on, I am sure you would like to have some idea of what the recommended intake of usable protein means in terms of the food you eat. Here are some comparisons, based on the hypothetical assumption that you would be getting all of your day's protein from one source:

TABLE III.
RECOMMENDED DAILY PROTEIN INTAKE

If you weigh:	to meet a day's allowance of usable protein:	YOU NEED: meat	fish	milk	eggs	dry beans	nuts
128 lb	35.8 g	7⅓ oz	8⅓ oz	5 cups	6	12¾ oz	12 oz
154 lb	43.1 g	9 oz	10 oz	6 cups	7	15⅓ oz	14⅓ oz

E. Protein Individuality

Before going on, a word of caution about putting too much stock in any figures purporting to deal with the "average" human being. R. J. Williams, a nutritionist who has devoted himself to the study of individual nutritional differences, illustrates dramatically the range of our "protein individuality." He points out that if beef were the only source of protein, one person's minimum protein needs could be met by two ounces of meat; yet another individual might require eight ounces.[1] Although over 98 percent of a population may not range more than 30 percent from an average requirement, these two possible extremes represent a *fourfold* difference in protein requirement! And requirements for other nutrients are found to be equally, or even more widely, disparate.

Even more surprising, perhaps, is the fact that the need for protein can vary within the individual. Certain physical stress (pain, for example) or psychological stress (even from exam pressure) can cause one's protein requirement to jump by as much as one-third over ordinary needs.[2]

The obvious conclusion is this: *the fact that your*

friend is thriving beautifully on a low-protein diet tells you nothing about a diet suited to your own body's needs. The best answer is to develop what Dr. Williams calls "body wisdom," which involves more than just being aware of how you feel—that is, your energy level, general health, and temperament. Certain nutritional deficiencies have been shown to affect negatively one's appetite and choice of foods; so just feeling "satisfied" is not enough. Part of "body wisdom" involves being a wise observer of your body's *condition*. Because nails, hair, and skin require newly synthesized protein for growth and health, their condition is usually a good indication of whether or not you are getting enough protein. Similarily, notice whether or not abrasions heal quickly. If they don't, you may be seriously lacking protein in your diet.

Now that we can estimate the amount of protein that human beings must have (and understand how, in part, it depends on the type of protein eaten), we're ready to consider the really practical question: what are the best protein sources and how can we make best use of them? Since there is a great deal of "mythology" surrounding protein sources, let's first get our thinking straight about the useful distinctions to be made among them.

F. Is Meat Necessary?

Those who insist on the superiority, in fact indispensability, of meat as a protein source base their argument on both the large quantity and the high quality of protein in meat. Plant protein is seen as inferior on both counts. The result is that animal and vegetable protein are thought of as comprising two separate categories. In fact, this is a common mistake in our thinking about protein. For our nutritional concern here, it is much more useful and accurate to visualize animal and vegetable protein as being on one continuum.

CHART 8
THE FOOD PROTEIN CONTINUUM

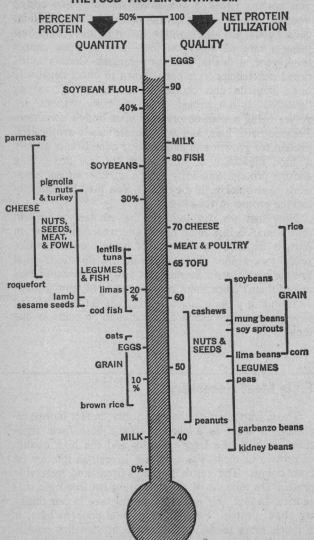

Chart 8, "The Food/Protein Continuum," will help you see the range of protein variability on two scales: protein quantity, based on the percent of protein in the food by weight; and usability, based on the NPU of the protein.

Quantity: When judging protein with quantity as the criterion, generalization is difficult. However, it is clear that plants rank highest, particularly in their processed forms. Soybean flour is over 40 percent protein. Next come certain cheeses, such as Parmesan, which is 36 percent protein. Meat follows, ranging between 20 and 30 percent. Dried beans, peas, and lentils are essentially in the same category; that is, between 20 and 25 percent protein. At the bottom end of the quantity scale we find examples of both animal and plant protein. We find grains here and, though it might surprise you, milk and eggs also. There are, of course, other plants—some fruits, for example—that contain too little protein to even appear on the scale. (We are concerned here only with plants that are widely used as sources of protein.)

Usability: The protein usability scale generally ranges from NPU values of about 40 to 94.[1] Clearly, animal protein occupies the highest rungs of this scale. Meat, however, is not at the top. It places slightly above the middle, with an average NPU of 67. At the top are eggs (NPU of 94) and milk (NPU of 82). The NPUs of plant proteins generally range lower on the continuum, between 40 and 70. However, protein in some plants, such as soybeans and whole rice, approach or overlap the NPU values for meat. But the general distribution of animal protein high on the NPU scale and plant protein lower on this scale tells us that the proportions of essential amino acids found in most animal protein more nearly match human body requirements than the proportions commonly found in plants. This means that in general you need to eat proportionately less animal protein than plant protein to be "covered" for the essential amino acid requirements.

But people don't have to depend on meat for protein and the correct supply of amino acids. There are several other alternatives:

(1) Eat large amounts of lower-quality plant protein, enough so that you will get an adequate amount of even the "limiting amino acids."

(2) Eat alternate animal-protein sources, such as dairy products.

(3) Eat a variety of plant proteins which have mutually complementary amino acid patterns.

When eating plant protein from a single plant source (such as beans or rice), you're likely to be limited in the amount of protein your body can utilize, because of a "limiting amino acid" (for beans the "limiting amino acids" are the sulfur-containing amino acids and for rice they are isoleucine and lysine). Consequently, a major drawback of the first alternative is that you would have to eat (and *waste!*) relatively enormous quantities of your protein source in order to ensure your daily protein requirement.

The advantage of the second choice is that dairy products have highly usable protein, in fact better values for protein utilization (NPU) than meat. But by itself, of course, this alternative is gastronomically dull; and moreover, since protein conversion even by dairy cattle entails some waste of protein, why rely on this alternative more than you have to?

The third alternative means eating daily (for practicality, in the *same meal*) different plant foods in which the amino acid deficiency of one item is supplemented by the amino acid contained in others. (Remember that the EAAs must be present simultaneously.) This diet is more efficient than the first alternative because the complementary effect of the mixture means that more of the protein *can be used* by the body (less is lost and converted to fuel). And it is more efficient than the second choice because it takes optimal advantage of more abundant plant protein.

G. Complementing Your Proteins

Obviously the best solution is to use both the second and third alternatives. This means combining different plant sources, or non-meat animal-protein sources with plant sources, in the *same meal*. Most people do this to some extent anyway, just as a matter of course. Eating a mixture of protein sources can increase the protein value of the meal; here's a case where *the whole is greater than the sum of its parts*. To repeat, this is true because the EAA deficiency in one food can be met by the EAA contained in another food. For example, the expected biological value of three parts white bread and one part cheddar cheese would be 64 if there were no complementary relationship. Yet, if eaten together, their actual biological value is 76![1] The "whole" is greater largely because cheese fills bread's lysine and isoleucine deficiencies. Such protein mixes *do not result in a perfect protein* that is fully utilizable by the body (remember that only egg is near perfect), but combinations can increase the protein quality as much as 50 percent above the average of the items eaten separately.

Eating wheat and beans together, for example, can increase by about 33 percent the protein actually usable by your body. Chart 9 will help you see why. It shows the four essential amino acids most likely to be deficient in plant protein. On each side, where beans and wheat are shown separately, we see large gaps in amino acid content as compared to egg protein. But if we put the two together, these gaps are closed.

To exploit this complementary effect, you can make dishes and plan meals so that the protein in one food fills the amino acid deficiencies in another food. A bit laborious, you say? It's not as hard as it sounds! And to prove it, I have included many recipes to guide (and tempt) you. But the real fun for you might be "inventing" your own complementary protein combinations.

CHART 9

DEMONSTRATING PROTEIN COMPLEMENTARITY

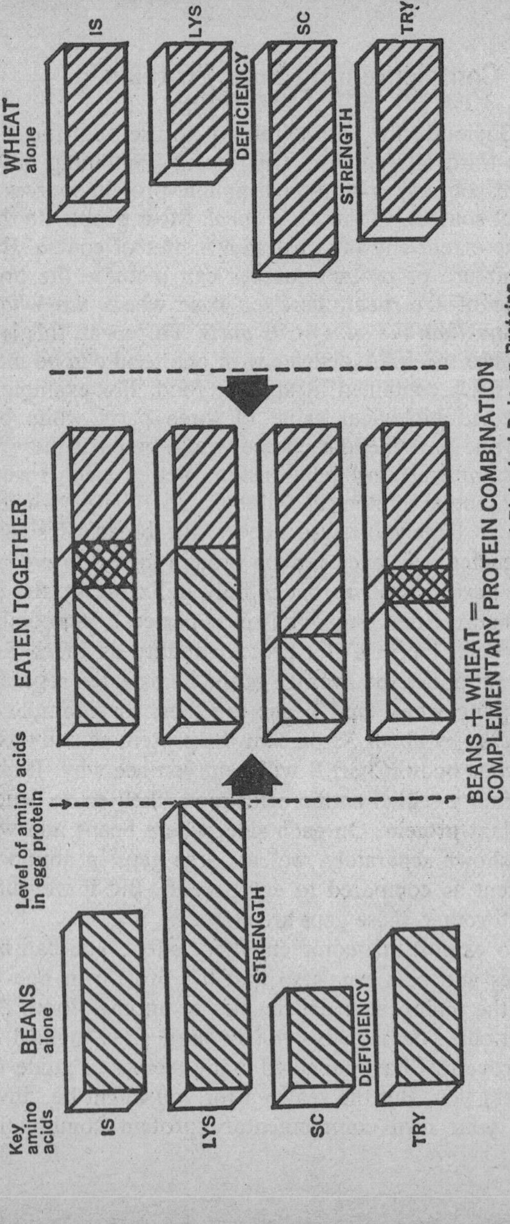

BEANS alone   EATEN TOGETHER   WHEAT alone

Level of amino acids in egg protein

Key amino acids

IS   LYS   SC   TRY

STRENGTH   DEFICIENCY

BEANS + WHEAT = COMPLEMENTARY PROTEIN COMBINATION

Source: Amino Acid Content of Foods and Biological Data on Proteins, Food and Agricultural Organization of the U.N., Rome, 1970.

H. Protein Isn't Everything

Many people who might otherwise rely more on plant sources for protein continue to eat great quantities of meat because they believe that only "good red meat" can supply the many vitamins and minerals that their bodies need. Are they right?

Actually, with the one exception of Vitamin B_{12}, non-meat sources* provide more than half of our intake of each of the 11 most frequently cited vitamins and minerals. And for the one exception, Vitamin B_{12}, meat is not the sole source; it is also found in all dairy products and in certain species of algae. Non-meat foods supply: (1) over 90 percent of our Vitamin C, and calcium; (2) 86 percent of our magnesium; (3) between 68 and 76 percent of our iron, riboflavin, thiamin, Vitamin A, and phosphorus; (4) almost 30 percent of our Vitamin B_{12}.[1]

Other important nutrients not covered in most nutrient breakdowns include potassium and magnesium. Although meat is a good source for potassium, there are non-meat sources that are even better. Meat contains from 290 to 390 milligrams (mg.) of potassium per 100 grams, but a baked potato has 503 milligrams and lima beans 422 milligrams. In the case of magnesium, meat is actually among the poorer sources. Rich sources include: cocoa, nuts, soybeans, whole grains, and green leafy vegetables.[2]

Since non-meat foods provide most of our intake of important vitamins and minerals—even in the typical American diet, in which they play "second fiddle" to meat—we can safely conclude that replacing some or all of our meat intake with plant and dairy products would not endanger but would enhance our intake of

---

* Nonmeat sources include all dairy and plant foods. Meat sources include meat, poultry, and fish.

these nutrients. All this is not to belittle the nutritional value of meat. My aim is only to provide a more realistic view of the wide variety of nutritious food sources in order to replace the culturally fixed idea of the absolute supremacy of meat.

In addition to protein, vitamins, and minerals, two other dietary factors have gained considerable medical attention since my book was published. The first is cholesterol. Recent understanding of the genetic basis for the body's regulation of triglyceride and cholesterol metabolism makes it highly probable that people will differ radically in the deleterious effects of high cholesterol intake. For example, a large proportion of people who have cholesterol levels of over 200 milligrams per milliliter (and not necessarily high triglyceride) are at increased risk of developing heart disease. A small portion of those people, especially men, who have a genetic condition that makes them unable to regulate cholesterol levels and/or triglyceride metabolism, and who have family histories of heart disease, will be at substantially greater risk.[3] With these observations in mind, it is well to heed the warning of Professor Jean Mayer of Harvard University:

> Anyone who doesn't know his cholesterol or whose cholesterol is over 200 should go very easy on eggs, i.e., no more than two a week. It is also important for boys 14 on up to taper off inasmuch as adolescence is a period during which there is usually considerable damage to arteries (80% of young Americans killed in Vietnam had serious arteriosclerotic damage).[4]

The message is clear: first, have your cholesterol checked; then you will *know* how closely to watch your cholesterol intake. If you do find it is too high (or if you don't know), remember that cholesterol is only found in animal foods, so that if you are reducing your intake of animal foods and replacing it with plant food, then you will probably also be lowering your cholesterol intake. Of commonly eaten foods, it is true that eggs have by far the most cholesterol. Cheese too is often considered a cholesterol culprit—it has only about 40 percent more cholesterol than beef. The important difference is, however, that while you might easily eat eight ounces of meat, you would never eat that much cheese in one meal. As a rule of thumb, if you eliminated one pound of meat a week from your diet, you could substitute one large egg or two-thirds of a pound of cheese and still take in no more cholesterol than the beef had given you. Also note that beef has more than six times the cholesterol of whole milk. Thus, for the same cholesterol that one pound of beef was giving you, you could drink three quarts of whole milk.[5]

In the recipes given later in the book, I have tried to moderate my use of eggs. In most recipes that call for eggs, one serving would generally represent no more than one-third of an egg. (Thus you could eat six servings of such dishes each week without exceeding Dr. Mayer's guideline.) I have also given a choice in many recipes as to how many eggs to use, so that you can make your own choice depending on your cholesterol level and your family's medical history.

The second factor to which much attention has recently turned is the fiber content of the diet. The low fiber content of the highly processed American diet has been linked with increased risk of intestinal blockage, appendicitis, and cancer of the lower intestine—a major killer of males in the United States. A plant-centered diet—one rich in whole grains, legumes, fresh fruits, and vegetables, as this book recommends—would have the additional value of providing plenty of roughage apparently needed by the body.

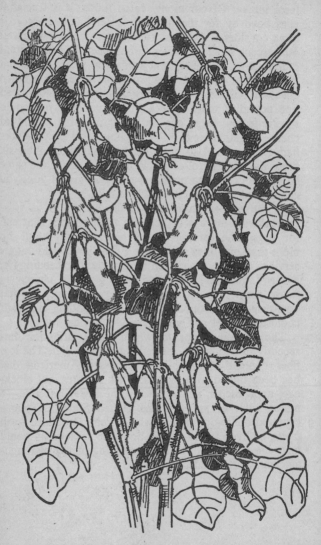

Soy beans

Part III

Eating from the Earth: Where to Get Protein Without Meat

Seafood

A. A Daily Guide

Now that you understand the body's need for protein and the importance of protein usability, this section will provide all the nutritional data on good protein sources for you to use in checking the adequacy of your own diet—old or new. The amino acid ratings in this section supply the raw material for your more complete understanding of the "whys" and "hows" of combining proteins in order to increase their usability. However, if you prefer to go directly to the meal-planning section, Part IV, you may skip these protein tables of section C for now without any loss in your ability to apply the basic principles of the book in your own kitchen.

1. The Calorie Criterion

Since most foods contain *some* protein, if you could consume an unlimited quantity of food every day, you would eventually fill your protein need! But, if you wish to get enough protein without putting on weight, a calorie guideline is necessary to define a good protein source.

My guideline is based on this formula: A man of 154 pounds should consume about 2700 calories a day and 43.1 grams of usable protein;* or 63 calories for each gram of protein. A woman of 128 pounds should

* If you would like to review the meaning of "usable" protein, turn back to Part II, sections C and D.

consume about 2000 calories a day and 35.8 grams of usable protein; or 56 calories for each gram of protein. Therefore, in order not to gain weight and still get enough protein, the calorie/protein ratio shouldn't exceed these limits; that is, an average ratio of about 60:1. In fact, some of your protein sources should be well below this ratio in order to make room in your diet for items like fruit, which provide calories and vitamins but essentially no protein.

With few exceptions, the foods in the protein tables observe the 60:1 ratio of calories to protein. Potato chips, for example, are 5 percent protein; but they were excluded because they have a ratio of about 179 calories per gram of usable protein. Similarly. English walnuts (about 88:1) and pecans (about 149:1) are not listed.

2. The Unprocessed Criterion

Only unprocessed or "less-processed" foods (such as whole wheat flour as opposed to white flour) are included in the tables because they are generally higher in protein and other nutrients. (See the Appendices F, G, and H for comparisons of whole wheat flour with white flour, brown with white rice, and a variety of sugar sources.)

3. The Protein Content Criterion

Finally, even though many more vegetables probably meet the caloric criterion, they were excluded if an *average* serving provides less than two grams of total protein.

B. How to Use the Tables

1. Your Protein Intake: The Right Amount?

The first two columns in the protein tables tell you what percent of your daily protein need is met by an average serving of a given food. The items are ranked in *decreasing* order according to the percent of their contribution to your daily protein requirement, both within each food category and by food category.* *To fulfill your protein allowance, these percentages must add up to 100 percent each day.*

These percentages reflect the recommended protein allowance of .28 gram of *usable* protein per pound of body weight. (Recall that this allowance includes a 30 percent increase above the minimum requirements to take individual differences into account.) The last three columns of the tables show you the basis on which I arrived at these percentages: the *total* grams of protein have been reduced by the NPU score[1] of the food in order to arrive at the grams of protein *your body can use*. This amount of usable protein I then divided by the daily protein allowance to get the percent of the daily protein allowance that an average serving fills. Simple enough.

To remind you of the importance of adjusting for protein usability, let me give you a graphic example. If, for instance, we considered that eating one-half ounce of egg protein was the same as eating one-half ounce of peanut protein, we would be greatly mistaken. The amino acid pattern of the egg protein (NPU of 94) is one that the body can use almost completely; but the body can only use half of the peanut protein (NPU of 43), because its amino acids deviate considerably from the body's one utilizable pattern. So if you eat one-half

---

* Except for meat and poultry, placed last, because they are primarily included for the sake of comparison with non-meat protein sources.

ounce each of egg and peanut protein, you get twice as much protein from the egg as from the peanut. The percentages shown in the charts have been calculated to correct for these differences in the availability of protein to your body.

The only difficulty in adjusting for differences in protein usability is that research to determine the NPU scores of food proteins is still rudimentary. Many plant foods have not been tested, and the NPU scores that we do "know" are often based on a limited number of experiments. We can hope that this research will progress. In the meantime, even with rough estimates of protein quality, we are on better ground than if our calculations were based on *total* protein, knowing full well that 5 to 70 percent of this total is not usable by the body.

The percentages in the first two columns apply to the average American adult—a 154-pound male and a 128-pound female. If you are not quite so average, use the following guideline for determining the appropriate protein intake for your body weight:

TABLE IV.
ARE YOU GETTING THE RIGHT AMOUNT OF PROTEIN FOR YOUR BODY?

In the following
Protein Tables (section C) . . .

	Male Adult		Female Adult	
if you weigh:	the %'s should add up to:	the %'s should add up to:	Total %'s if pregnant:	Total %'s if nursing mother:
108		85	145	125
118	75	90	155	130
128	85	100	165	140
138	90	110	170	145
148	95	115	180	155
154	100	120	185	160
164	105	130	190	165
174	115	135	200	175
184	120	—	—	—
194	125	—	—	—

For ages 15 to 18, add 10 to the percentage total given for your weight in Table IV above.

For children (either sex), use the second column on each protein table in section C. If a child, aged 1–3, with an approximate weight of 28 pounds, is getting enough protein, the percentages should add up to 50 percent for the day. For ages 4–6, weight approximately 44 pounds, percentages should add up to 65 percent. And for ages 7–10, weight approximately 66 pounds, percentages should add up to 78 percent.

Add up your protein intake for a few days to see whether or not you are meeting your protein allowance. If you're not, use the tables to figure out ways to increase your intake and let it become a habit!

2. Mixing Your Own Proteins

Next to the percentages in the tables are letter ratings which allow you to make up your own complementary protein combinations. The letter ratings indicate how well each type of food supplies you with a key amino acid. (Of the eight essential amino acids, only the four likely to be deficient in a diet of non-meat protein are shown here.) Since egg protein is considered to be the most nearly perfect protein, the ratings are based on how closely the particular amino acid content of a food matches the amount of that amino acid found in egg protein.* Thus:

Letter Ratings: Percent of Egg Amino Acid Content

A + $\geq$ 100	C = 40–60
A = 80–100	D = 20–40
B = 60–80	E = 1–20

---

* The amino acid content of egg protein used by scientists as the model is that established by the U.N. Expert Group, reported in *Protein Requirements* (WHO, FAO), 1965.

Using the protein tables of section C, you can match the deficiencies in some foods (C and D ratings) with adequacies (A and B ratings) in other foods in order to achieve higher biological values than those of the same foods eaten separately. Discovering the patterns of amino acid strengths and weaknesses in the different food groups will enable you to do your own "protein matching." To help you I provide two guides:

(1) For foods having no serious amino acid deficiencies, such as seafood (Protein Table I), dairy products (Protein Table II), and meat and poultry (Protein Table IX), I have emphasized their particular strengths by putting their **A+** ratings in boldface. These foods need no supplementation from other foods but make excellent supplements themselves.

(2) All the other protein tables have foods with serious amino acid deficiencies. The one or two most important weaknesses of each food are indicated by boxed letters. Compensation for these deficiencies can come either from the foods in category (1) above or from other foods having an *opposite* pattern of amino acid deficiency. Rather than concentrating on the names of amino acids, it might be easier simply to note the columns in which weaknesses tend to occur.

In Part IV, section C, "It Pays to Mix Your Own," there are two illustrations to help you. One, page 153, shows in summary form how the major food groups complement each other. The other, page 154, provides the exact proportions of combinations that have been scientifically tested to improve protein usability. However, if you wish to "do it yourself" and, therefore, understand more fully the basis for making these combinations, I have provided **"Tips for complementing . . ."** following each of the nine protein tables that now follow.

C. Protein Tables and Tips for Complementing Protein

Protein Table I. SEAFOOD

Average Serving of Seafood, 3½ oz (100 g), in Decreasing Order of Usable Protein	Percent of Daily Protein Allowance in an Average Serving		Ratings of Amino Acid Content as Compared to Egg Protein				Total Grams of Protein	NPU	Grams of Protein Your Body Can Use[2]
	M	F.	Tryp.	Iso.	Lys.	SC.[1]			
					STRENGTH				
1. Tuna,* canned in oil, drained, ⅝ cup	44%	53%	B	B	A+	B	24	(80)	19
2. Mackerel, Pacific	41	50	B	B	A+	B	22	(80)	18
3. Halibut	39	47	B	B	A+	C	21	(80)	17
4. Humpback salmon	37	45	B	B	A+	B[3]	20	(80)	16
5. Swordfish[3]	35	42	B	B	A+	B[3]	19	(80)	15
6. Striped bass	35	42	B	B	A+	B	19	(80)	15
7. Rockfish	35	42	B	A	A+	B	19	(80)	15
8. Shad	35	42	B	B	A+	B[4]	19	(~80)[5]	15
9. Shrimp									
10. Sardines, Atlantic, 8 med., canned in oil	32	39	B	A	A+	B	21	(69)	14
11. Carp	32	39	B	B	A+	A[3]	18	(80)	14
12. Catfish	32	39	B	B	A+	A	18	(80)	14

*Warning: large ocean-going fish like blue-fin tuna and swordfish, which are at the end of long food chains, have shown to be heavily contaminated with mercury. See page 37 for exact data.

Seafood Continued

Average Serving of Seafood, 3½ oz (100 g), in Decreasing Order of Usable Protein	Percent of Daily Protein Allowance in an Average Serving		Ratings of Amino Acid Content as Compared to Egg Protein				Total Grams of Protein	NPU	Grams of Protein Your Body Can Use²
	M	F	Tryp.	Iso.	Lys.	SC.¹			
					STRENGTH →				
13. Cod	32%	39%	B	B	A+	A	18	(80)	14
14. Pacific herring	32	39	B	A	A+	B	18	(80)	14
15. Haddock	32	39	B	B	A+	A	18	(80)	14
16. Crab	32	39	B	B	A+	B⁴	17	(~80)	14
17. Northern lobster	32	39	B	B	A+	B⁴	17	(~80)	14
18. Squid	30	36	A	B	A+	B	16	(~80)	13
19. Scallops, 2 or 3	28	34	A	B	A+	B	15	(80)	12
20. Flounder or sole	28	34	B	B	A+	C	15	(~80)	12
21. Clams, 4 large, 9 small	26	31	A	B	A+	B	14	(~80)	11
22. Oysters, 2 to 4	21	25	A	B	A+	B	11	(~80)	9

¹Amino acids: Tryp. = Tryptophan; Iso. = Isoleucine; Lys. = Lysine; SC. = Sulphur-containing amino acids. These are the four essential amino acids likely to be deficient in plant protein.
²Loss calculated from the Net Protein Utilization score (NPU). See page 68 for an explanation of NPU.
³Also slightly deficient in the aromatic amino acids, phenylalanine, and tyrosine.
⁴Also slightly deficient in valine.
⁵~ = estimated.

Tips for complementing other foods with seafood

The lysine strength (A+) of seafood means that it can complement well the protein of foods low in lysine, such as grains and certain nuts and seeds.

Protein Table II. DAIRY PRODUCTS

Average Serving of Dairy Products	Percent of Daily Protein Allowance in an Average Serving		Ratings of Amino Acid Content as Compared to Egg Protein				Total Grams of Protein	NPU	Grams of Protein Your Body Can Use
	M	F	Tryp.	Iso.	Lys.	SC.¹			
					STRENGTH				
1. Cottage cheese, 6 tbsp, 3½ oz (100 g)									
Uncreamed	30	36	B	A	A+	B	17	(~75)	13
Creamed	26	31	B	A	A+	B	14		11
2. Egg white, dried, powdered, ½ oz (14 g)	21	25	A+	B	A+	A+	11	(83)	9
3. Milk, non-fat dry solids, 4 tbsp, 1 oz (5½ tbsp inst.)	19	22	A	B	A+	B	10	(82)	8
4. Parmesan cheese, 1 inch sq, 1 oz (28 g)	16	20	B	A	A+	B	10	(~70)	7
5. Milk, skim, whole or buttermilk, 1 c (244 g)	16	20	A	A	A+	B	9	(82)	7
6. Yogurt from skim milk, 1 c (244 g)	16	20	A	A	A+	B	8	(82)	7
7. Swiss cheese, 1 inch sq, 1 oz (28 g)	14	17	B	A	A+	B	8	(~70)	6

Dairy Products Continued

Average Serving of Dairy Products	Percent of Daily Protein Allowance in an Average Serving		Ratings of Amino Acid Content as Compared to Egg Protein					Total Grams of Protein	NPU	Grams of Protein Your Body Can Use
	M	F	Tryp.	Iso.	Lys.	SC.[1]				
					STRENGTH					
8. Edam cheese, 1 inch sq, 1 oz (28 g)	14	17	B	A	A+	B	8	(~70)	6
9. Egg, 1 medium (48 g)	14	17	A	A	A+	A	6	(94)	6
10. Ricotta cheese, ¼ c (60 g)	12	14	B	A	A+	B	7	(~75)	5
11. Cheddar cheese, 1 inch sq, 1 oz (28 g)	12	14	B	A	A+	B	7	(70)	5
12. Roquefort cheese or Blue mold, 1 inch sq, 1 oz (28 g)	9	11	B	A	A+	B	6	(~70)	4
13. Camembert cheese, 1 inch sq, 1 oz (28 g)	9	11	B	A	A+	B	5	(~70)	4
14. Ice cream, about ⅙ pint (100 g)	9	11	A	A	A+	B	5	(~82)	4

The following dairy products are not good protein sources because they contain too many calories for the amount of protein you get: cream, sour cream, cream cheese, butter (no protein).

[1]See page 130 for an explanation of the selection of good protein sources based on their calorie-to-protein ratio.

Tips for using dairy products to complement the protein in other foods

1. **Amino Acid Makeup:** dairy products have excellent amino acid ratings, as you would suppose from their high NPU scores. Thus they make good supplements to any food. But dairy products have notable amino acid strengths in isoleucine, and especially in lysine. These strengths can be used to advantage in combination with cereal grains (Protein Table V), which are low in both of these same amino acids. And, it doesn't take much! Only two tablespoons of non-fat dried milk added to one cup of wheat or rye flour increases the protein quality about 45 percent. Thus, bread with cheese, cheese-rice casseroles, and cereal with milk are all good protein mixes. These same amino acid strengths allow dairy products to complement the protein of nuts and seeds (Protein Table IV): sesame, peanuts, black walnuts, etc.

2. Experimentally determined complementary protein mixes include milk products:

plus Grains, for example:
>Milk + Rice
>Milk + Wheat
>Milk + Corn + Soy
>Milk + Wheat + Peanuts

plus Nuts and seeds, for example:
>Milk + Peanuts
>Milk + Sesame

plus Legumes, for example:
>Milk + Beans

plus Potatoes:
>Milk + Potatoes

Protein Table III. LEGUMES: Dried Beans, Peas, and Lentils

Average Serving of Legumes, ¼–⅓ c dry¹ (Approx. 50 g)	Percent of Daily Protein Allowance in an Average Serving		Ratings of Amino Acid Content as Compared to Egg Protein				Total Grams of Protein	NPU	Grams of Protein Your Body Can Use
	M	F	Tryp.	Iso.	Lys.	SC.¹			
	If complemented, add 5%		DEFICIENCY →			DEFICIENCY →			
1. Soybeans or soy grits	23	28	A	B	A	[C]²	17	(61)	10
2. Mung beans	16	20	[C]	[C]	A+	[D]	12	(57)	7
3. Broad beans	14	17	[C]	B	A	[D]	13	(48)	6
4. Peas	14	17	B	A+	A+	[D]	12	(47)	6
5. Black beans	12	14	B	[C]	A	[D]	12	(42)	5
6. Cowpeas (black-eyed)	12	14	[C]	B	A+	[C]	12	(45)	5
7. Kidney beans	12	14	[C]	B	A+	[C]	11	(38)	5
8. Chick-peas (garbanzos)	12	14	[C]	B	A+	[C]	10	(43)	5
9. Lima beans	12	14	[C]	B	A+	[C]	10	(52)	5
10. Tofu (soybean curd), wet weight, 3½ oz, 2"x2"x2½"	12	14	A	B	A	[C]	8	(65)	5
11. Lentils	9	11	[C]	B	A+	[D]	13	(30)	4
12. Other common beans, navy, pea bean, white	9	11	[C]	B	A+	[D]²	11	(38)	4

¹Makes ¾–1 c when cooked. See pages 93–94 for an explanation of boxed letters.

²Also deficient in valine.

Tips for complementing the protein in legumes

1. Amino Acid Makeup: notice in Protein Table III that the major amino acid deficiencies of legumes appear in the two **outside** columns: tryptophan and the sulfur-containing amino acids. But among the nuts and seeds in Protein Table IV and among the grains in Protein Table V, deficiencies appear most frequently in the two **inside** columns: isoleucine and lysine. It is now clear why legume protein, on the one hand, and the protein in grains and certain nuts and seeds, on the other hand, complement each other. Having exactly the opposite strengths and weaknesses, in combination they become more complete proteins.

2. Experimentally determined complementary protein mixes include legumes:

plus Grains, for example:

> Legumes + Rice
> Soybeans + Rice + Wheat
> Beans + Wheat
> Soybeans + Corn + Milk
> Beans + Corn
> Soybeans + Wheat + Sesame

plus Dairy products, for example:

> Beans + Milk

plus Nuts and seeds, for example:

> Soybeans + Peanuts* + Sesame
> Soybeans + Peanuts* +
>   Wheat + Rice
> Soybeans + Sesame + Wheat

---

* Peanuts are **botanically** classified as legumes.

Protein Table IV. NUTS AND SEEDS

Average Serving of Nuts and Seeds, Approx. 1 oz (28 g)	Percent of Daily Protein Allowance in an Average Serving		Ratings of Amino Acid Content as Compared to Egg Protein				Total Grams of Protein	NPU	Grams of Protein Your Body Can Use
	M	F	Tryp.	Iso.	Lys.	SC.¹			
	If complemented, add 3–4%			DEFICIENCY →	DEFICIENCY →				
1. Pignolia nuts, 2½ tbsp	12	14	—¹	—	—	—	9	(~50)	5
2. Pumpkin and squash seeds, 2 tbsp	12	14	A	B	B	—	8	(~60)	5
	If complemented, add 2–3%								
3. Sunflower seeds, 3 tbsp, or sunflower meal, 4 tbsp	9	11	A	B	C	B	7	(58)	4
4. Peanuts, 2 tbsp	7	8	B	C	C	C²	8	(43)	3
5. Peanut butter, 2 tbsp	7	8	B	C	C	C²	8	(43)	3
6. Cashews, 12–16 nuts	7	8	A+	B	B	B	5	(58)	3
7. Sesame seeds, 3 tbsp, or sesame meal, 4 tbsp	7	8	A	C	C	A	5	(53)	3
8. Pistachio nuts, 3 tbsp	7	8	B	C	B	B²	5	(~50)	3
9. Black walnuts,³ 4 tbsp, 16–20 halves	7	8	B	C	D	B	6	(~50)	3
10. Brazil nuts, 8 medium	4	5	A+	C	C	A+	4	(50)	2

The following nuts are not good protein sources because they contain too many calories for the amount of protein you get: pecans, chestnuts, coconuts, filberts, hazelnuts, macadamia nuts, almonds, pine nuts, English walnuts.

¹Amino acid content unknown.
²Also deficient in threonine.
³Black walnuts have about 40 percent more protein than English walnuts.

Tips for complementing the protein in nuts and seeds

1. **Amino Acid Makeup:** the amino acid pattern that emerges among the nuts and seeds is one of deficiency in the two **inside** columns, isoleucine and lysine, and strength in the two **outside** columns, tryptophan and the sulfur-containing amino acids. Sesame seed strikingly exemplifies this contrast. Seeds and many nuts, therefore, make good complements of legumes, which have just the opposite pattern—as you recall from Protein Table III.

Remember also the potential of dairy products to fill the amino acid "gaps" of nuts and seeds. The strength of dairy products in the two **inside** columns, isoleucine and lysine, means they have exactly what is needed by the nuts and seeds. It is not at all surprising, then, that experimentation has resulted in the complementary combinations below.

2. Experimentally determined complementary protein mixes include nuts and seeds:

plus Legumes, for example:
> Peanuts* + Sesame + Soybeans
> Sesame + Beans
> Sesame + Soybeans + Wheat

plus Dairy products, for example:
> Peanuts + Milk

plus Other nuts or seeds, for example:
> Peanuts + Sunflower seeds

plus Grains (because grains and nuts and seeds are low in the same amino acids, their complementarity seems to depend usually on the presence of legumes or dairy products), for example:
> Peanuts + Wheat + Milk
> Sesame + Wheat + Soybeans
> Exception: Sesame + Rice

* Peanuts are **botanically** classified as legumes.

Protein Table V. GRAINS, CEREALS, AND THEIR PRODUCTS

Average Serving of Grains, Cereals, and Their Products[1]	Percent of Daily Protein Allowance in an Average Serving		Ratings of Amino Acid Content as Compared to Egg Protein				Total Grams of Protein	NPU	Grams of Protein Your Body Can Use
	M	F	Tryp.	Iso.	Lys.	SC.			
	If complemented, add 2–3%			DEFICIENCY → →					
1. Triticale	14	17	–[2]	–	–	–	10	(~60)[3]	6
2. Wheat, whole grain hard red spring, ⅓ c (55–60 g)	12	15	B	C	C	B	8	(60)	5
3. Rye, whole grain, ⅓ c (55–60 g)	9	11	C	C	C	B	7	(58)	4
4. Egg noodles, cooked tender, 1 c (160 g)	9	11	B	B	C	C	7	(~60)	4
5. Bulgur (parboiled wheat), ⅓ c (50–55 g), or Cracked wheat cereal, ½ c (35–40 g)	9	11	B	C	C	B	6	(~60)	4
6. Barley, pot or Scotch, ⅓ c (60–65 g)	9	11	A	C	C	B	6	(60)	4
7. Millet, ½ c (55–60 g)	7	8	A+	B	C	A	6	(~55)	3
8. Spaghetti or Macaroni cooked tender, 1 c (140–150 g)	7	8	B	B	C	C	5	(~50)	3

Grains Continued

Average Serving of Grains, Cereals, and Their Products	Percent of Daily Protein Allowance in an Average Serving		Ratings of Amino Acid Content as Compared to Egg Protein				Total Grams of Protein	NPU	Grams of Protein Your Body Can Use
	M	F	Tryp.	Iso.	Lys.	SC.			
				← DEFICIENCY →					
9. Oatmeal, ⅓ c (30–35 g)	7	8	B			B	4	(66)	3
10. Rice, ⅓ c (60–65 g)									
a. Brown	7	8	B	C	C	B	5	(70)	3
b. Parboiled (converted)	7	8	B	B	C	A	5	(~70)	3
c. Milled, polished	5	6	A	B	C	B	4	(57)	2
11. Wheat germ, commercial, 2 level tbsp (11–12 g)	5	6	C	B	A+	B	3	(67)	2
12. Bread, commercial, 1 slice, whole wheat or rye	2	3	—	—	—	—'	2.4	(~45)	1.2
13. Wheat bran, crude, 2 round tbsp (10 g)	2	3	A	C	B	A	1.6	(55)	0.9

¹Raw unless otherwise stated.
²Amino acid pattern unknown.
³At least one triticale producer claimed a usability score (PER) comparable to soybeans.

Protein Table VI. FLOUR

For ease in calculating the amount of protein in the bread you make, protein values for flours are given here per cup rather than per average serving.

One Cup of Flour	Ratings of Amino Acid Content as Compared to Egg Protein				Total Grams of Protein	NPU	Grams of Protein Your Body Can Use	If complemented, add usable grams!
	Tryp.	Iso.	Lys.	SC.				
		DEFICIENCY						
1. Soybean flour, defatted (138 g)	A	B	A	C[2]	65	(61)	40	5
2. Gluten flour (140 g)	B	B	D	B[3]	85	(39)	23	?
3. Peanut flour, defatted (100 g)	B	C	C	C	48	(43)	21	9
4. Soybean flour, full fat (72 g)	A	B	A	C	26	(61)	16	3
5. Whole wheat flour, or Cracked wheat cereal (120 g) (see Appendix F for comparison with white flour)	B	C	D	B	16	(60)	10	2

Flour Continued

One Cup of Flour	Ratings of Amino Acid Content as Compared to Egg Protein				Total Grams of Protein	NPU	Grams of Protein Your Body Can Use	If complemented, add usable grams[1]
	Tryp.	Iso.	Lys.	SC.				
		DEFICIENCY						
		➡	➡					
6. Rye flour, dark[4] (119 g)	C	C	C	B	16	(58)	9	2
7. Buckwheat flour, dark[4] (100 g)	B	C	C	B	12	(65)	8	2
8. Oatmeal (80 g)	B	C	C	B	11	(66)	7	1
9. Barley flour (112 g)	B	C	C	B	11	(60)	7	2
10. Cornmeal, whole ground (118 g)	C	C	C	B	10	(51)	5	2
11. Wheat bran, crude (55 g)	A	C	B	A	9	(55)	5	1

[1]Approximate amount of protein saved by complementing the protein in the flour. Refer to the beginning of Table V for tips on complementing grain protein.
[2]Also slightly deficient in valine.
[3]Also deficient in threonine.
[4]Both dark rye and dark buckwheat flours have almost twice as much protein as the light varieties.

Tips for complementing the protein in grains, cereals, and their products

1. **Amino Acid Makeup:** Like many nuts and seeds on the previous protein table, the amino acid deficiencies of grains, cereals, and their products, including flour (Protein Table VI), generally appear in the two **inside** columns, isoleucine and lysine. (This pattern is broken primarily by processed cereal products and by legume flours that I have included here only for convenience.) As we have already noted, legumes are the obvious match for grains because they have the reverse pattern of deficiencies. Except for black-eyed peas and mung beans, legumes are moderately strong in the second column, isoleucine; and without exception legumes are very strong in the third column, lysine. Perhaps the simplest way to regularly use legumes to complement grains is merely to add about two tablespoons of soy grits (partially cooked, cracked soybeans) to every cup of grain—in any dish from your morning oatmeal to your supper casserole. The dish will taste better too. Certain commercial cereals such as "Protein Plus" have already added soy grits for you. So be sure to check the labels of commercially made cereals for a fortuitous complementary protein combination!

For the same reasons—strengths in both center columns, isoleucine and lysine—milk products make good complements to grains. But there's a "natural" complement that you might not notice. Yeast, on Protein Table VIII, is also well endowed with these two amino acids in which grains are deficient. Nutritional, or brewer's, yeast, as it is called, can be mixed into breads and pancakes or sprinkled on breakfast cereals.

2. Experimentally determined complementary protein mixes include grains:

plus Legumes, for example:

> Rice + Legumes
> Corn + Legumes
> Wheat + Legumes

plus Dairy products, for example:
> Rice + Milk
> Wheat + Cheese
> Wheat + Milk

plus Nuts and seeds (because grains and nuts and seeds are low in the same amino acids, their complementarity seems to depend usually on the presence of legumes or dairy products), for example:
> Wheat + Peanuts* + Milk
> Wheat + Sesame + Soybean
> Exception: Rice + Sesame

plus Yeast, for example:
> Rice + Brewer's yeast

---

* Peanuts are **botanically** classified as legumes.

Legumes

Protein Table VII. VEGETABLES

Average Serving of Vegetables Based on a Fresh, Uncooked Weight of 3½ oz (100 g)[1]	Percent of Daily Protein Allowance in an Average Serving		Ratings of Amino Acid Content as Compared to Egg Protein				Total Grams of Protein	NPU	Grams of Protein Your Body Can Use
	M	F	Tryp.	Iso.	Lys.	SC.			
	If complemented, add 2–5%		DEFICIENCY	DEFICIENCY		DEFICIENCY			
1. Lima beans, green, 4 rounded tbsp, about ½ c when cooked	9	11	A	A	A	D	8	(~52)	4
2. Soybean sprouts, 1 c	7	8	—	C	C	F	6	(56)	3
3. Peas, green, ¾ c, shelled	7	8	B	B	A+	D	6	(53)	3
4. Brussels sprouts, 9 med.	7	8	B	B	A	D	5	(<60)[2]	3
5. Corn, one medium ear	7	8	D	C	C	B	4	(72)	3
	If complemented, add 1–2%								
6. Broccoli, 1 stalk, 5½ inches	5	6	B	B	B	C	4	(<60)	2–3
7. Kale, w/stems, ¾ c when cooked	5	6	B	C	C	D	4	(54)	2
8. Collards, ½ c when cooked	5	6	A	C	A	C	4	(~45)	2
9. Mushrooms, 10 small, 4 large	5	6	B	D	B	A[3]	3	(72)	2
10. Asparagus, 5–6 spears	3	4	B	D	B	D	3	(<60)	1.8
11. Artichoke, ½ large bud	3	4	—	—	—	—	3	(<60)	1.8
12. Cauliflower, 1 c flower pieces	3	4	A	B	A	D	3	(<60)	1.8

Vegetables Continued

Average Serving of Vegetables Based on a Fresh, Uncooked Weight of 3½ oz (100 g)[1]	Percent of Daily Protein Allowance in an Average Serving		Ratings of Amino Acid Content as Compared to Egg Protein				Total Grams of Protein	NPU	Grams of Protein Your Body Can Use
	M	F	Tryp.	Iso.	Lys.	SC.			
	If complemented, add 1–2%		DEFICIENCY			DEFICIENCY			
13. Spinach, ½ c when cooked	3	4	A	B	A+	B	3	(~50)	1.5
14. Turnip greens, ½ c when cooked	3	4	A	C	B	D	3	(45)	1.4
15. Mung bean sprouts, 1 c (100 g)	3	4	–	–	–	–	4	(36)	1.4
16. Mustard greens, ½ c when cooked	3	4	A+	C	B	C	3	(~45)	1.4
17. Potato, white, ½ med. baking potato	3	3	A	C	B	D	2	(60)	1.2
18. Okra, 8–9 pods, 3 inch long	2	3	B	B	B	C	2	(<60)	1.2
19. Chard, 3/5 c when cooked	2	3	B	B	B	–	2	(~50)	1

[1]Shopping hint: 100 g (or 3½ oz) is equivalent to slightly less than ¼ lb on the grocery scale.
[2]Where the NPU of a vegetable is unknown, I have judged it to be less than 60 (<60), based on typical NPU scores of other vegetables.
[3]The SC. content of mushrooms is disputed in my sources. I chose the high (A) level because it is in line with the unusually high NPU (72) of mushrooms.

Tips for complementing the protein in fresh vegetables

Since the most striking feature of fresh vegetables is their very low ratings in the last amino acid column, sulfur-containing amino acids, you would first want to look for foods with a high rating in that column. In Protein Table IV we find **sesame seeds** and **Brazil nuts** —both unusually strong (A and A+ rating) in the last column. Sesame and Brazils would probably serve best as complements to those fresh vegetables such as lima beans, green peas, Brussels sprouts, and cauliflower, which are very deficient in the last column while strong (A or B rating) in the second column, isoleucine. This is true because sesame and Brazils are themselves somewhat weak (C rating) in the second column.

In Protein Table V, among the grains, we can also find some possible complements to these fresh vegetables. **Millet** and **parboiled rice** (converted) stand out as exceptions among the grains; they are both very strong (A rating) in the last column, sulfur-containing, and moderately strong (B rating) in the second column, isoleucine. They, therefore, might well complement the protein in many fresh vegetables, especially the greens, which have just the opposite pattern.

Some vegetables might complement the protein in other vegetables. **Mushrooms,** high (A rating) in the last column, sulfur-containing, could be combined with lima beans, green peas, Brussels sprouts, broccoli, or cauliflower—all lacking in this amino acid.

Protein Table VIII. NUTRITIONAL ADDITIVES

Average Serving of Nutritional Additive	Percent of Daily Protein Allowance in an Average Serving		Ratings of Amino Acid Content as Compared to Egg Protein				Total Grams of Protein	NPU	Grams of Protein Your Body Can Use
	M	F	Tryp.	Iso.	Lys.	S.C.			
				STRENGTH →					
1. Egg white, dried, powdered, ½ oz (14 g)	21	25	A+	B	A+	A+	11	(83)	9
2. "Tiger's Milk," ¼ c, 1 oz (28 g)	14	17	—	—	—	—	8	(~75)	6
3. Brewer's yeast, powder, 1 level tbsp (9–10 g)	5	6	B	A	A+	C	4	(50)	2
4. Wheat germ, commercial, 2 level tbsp (11–12 g)	5	6	C	B	A+	B	3	(67)	2

Tip for complementing other foods with the protein in nutritional additives

Amino acid strength in the two center columns (isoleucine and, especially, lysine) make nutritional additives likely complements for foods having the opposite amino acid pattern. Likely complementary protein combinations include nutritional additives:

See Table:

plus Certain nuts and seeds, for example:
                    sesame seed, black walnuts   IV

plus Many grains, for example:
                    wheat, barley, oatmeal, rice   V

An experimentally determined complementary protein combination is nutritional yeast:

plus Rice

Rice and Legumes

Protein Table IX. MEAT AND POULTRY

Average Serving of Meat and Poultry, Cooked, 3½ oz (100 g)	Percent of Daily Protein Allowance in an Average Serving		Ratings of Amino Acid Content as Compared to Egg Protein				Total Grams of Protein	NPU	Grams of Protein Your Body Can Use
	M	F	Tryp.	Iso.	Lys.	SC.			
					STRENGTH				
1. Turkey, roasted, 3 slices, 3"x2½"x¼"	50	61	—	B	A+	B	31	(~70)	22
2. Pork, loin chop, lean and fat	44	53	A	A	A+	B¹	29	(~67)	19
3. Porterhouse steak, lean and marbled only (½ lb raw)	39	47	B	B	A+	B¹	25	(67)	17
4. Hamburger, medium (¼ lb raw)	39	47	B	B	A+	B¹	26	(67)	17
5. Chicken, fryer, breast	35	42	B	A	A+	B	23	(~65)	15
6. Lamb, rib chop, lean and fat	30	36	B	B	A+	B¹	20	(~65)	13

¹Also slightly deficient in valine.

**Tips for using meat and poultry to complement
the protein in plant food**

High amino acid ratings (especially lysine) give even
small portions of meat and poultry the ability to complement plant foods, particularly those, such as grains,
which are low in lysine.

Turkey apparently surpasses all other meat and poultry
in its ability to complement plant protein. Experiments
show that if you add only **one-fifth** as much turkey to a
meal of wheat, peanuts, or black-eyed peas, the protein
quality of the combination will be the same as if the
entire meal had been beef![1]

D. How the Food Groups Rate— Protein-Wise

1. Seafood

Seafood rates first place as a source of protein. Fish
is near meat in protein content and superior to meat in
protein usability (NPU), except for shark and skate.
Some fish, like cod and haddock (#13 and #15 on
Protein Table I), are practically *pure* protein; that is,
they contain *no* carbohydrates and only about .1 percent fat. Though the average protein portion I have
given is small (less than ¼ pound), even at this level
some fish can fill 40–50 percent of your daily allowance. It doesn't take much: even small chunks of fish
in soups and lightly cooked vegetable mixes can give
the dish a taste and protein boost.

The next-to-the-last column of the table tells you
about the protein usability of seafood: the high NPU of
most fish, 80, reflects excellent amino acid ratings.
Notice particularly the high lysine content (A+ rating)
of seafood. It is now easy to explain why fish and rice

are successfully eaten as a staple by so many people. Rice, as you will see, is deficient in lysine and isoleucine—defects which seafood can effectively remedy.

I have given the values for raw as opposed to cooked seafood only because the best data available to me was in this form. No significant amount of protein is lost in cooking seafood.

2. Dairy Products

In Part II you may have been surprised to discover that dairy products appear low on the quantity scale of the "Food Protein Continuum." It is true that their percent protein on a weight basis is low. However, the fact that milk (#5 in Protein Table II) is only 4 percent protein and eggs (#9) are only 13 percent protein should not mislead you. Remember that the quality of these products is higher than any other food. On the right side of Table II, you can read their NPU scores —the measures of protein usability. The NPU of milk is over 80 and that of egg is 94 as compared to beef, for example, with an NPU of 67.

An example will remind you of the importance of NPU. Although eggs *appear* to have much *less* protein than beans (that is, eggs are only 13 percent protein, while beans are 21 percent protein), as far as your body is concerned their protein content is nearly equal. Why? Because the high NPU of eggs means that its protein is almost fully used by the body while the low NPU of beans makes its protein only partly available.

Also, the relatively low protein content of some dairy products is made up for by the fact that they are in forms that we normally eat in large quantities. For example, two cups of milk (#5 on Table II) supplies more than one-third of your daily protein allowance. Let's compare this with another food, noodles (#4 on Protein Table V), whose protein content is *three times* that of milk. To get the same proportions of your daily protein allowance from noodles as from two cups of milk, you would have to eat *four* cups of cooked noodles. The point is that whereas you might easily drink two cups of milk a day, you are not likely to eat four cups of noodles!

You will discover in the protein cost and calorie comparisons following the protein tables (Table V and Chart 10) that dairy products fare quite well on these counts also. And dairy products have another virtue to recommend them. They are our major source of calcium. This nutritional strength takes on special importance in light of the fact that the majority of American women consume considerably less than the recommended allowance of calcium. But some people hesitate to increase their intake of dairy products because of their fat content. This shouldn't be a stumbling block—not when there are so many delicious ways to enjoy *low-fat* dairy products.

3. Legumes: Dried Beans, Peas, and Lentils

Legumes are one of the earliest crops cultivated by man. Even in biblical times their nutritional value was known. When Daniel and other favored children of Israel were offered the meat usually reserved only for the King of Babylon, Daniel refused. He asked only for pulses (legumes) and water. After ten days, the Bible passage relates, the faces of the children "appeared fairer and fatter than all the children that ate of the king's meat." This is not too surprising, because the protein content of some legumes is actually equal to, or greater than, that of meat! But maybe you are registering surprise that anyone would *choose* legumes. It is true that dried beans and peas can be the dullest food in the world, but they can also be the basis of the most savory dishes in your menu. Lentils, peas, black beans, and soybeans make delicious and satisfying soups. (See *The Natural Foods Cookbook*, pp. 68–70; for details, see "Recommended Paperback Cookbooks" at the end of this book.) Kidney beans and garbanzos (chick-peas) make a great cold salad or they can top off a fresh green salad. Peabeans with maple syrup is the old favorite: Boston baked beans.

Since legumes are all at least 20 percent protein, why don't they contribute even more to meeting our daily protein allowance than the typical 10–20 percent indicated on the table? The answer is twofold: first, their NPU scores are on the average lower than any other food group recommended as a protein source. Lentils (#11 in Protein Table III) have the lowest NPU score, 30, of any food included in these tables. But legumes also include some of the highest-quality plant protein. Soybeans and mung beans (#1 and #2) have NPU scores of 61 and 57 respectively—reflecting protein usability approaching that of meat. (Note that soybean curd, tofu, has an even higher NPU, 65, than the untreated soybean.) Second, we tend to eat legumes in small quantities. A serving of three-fourths cup of legumes actually weighs only 50 grams before cooking. We usually eat other high-protein food, like meat, in quantities at least twice this amount. But remember that the percentages I have given you here are for legumes eaten *without* the benefit of supplementation with other protein sources. Eating legumes with cereals can make the protein *in both* more valuable to you, increasing the availability of their combined protein content as much as 40 percent.

Before leaving legumes, however, there is one caveat about soybeans: they should always be well cooked, since the cooking destroys an enzyme which limits protein digestion.

4. Nuts and Seeds

Nuts and seeds follow legumes in their ability to meet your daily protein need. They rank behind legumes only because we tend to eat them in much smaller quantities and they, therefore, contribute less to our dietary needs. Actually, they are as rich in protein as the legumes and they often have higher NPU values.

First let's compare the two seeds, sesame and sunflower. Sunflower seed is definitely richer in protein than is sesame—24 percent as compared to 19 percent. The usability of sunflower protein is also better than sesame protein; this is probably the result of the lower lysine and isoleucine content of sesame seed. Experimentally, sunflower seeds show even greater ability to promote growth than meat. Both types of seed have higher NPU scores than most legumes.

You might also wish to note that sesame seeds lose most of their calcium, iron, thiamine, and all of their sodium, potassium, and Vitamin A when they are decorticated. To avoid this loss you can purchase the "unhulled" variety. However, some studies have shown that in order for the body to digest the sesame seed it must be ground. This can be done in any good blender or with a mortar and pestle.

Now look at the nuts. The quantity and usability of their protein is generally lower than the seed meals. A surprise is cashew nuts, whose NPU matches sunflower seeds (and nearly equals soybeans). If you find that your favorite nuts (such as pecans or English walnuts) are not listed here, it's because they are too calorific! To illustrate: if you (a woman) wanted to get your daily protein allowance solely from pecans (hypothetical, of course), you would have to consume almost one and a half pounds of pecans, which contain over 4000 calories—or about twice what you should consume. This illustrates the rationale I have used for including only those items which can provide protein without exceeding caloric needs. The one exception here is Brazil nuts, which have been included because of their unusual strength in the sulfur-containing amino acids (rare in plant protein). For a complete analysis of the calorie "cost" of the foods given here, see Chart 10.

Finally, notice that the portions given here are quite conservative. A one-ounce serving of peanuts provides

7 to 8 percent of your daily protein needs. But if you ate a 10¢ package of peanuts (one and a half ounces), you would actually be fulfilling 10 to 12 percent of your daily allowance.

5. Grains, Cereals, and Their Products

Cereals provide almost half the protein in the world's diet. This might surprise you, since the percent of protein in cereals is not high. Someone must be eating a lot of grain! Not us, of course, but other people in the world.

Let's take a look at grains from several points of view. First, as to the *quantity* of protein they contain. Among the various grains we find wide differences. In first place is triticale, a newly developed cross between rye and wheat which is reported to have 16–17 percent protein. Wheat, rye, and oats have from 30 to 35 percent *more* protein by weight than rice, corn, barley, and millet. The protein content of one type of grain can also vary significantly: wheat, for example, ranges between 9 and 14 percent protein. The values you find for wheat in Protein Tables V and VI are based on the highest-protein wheat: hard red spring wheat. You may wish to check the labeling on wheat products to see what type of wheat is used. Durum wheat, often used in pasta, has the second-highest protein content, 13 percent.

These differences may suggest to you that if rice is a staple in your diet, you may wish to increase the protein content by adding some whole wheat, rye, or oats. Did you know that you can cook whole-grain wheat, oats, and rye in the same way that you do rice? The mix has a nutty, rich flavor which you may prefer to rice alone.

Oatmeal is low (#9) on Table V only because we usually eat it in a rolled form that is much lighter than the whole grains. (Less weight: therefore, less protein.)

But what about the usability of cereal protein? Their NPU values generally range from the low 50's to the low 60's, but there are some important exceptions. The NPU of whole rice, 70, is probably the highest of any of the whole grains and equal to the NPU of beef! Wheat germ and rice germ (not listed) come next, with NPUs of 67. Oatmeal and buckwheat follow, with NPUs of 66 and 65 respectively. These values are higher than most vegetable protein and are comparable to the quality of beef. On the other hand, the lowest NPU of cereal products is that of wheat gluten (#2 under "Flour," Protein Table VI). Although gluten flour is 41 percent protein, its NPU of 39 means that only about *one-third* of its protein is available to the body. A deficiency of lysine (D rating) appears to be the culprit. These differences in usability and quantity among the grains mean that the price you pay and the calories you have to eat to get a given amount of protein also vary significantly. You may wish to take careful note of these differences on the protein cost table and calorie "cost" chart in Part IV.

Cereal products such as bulgur (#5 on Table V) may stump you if you've only read traditional cookbooks. Bulgur is partially cooked, usually cracked wheat. Its processing is both an asset and a liability. Thus, while the lysine in bulgur is more available than that in whole wheat, from 2 to 28 percent of its B vitamins are destroyed.

6. Vegetables

A glance at Protein Table VII will show you that vegetables, in general, will not be large contributors to your daily protein intake. On a moisture-free basis, some green vegetables have a protein content equivalent to nuts, seeds, and beans. But their water content gives them bulk that limits their usefulness in our diets—as protein suppliers, that is. However, don't forget their valuable role in providing essential vitamins and minerals! So if you enjoy these vegetables, eat lots of them. Whereas I have given one-half cup of cooked greens as an average serving, you may enjoy twice this amount. With the exception of potato, all these vegetables are low in calories; so there is no need to limit your intake on this account.

The NPU scores of these vegetables provide some interesting surprises. Among the legumes in Table III, we saw that mung beans had an NPU of 57. But here, as mung bean sprouts, their NPU is only 36. Soybean sprouts also take a slight dip in NPU, with 56 as compared to 61 for the dried bean.

To increase the protein content and taste interest of vegetable dishes, experiment with milk- and cheese-based sauces. I have discovered that buttermilk makes an excellent sauce base. Since it is already somewhat thick, one needn't add as much flour. In addition, its tartness highlights many green vegetables.

Also, sliced or crumbled hard-boiled egg is very tasty on green vegetables such as spinach or asparagus. Adding nuts is another way to increase the protein value of vegetable dishes. Your favorite vegetable dishes in Chinese restaurants probably include walnuts or cashews. Why not do the same? Broccoli, peas, and cauliflower are especially good with nuts.

The following vegetables *cannot* be considered protein sources, because they contain less than 2 percent protein: snap beans, beets, burdock, cabbage, eggplant, lettuce, onions, green peppers, pumpkin, radishes, rhubarb, squash, sweet potatoes, tomatoes, and turnips. Many, however, should be included in the diet as sources of vitamins and minerals.

7. Nutritional Additives

If you have doubts about the adequacy of your protein intake, even a small amount of the first two items in the nutritional additives protein table (VIII) can give you a real protein boost. Only one tablespoon of dried egg white or one-fourth cup of "Tiger's Milk" mixed into your favorite drink can fill 14 to 17 percent of your daily protein need.

The other two nutritional additives (#3 and #4 in the table) are used by most people because of their high vitamin and mineral content. (Yeast is from two to ten times richer than wheat germ in these nutrients.) I have included them because a very small amount (one or two tablespoons) can meet 5 percent of your protein allowance and, second, because of their amino acid strengths.

8. For Comparison: Meat and Poultry

Notice, on Protein Table IX, that only three and a half ounces of meat contribute from 30 to 61 percent of your daily protein allowance. These figures make very clear that the enormous quantities of meat we now consume are hardly needed! In Eastern cuisine, small amounts of meat supplement staple vegetable dishes. This dietary tradition, although perhaps determined by the limited availability of meat, more correctly reflects the body's actual needs.

Gelatin, an animal protein, is often recommended as a protein supplement. Actually, it should be your last choice. Several important amino acids are virtually lacking in gelatin. It has an NPU of 2! Moreover, gelatin can *reduce* the usability of the protein in food eaten with it.

E. Getting the Most Protein for the Least Calories

Chart 10 tells you the number of calories you have to consume in order to get one gram of usable protein from selected food sources. The term "usable protein" means that the protein content has been reduced according to the NPU of the food.

You are all aware of the fact that being overweight is in some way associated with higher risks of dying. (Or, if you're not, you might ask a life insurance salesman. I'm sure he would know!) What might be less familiar to you is the fact that American men who are only *10 percent* overweight eventually exhibit a *20 percent* greater risk of dying before their time than do men of normal weight.[1] Thus even a modest increase in body weight involves much more than a question of looking good. It is a question of good health. So this guide is for those who wish to stay within calorie bounds without jeopardizing protein intake.

Recall that calorie "cost" was one of the criteria used in selecting good protein sources. With few exceptions, only those foods which can give you enough protein without exceeding your daily caloric needs have been included. In Appendix B you'll find the exact number of calories per gram of usable protein for each food item.

Now, let's look at Chart 10. Notice that as you trace food items down the chart, the number of calories increases. Arrayed across the chart are the non-meat food groups chosen as good protein sources. As you read from left to right, the average calorie "cost" of the items in each group increases—seafood being the least calorific, while seeds and nuts have the highest calorie "cost." Thus it is easy to see how the food groups compare as calorie contributors. Now let's take each food group and discuss its special features—from a calorie point of view.

1. Seafood

Seafood is inevitably in first place. It could hardly miss. Two items in this group, haddock and cod, are essentially pure protein. Every gram of protein itself contains four calories. Therefore, four calories per gram

CHART 10
CALORIE "COST" PER GRAM

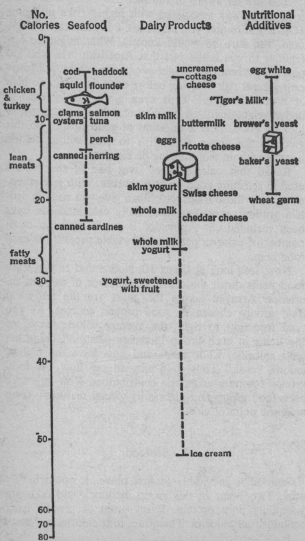

| No. Calories | Seafood | Dairy Products | Nutritional Additives |

0

cod — haddock
squid | flounder

uncreamed cottage cheese

egg white

"Tiger's Milk"

chicken & turkey

clams oysters | salmon tuna

skim milk

buttermilk

brewer's yeast

10

perch

eggs | ricotta cheese

lean meats

canned | herring

baker's yeast

skim yogurt | Swiss cheese

whole milk | cheddar cheese

wheat germ

20

canned sardines

whole milk yogurt

fatty meats

30

yogurt, sweetened with fruit

40

50

ice cream

60
70
80

OF USABLE PROTEIN

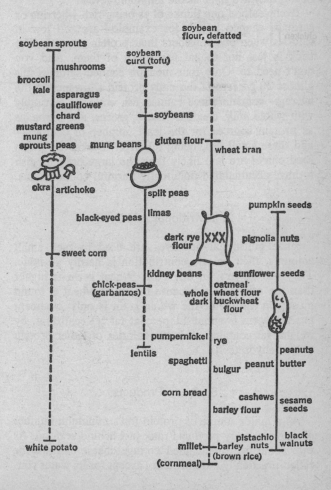

Vegetables	Legumes	Grains, Cereals, & Flours	Seeds & Nuts

soybean flour, defatted

soybean sprouts

soybean curd (tofu)

mushrooms

broccoli
kale

asparagus
cauliflower
chard
mustard greens
mung sprouts

soybeans

mung beans | gluten flour

wheat bran

okra | artichoke

peas

split peas

black-eyed peas | limas

pumpkin seeds

dark rye flour

pignolia nuts

sweet corn

kidney beans

sunflower seeds

chick-peas (garbanzos)

oatmeal
whole dark | wheat flour
buckwheat flour

pumpernickel | rye

peanuts

lentils

spaghetti

bulgur | peanut butter

corn bread

cashews | sesame seeds

barley flour

pistachio nuts

black walnuts

millet | barley
(brown rice)

(cornmeal)

white potato

of protein is the minimum that any food could have. (Each gram of pure carbohydrate also contains four calories, while each gram of fat has nine calories. Thus, by weight, fats have over twice as many calories as protein or carbohydrates.) Since haddock and cod contain no carbohydrates and an almost unmeasurable amount of fat, they are right at the minimum level.

Even seafood one thinks of as being rich—herring or sardines canned in oil, for example—are *still* low in calories when one considers their protein strength. The trick is just not to eat too much of them. And you don't need to. Only four medium canned sardines fills almost 20 percent of the daily protein allowance of the average woman. These canned fish compare favorably with whole milk, cheddar cheese, greens, and soybeans as protein sources for the least number of calories— and these small fish, being relatively low on the ocean food chain, are less likely than the large predator fish to have accumulated potentially harmful contaminants.

2. Nutritional Additives

Since nutritional additives are used in such small amounts, their caloric contribution is hardly an issue. They are all low, in any case. Wheat germ is higher than the others only because the oil in wheat is found mostly in the germ: the whole grain is only 2 percent fat; the germ is about 11 percent fat. (Recall that, by weight, fat contains twice the calories of either protein or carbohydrates.)

3. Dairy Products

As a major source of protein for a minimum number of calories, dairy products rank just behind seafood. As with some fish, uncreamed cottage cheese can also be called practically pure protein (except for its water content, of course). It is less than 1 percent fat and only 3 percent carbohydrate.

Notice that skim milk and buttermilk have fewer calories per gram of usable protein than even plain yogurt. But notice here that commercial, sweetened yogurt, advertised as a good "diet" food, is not in fact outstanding as a low-calorie source of protein: it places well down the chart.

One tends to think of cheese as calorie laden because we are aware of its high fat content (26 to 30 percent fat). So you might well be surprised to find cheeses ranking near yogurt and whole milk on this chart. The answer is their extraordinarly high protein content. Cheese is from 18 to 36 percent protein as compared to only 4 percent for milk! This means that you need eat only a very small amount. A two-ounce piece of cheese supplies about 30 percent of your daily protein allowance, but only about 10 percent (200 calories) of the average woman's calorie allowance.

4. Vegetables

Fresh vegetables rate well on this scale for exactly the opposite reason as does cheese. Their fat content is virtually zero but their protein content is not high either, so you have to eat lots of them to get a significant amount of protein. But that's all right, calorie-wise. You would have to eat three-quarters of a pound of broccoli, for example, before you would consume the number of calories contained in a one-inch cube of cheese.

But even among the low-calorie vegetables there are some real differences. Soybean sprouts, mushrooms, and broccoli have about half as many calories for every gram of usable protein as do peas and okra. Sweet corn contributes more calories than all of these, and the potato is right at the calorie limit for a good protein source.

5. Legumes: Dried Beans, Peas, and Lentils

From a caloric point of view, we find wide variability among legumes. Soybean curd (tofu) has the fewest calories for the amount of usable protein, largely because most of the fat is removed in its processing. Tofu is truly an excellent protein source. Lightly sautéed, with a fresh vegetable accompaniment, one could easily eat seven ounces of tofu and fulfill 25 to 30 percent of a day's need for protein—at the cost of only about 5 to 7 percent of a day's calorie allotment. I have included several tofu dishes among the recipes given later in this book.

The wide variation among the dried legumes is not due, however, to differential fat content, or even to the amount of protein contained (except for soybeans, whose protein content is well above the others). The wide range reflects primarily differences in protein *usability*. Lentils, for example, place far down the scale because they have the lowest NPU score. Low NPU means less usable protein. The result is that you or I have to eat more of the food (and hence more calories) to get a given amount of protein.

Legumes are another category of food (like cheese) that many people think of as being "fattening." Yet, in relation to the amount of protein you are getting, soybeans actually are on a par with green vegetables! Most of the legumes have between one-half and two-thirds of the maximum allowable calories per gram of usable protein. And this is pretty good. It means that you could conceivably eat all of your daily protein allowance in the form of legumes and still have left one-half to one-third of your daily calorie allowance for other good things.

6. Grains, Cereals, and Their Products

Part of the reason for the wide range here in calories per gram of usable protein is that I've included some legume flours with the grains—since they too are used in baking. Defatted soybean flour is the clear-cut winner, with only 11 calories per gram of usable protein, making it similar to skim milk from the calorie-to-protein point of view. Gluten flour would be quite near it, if it were not for its low NPU score. Gluten's low quality reduces the amount of usable protein, causing it to drop to the level of whole milk or cheddar cheese.

The variability among the true whole grains and their products is for the most part attributable to differences in protein content; that is, their percent on a weight basis. For this reason, you would have to eat more calories to get a given amount of protein from barley, millet, rice, or cornmeal than you would from dark rye, oatmeal, or whole wheat. In fact, judged by the calorie criterion I have adopted, cornmeal and rice should not be considered as good protein sources at all! Rice has about 69 calories per gram of usable protein, and cornmeal has approximately 80. I have included both because they are so widely eaten as protein sources. To compensate for their failings, I encourage their use in combination with other foods that increase both their protein content (such as egg in cornbread) and their protein usability (rice plus beans, for example).

7. Nuts and Seeds

Nuts and seeds are all located on the lower half of the chart, meaning that they all have between 30 and 60 calories per gram of usable protein. But, like cheese and legumes, these particular seeds and nuts are so rich in protein that, even with a high fat content, they are no more calorific per gram of usable protein than are the whole grains. (Many nuts have been excluded because their calorie-to-usable-protein ratio exceeds 60:1. These are listed at the end of Protein Table IV.)

You might be surprised to see sunflower seeds and sesame seeds so widely separated on the chart; sesame having significantly more calories per gram of usable protein than sunflower seeds (57 compared to 40). The reason is threefold. In comparison with sunflower seeds, sesame seed has a slightly higher fat content, a 20 percent lower protein content, and a lower NPU score.

F. Your Protein Dollar: A Cost Comparison

Table V, on protein cost, tells you how much it would cost to fill all of a day's protein allowance from a single food source eaten alone.* The prices are based on the grams of protein in the food, with an adjustment for protein usability. In other words, the price is based on the grams of protein your body can *use*, not on the total grams of protein. Of course, the chart is for the purpose of comparison. I'm not expecting you to eat your daily protein allowance in only one food!

Although prices have about doubled since 1971 on many items, the basic pattern that emerges on this table is the same as in the first edition. In Appendix C, I have included both the exact cost for one day's protein allowance and the cost per pound I paid for the food. If you wish, compare the price per pound you are paying and adjust for any major difference. The variations in price are quite large, according to what part of the country you live in and the type of store you shop in. These prices were collected in Fort Worth, Texas, in late 1974 and probably represent a middle range of cost. (Appendix C also includes additional items that would not fit on the Table V.)

The costs range down the table from about 25¢ to about $3.50. The contrasts among the food groups are not as distinct as those on the calorie-to-protein chart

---

* The cost is based on 43.1 grams of *usable* protein, the daily allowance for the average American male, weighing 154 pounds. "Usable" protein means that the total grams of protein have been reduced by the NPU score to the level the body can actually use.

TABLE V. PROTEIN COST

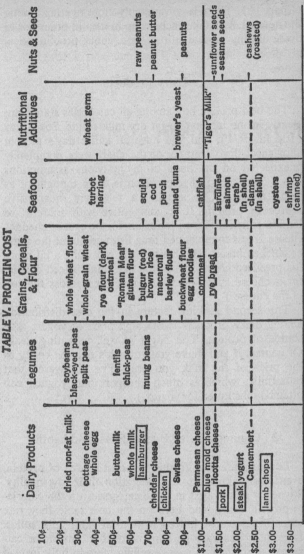

(Chart 10). There is considerably more overlap among the items. Let us take each group in turn in order not to overlook any critical information about protein price.

1. Dairy Products

The best protein buy among all categories stands out clearly in the table: non-fat dry milk solids. 26¢ a day (10¢ in 1971), and you have an entire day's protein allowance! Two features of the chart were completely unexpected on the basis of my previous assumptions about food costs: cheese, which is often thought of as being expensive, is actually a relatively *in*expensive source of protein. It is competitive with sources we tend to consider cheap; for example, the cost of cheddar cheese is less than canned tuna fish and about the same as chicken breast. (Of course, you pay quite a bit more for presliced cheese. So if you like thinly sliced cheese, try a cheese slicer—the kind that runs across the top of the cheese.)

The second striking feature in the cost distribution among dairy products is the high price of yogurt as a source of protein. You might as well be eating steak! Of course, if you make your own it's only as costly as the price of the milk you use. (I've discovered that buttermilk, which is much cheaper than yogurt, can often be substituted for yogurt.)

2. Legumes: Dried Beans, Peas, and Lentils

Legumes are a uniformly low-cost source of protein, even after taking into consideration their low quality. Soybeans placed first in three categories on the calorie-to-protein chart, and here on the cost table they rate second, very close indeed to non-fat skim milk solids. Legume prices vary perhaps more than any other category, so try to find a store selling them in bulk instead of small prepackaged units that invariably cost more.

3. Grains, Cereals, and Their Products

The price of a day's protein allowance from most of the grains and their products ranges between 30¢ and $1—with wheat and rye at the low end and millet and cornmeal at the high end. This positioning reflects both the higher usability and quantity of protein in wheat, rye, and oats. Triticale, the new wheat-rye hybrid, is believed to exceed its parents in both usability and quantity of protein, and is a good buy at anything like wheat prices. As you can see, grains are as cheap a source of protein as legumes.

I have included the commercial cereal "Roman Meal" to show that such products can sometimes be less expensive than staples like cornmeal. In this case, the low protein-price is due to processed flaxseed, a very high protein oilseed, contained in "Roman Meal." But, as you know, not all commercial cereals are a bargain.

4. Seafood

Certain seafood are a real cost surprise: tuna, that old cheap-meal standby, is actually more expensive than perch.* Crab, often reserved for only the most special meal, is still only slightly less expensive than many steaks. But the least expensive of the fish, such as perch, cod, or turbot, are nearly as cheap a means of getting one's daily protein allowance as are beans.

5. Nutritional Additives

Although brewer's yeast does not rate as well, cost-wise, as wheat germ, remember that brewer's yeast is

---

* Swordfish, which was used instead of perch in the first edition, in this comparison, has now been withdrawn from the American market as the extent of its mercury pollution has become apparent.

much richer in vitamin and mineral content. Because of its high protein content of 30 percent, "Tiger's Milk," a commercial mixture of milk and soy protein, is not as expensive a source of protein as you might think, when first confronted with its high price on the grocery shelf. But it's not cheap either. If you are concerned primarily with getting additional protein (and not the extra vitamins and minerals put in "Tiger's Milk"), you are considerably better off using non-fat dry milk instead of an additive; it is *much* cheaper and slightly richer in protein.

6. Nuts and Seeds

In this food group we find some of the highest-priced protein sources. Pistachio nuts in the shell are off the chart altogether, costing more than $5 for a day's protein quota. But don't shun such delights as cashews and black walnuts because they're costly—just use them sparingly. Only a small amount can turn the simplest vegetable recipe into a special dish. But the only *really* good buys are peanuts and the seeds.

Another point worth noticing is the difference between the roasted and raw peanuts. Raw peanuts are significantly cheaper than their roasted counterparts. The same thing was true for raw cashews (in the San Francisco Bay area) in 1971, and probably is today.

Part IV

Eating from the Earth: How to Get Protein Without Meat

Rice

A. What Is a Meal Without Meat?

I mean that literally. What *is* a meal without meat? Many of us have a hard time imagining menus without it. When we asked our mothers "What's for supper, Mom?" the shorthand answer always came back "Pork chops" . . . "Chicken" . . . "Meat loaf." The meat course defined the meal.

These menus that many of us take so for granted are inherited from our physically active forebears. But in our mechanized society we need many fewer calories each day than our great-grandparents, who worked the fields, carried water, and washed by hand. This fact has become well known, if not well heeded. The trouble is that it is virtually impossible to avoid consuming too many calories per meal as long as one defines it as meat-vegetable-starch-salad-bread-and-dessert. It just can't add up any other way than *too much.*

But once we leave meat, the center of the menu, out of the equation, then the whole pattern of habit falls apart. Anything goes. Then you are free to respond to your own appetite in planning menus. We have found in our family and with non-meat-eating friends that what seems most natural is a meal of one dish into which we have put our care and imagination, accompanied by one simple side dish such as salad, good hearty bread, or steamed vegetable. Therefore, the majority of the recipes in the book and all those in the first section of the recipes are not merely main-dish ideas but are really "meal-dish" ideas—meals in themselves with (if you choose) the addition of a simple salad, etc.

And there is much more flexibility in meal planning if we rethink our notion of when and how we take in our daily protein allowance. Here I do not mean merely going from meat to non-meat sources. We must get rid of the notion that protein comes from one large, important item at mealtime and that the rest of our diet is filler in order to get calories or vitamins. Instead, if almost everything we eat has some protein in it, our protein intake will add up to fill our protein need over the course of the day. In other words, baked goods can easily have soy or milk in them, salads and salad dressings can be made with all kinds of dairy products. Nuts and seeds and dairy foods can enrich any vegetable dish. Even desserts don't have to be empty calories but can be a rich protein source too. If we make everything we eat count nutritionally, then we don't have to have one piece of meat that in itself will supply all our protein.

Eating with less meat has appeal from many angles. As Maya Pines (author of the article "Meatless, Guiltless" to which I referred earlier) noted, she has never seen a fat vegetarian. In our own experience there is truth to this: after losing the pounds that we had always wanted to lose, we find it easier to maintain our ideal weights. The dishes are satisfying and the bulk of plant foods is more filling, so that we just don't overeat. (Our appetite for sweets has declined markedly also.)

But there are other non-health-related, purely pleasure-related returns from non-meat-centered eating. For one thing, it can be more fun. You will find a greater variety of textures, colors, and tastes in plant foods that are more satisfying to handle, touch, and smell than that slab of meat. And because there is no Betty Crocker of plant foods, telling you what a dish *should* be like, you'll find that you soon become more experimental. I recall the first non-meat dinner party I gave for my husband's birthday. I made a walnut-cheddar loaf. Never too confident of my own cooking, I was comforted by the notion that no one would be comparing my dish with Julia Child's version. Who else ever tasted walnut-cheddar loaf! After you become comfortable with the ingredients, you will become a creator, taking foods that are in season and on hand and creating your own favorites. (A meal without meat is more than a kitchen without grease!)

But let me offer one important caveat that I also included in the first edition of this book: don't expect yourself to change overnight! Why not start with one new menu a week, or one new ingredient, until you gradually build up a "repertoire" of dishes you enjoy. The notion of suddenly changing lifelong habits of any kind on the basis of new understanding does not strike me as very realistic or even desirable—however great the revelation! As least this is not the way it has worked in my family. The change went something like this: the more we learned about the "costliness" of meat on so many grounds, and the more we discovered the delicious possibilities of foods we had always neglected, the less important meat became, and eventually the less attractive. Never did we swear off meat, vowing to make this a great sacrifice for the sake of mankind! Rather, meat began to play a smaller and smaller role in our diet as it was displaced by new and, frankly, more interesting ways of meeting our daily protein need.

B. "But It Takes Too Much Time . . ."

This is the most common reaction to my cooking suggestions. After all, there are no prepackaged, instant complementary protein combinations on the grocery shelf! I used to resist making even so-called "quick" breads from scratch. How could they be as quick as a ready-made mix? But I began to want to make dishes that demanded I start from scratch. I decided to test myself. How much more time did it actually take to make my cornbread recipe than using a commercial cornbread mix? I was surprised to find that it hardly

took any more time at all! *Both* required that I get out
bowls and utensils, mix the batter, oil the baking pan,
pour the batter, put it in the oven, clean the mixing
utensils and then the baking pan. The only difference
was that, for my recipe, I had to combine a few more
ingredients—a really minor part of the whole operation.

But people continue to tell me that they can't wait
for the long cooking time necessary when using whole
foods, can't take time to chop fresh vegetables and
hand-make exotic ethnic dishes. But while the actual
time using my stove may be longer than it takes
to fry a hamburger, I am sure that I do not spend
any more of my time on food than they do. So
what is the secret? Part of the answer is that there
is more to feeding oneself or a family than just putting together the meals. There is: (1) knowing what
to have on hand for easy meals; (2) shopping; plus
(3) kitchen layout and time-saving utensils.

1. What to Have on Hand

Part of cooking quickly with no fret and bother is
knowing what to have on hand. There are probably
certain foods that you always have, that you shop for
automatically because you know that if you have these
basic ingredients, you can always produce a good meal.
As you begin to change your eating habits, your buying
and stocking habits will change too. To help you, I
have made a list of the 25 items that I am virtually
never without. Many of these foods are probably in
your kitchen right now, but perhaps it never occurred
to you that you could build a meal on many of them.
Of course, in each of these categories there are many,
many more possibilities, but with these 25 items you
could make *any* of the recipes in this book. (You
might have to substitute a little, but that is part of the
fun!)

Again, I am not suggesting that you go out and buy
a whole lot of new ingredients all at once. If you have

a friend who uses whole grains, legumes, and seeds, ask if you might just have some samples to get you started. (That's how I got started, with the help of a dear friend: Ellen Ewald.) If you are not that lucky, then perhaps you might find a friend who would also like to experiment. Together you might buy one-pound quantities of a few new things, split them, then compare experiences and reactions to your new menus. This way you will not be making such a big initial investment that you will feel it *has* to "work" all at once! Or, if you are on your own, just find one recipe that looks good to you. Buy any ingredient you don't already have, then try discovering all the other possibilities for that same ingredient. You'll be amazed at the variety that is possible when cooking with plant foods!

Here are my basic pantry items for easy meals, with some tips on how I use them:*

(A) *Dairy Products*

1. *Non-Fat Dry Milk:* use in hot cereal, any baked goods, soups, blender drinks, white sauces.

2. *Cottage Cheese:* the basis of sauces, salad dressings, casseroles, and pancake filling, or simply as a spread for toast.

3. *Plain Yogurt or Buttermilk:* as dressing for fruit salad, basis of cold summer blender soups, dessert topping, and sauces for main dishes (especially curries). Note that buttermilk is much cheaper and you can substitute it for yogurt, in many cases.

(B) *Quick-Cooking Grain Products*

1. *Bulgur* (partially cooked, i.e., parboiled wheat, usually cracked): for breakfast cereal, dinner grain, soup thickener, cold salad with vegetables. (Couscous

---

* For "Basic Cooking Instructions," see Appendix A at the end of the book.

is similar to but more refined and usually more expensive than bulgur.) Bulgur has a nutty flavor that can be enhanced by sautéeing it before steaming.

2. *Soy Grits** (partially cooked, cracked soy beans): use in hot cereals, baked goods, in small amounts with other grains, in spaghetti sauce or bean chili, soups— or in just about anything for extra protein. (Soy grits have a very mild taste and absorb the flavor of whatever they are cooked with.)

3. *Flours* (whole wheat, soy, corn): endless possibilities!

(C) *Nuts and Seeds*

1. *Sunflower and Ground Sesame Seeds* (nutritionists have advised that sesame seeds should be ground for digestibility; this can be easily done in the blender or with a mortar and pestel): use in baked goods, salads, toasted as attractive topping, in casseroles, in stuffing, granola, with peanuts for snacking. (Toasting lightly brings out the flavor.)

2. *Peanuts and Peanut Butter:* use in bean croquettes, casseroles, salads, cookies, candy, spaghetti and vegetable sauce, and curries.

(D) *Quick-Cooking Legumes*

1. *Split Peas* (green or yellow): use in soups, curries, sauces, rice, rice patties, loaves.
2. *Lentils:* same uses.

(E) *Fresh Foods*

These are fresh foods that keep well. From these three foods you can, as a friend has put it, always create a meal out of nothing.

1. *Carrots:* use in carrot-and-onion soup, in bread, grain dishes, carrot salad, curries.

* Also called soy granules.

2. *Onions:* use in French onion soup, casseroles, curries.

3. *Potatoes:* use in in soups, salads, casseroles, pancakes.

(F) *Canned Foods*

1. *Kidney Beans and Garbanzo Beans:* use in stews, chili, tacos, puréed in pita,* curries. (I use canned beans only when I am really rushed and have emptied my freezer store of leftover cooked beans.)

2. *Tomatoes:* use in soups, casseroles.

3. *Spaghetti Sauce:* use in pasta dishes, as topping for bean croquettes, eggplant platters.

4. *Tuna Fish:* use in casseroles, sandwiches, salads, rice fritters.

5. *Minced Clams:* use in chowder, spaghetti sauce, dips, spreads, corn-clam fritters.

6. *Beets:* add beautiful color and interest to vegetable, tuna, lettuce, or spinach salads.

7. *Corn:* use in casseroles, fritters, soups, stews, pancakes.

8. *Sweet Peas:* use in salads, soups, casseroles.

(G) *Freezer Foods*

1. *Leftover Beans:* always cook at least twice what the recipe calls for and store the rest for instant meals.

2. *Middle Eastern Flatbread (Pita) and Tortillas:* use not only for authentic foreign dishes but for instant sandwiches with all types of fillings.

3. *Frozen Peas:* add color, taste, and nutrition to soups, stew, salads, etc.

(H) *Seasonings*

1. *Powdered Vegetable Seasoning:* use in just about anything! (Look around and you can find vegetable

---

* Middle Eastern flatbread.

seasonings that are made from natural ingredients and without preservatives. If nowhere else, your health food store will carry these. Use with water whenever the recipe calls for seasoned stock and you have none, or sprinkle on whenever you think extra flavor might be needed.)

2. Shopping

Using lots of whole-grain flours, peas, beans, lentils, nuts, and seeds means that I can buy most of my staples in large quantities. This means I shop less frequently. Try to find a natural foods store that sells food in bulk intead of in small, prepackaged units. It is usually cheaper this way and you consume less paper and plastic too.

Of course, even less time would be required if you could buy these whole-food items at your neighborhood supermarket. So don't just accept these foods as too offbeat to be easily available. Ask your market manager why he does not have brown rice, soy flour, whole wheat flour, and interesting varieties of beans, cracked wheat, etc.? If he says there is not enough demand, tell him that you can get ten people who would buy five pounds a month and he might begin to change his mind.

It is only you and I who can create the demand for plant food and thus make it commercially feasible to gear our vast American acreage to feeding people instead of animals.

3. Kitchen Shortcuts

(A) *Keeping It All Within Reach*

Preparation time is, of course, not just how long something takes to cook. It's getting the ingredients to the cooking stage. That's why the organization of your kitchen is all-important.

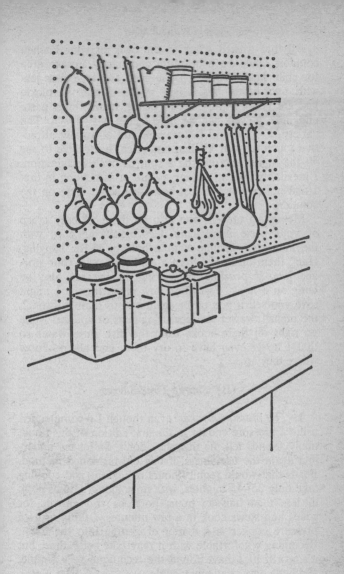

All that wasted space in the back of your kitchen counters could be a beautiful and handy storage area for your whole foods. All you need are large glass jars with tight-fitting lids. Giant peanut butter or pickle jars are good. Flours, seeds, beans, lentils, even pasta and milk power, can be here within easy reach. The variety of color and texture will add a visually attractive touch to your kitchen too. Also, being able to *see* all the ingredients can be a spur to one's imagination. I inevitably end up tossing a little of something in that I had not planned to just because I see it there on the counter.

Measuring utensils can also be there, in easy grasp of your basic ingredients. Get measuring cups with the long stem handle with a hole in it for hanging. Hang them on hooks from a cupboard over your storage jars, if possible. Measuring spoons can also be hung on a hook. Just think how much time you might save yourself if you never again had to fumble through the utensil drawer for measuring cups or spoons! Mine go right on their hooks from the dish rinse water so that I never even have to dry them and always know where they are.

(B) *Simple Time-Savers*

1. *The pressure cooker:* even though I recommended using a pressure cooker in the first edition of this book, many friends tell me that they don't. So let me underline again the usefulness of this old-fashioned method. Beans that would require hours of soaking and cooking take only 35–45 minutes, with no soaking. Grains cook in less than half an hour; potatoes and carrots for soups and stews cook in a few minutes. I think using a pressure cooker is a matter of getting into the habit. Becoming comfortable with it may take some time, but it's worth it! I have found the technique very simple, and have never had any trouble.

I also devised a foolproof method for pressure cooking grains. I bought a stainless-steel mixing bowl that fits inside my pressure cooker and is about one inch shorter than the inside height of the cooker. I fill the pressure cooker with about three inches of water. I then put the grain or beans I am cooking in the stainless bowl, with water to cover, plus about one inch. I

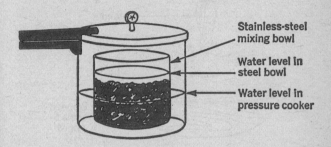

Stainless-steel mixing bowl

Water level in steel bowl

Water level in pressure cooker

then put the stainless bowl inside the cooker and cook it as anyone would with the pressure cooker. This method is quick—I never have to measure the water, because I just add water to a level one inch above the food. And it is impossible to scorch the food, because there is a layer of water between the stainless bowl and the pressure cooker. See illustration. You can also use this method to cook two items separately in the same pressure cooker. Simply put one food in the pressure cooker, with water in the same proportion of water as you would ordinarily use in a pressure cooker, and the other ingredient in the stainless-steel bowl, with water to cover, plus about one inch.

If you don't want to try it "my style," simply follow the basic cooking instructions that come with your pressure cooker or that you'll find at the end of this book under "Basic Cooking Instructions."

2. *Vegetable choppers:* never again pass over a recipe because you don't want to take the time to chop vegetables with a knife. You don't have to—if you are not as adept with a knife as Julia Child, then you'll want a vegetable chopper. I have a plunger-style blade

in a round plastic case which I have found to work well. Even simpler is a combination chopping blade and gently contoured wooden bowl. The great advantage here is that the ingredients are neatly contained inside the bowl while you chop. See my illustration.

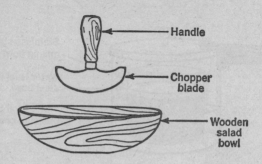

C. It Pays to Mix Your Own: Combining Non-Meat Foods to Increase Protein Values

The theory of protein complementarity that we learned in Part II is applied in the following section in over 100 recipes. But before turning to the recipes that have already been developed, let me illustrate for you how easy it is to come up with your own complementary protein combinations—and how much difference it can make in the amount of protein your body can actually use.

First look at Chart 11, "Summary of Complementary Protein Relationships." You will find that the four basic groups are easy to remember and use, as are the three basic combinations:

1. Grains (cereal, pasta, rice, or corn, etc.) + Legumes (beans, peas, or lentils).
2. Grains + Milk Products.
3. Seeds (sesame or sunflower) + Legumes (beans, peas, or lentils).

CHART 11
SUMMARY OF COMPLEMENTARY PROTEIN RELATIONSHIPS

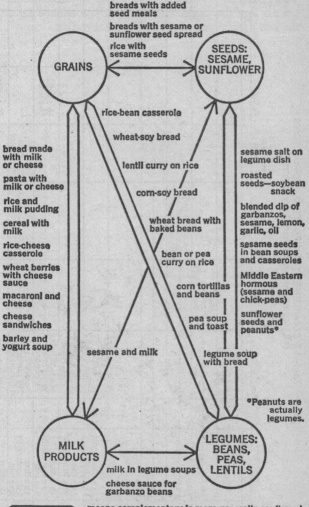

GRAINS

SEEDS: SESAME, SUNFLOWER

breads with added
seed meals

breads with sesame or
sunflower seed spread

rice with
sesame seeds

rice-bean casserole

wheat-soy bread

lentil curry on rice

corn-soy bread

wheat bread with
baked beans

bean or pea
curry on rice

corn tortillas
and beans

pea soup
and toast

legume soup
with bread

bread made
with milk
or cheese

pasta with
milk or cheese

rice and
milk pudding

cereal with
milk

rice-cheese
casserole

wheat berries
with cheese
sauce

macaroni and
cheese

cheese
sandwiches

barley and
yogurt soup

sesame salt on
legume dish

roasted
seeds—soybean
snack

blended dip of
garbanzos,
sesame, lemon,
garlic, oil

sesame seeds
in bean soups
and casseroles

Middle Eastern
hormous
(sesame and
chick-peas)

sunflower
seeds and
peanuts*

sesame and milk

*Peanuts are
actually
legumes.

MILK PRODUCTS

LEGUMES: BEANS, PEAS, LENTILS

milk in legume soups

cheese sauce for
garbanzo beans

means complementary is more generally confirmed
between several items in each group.

means complementary relationship is demonstrated
only between a few items in each group.

Table VI. COMPLEMENTARY PROTEIN PROPORTIONS*
(all ingredients uncooked, dry measure)

Beans/ peas	Soybeans[1]	Rice[2]	Wheat[3]	Corn	Milk[4]	Sesame or Sunflower Seeds	Peanuts	Misc.	Approximate Increase in Usable Protein by Combining
1 c†		2⅔ c							43%
½ c	←	→	3 c w/w flour 2½ c bulgur 1 loaf bread						33%
¼ c	←	—	→	1 c meal 6–7 tortillas 1 lb canned corn					50%
1 c	←	—	—	→	2 c milk/yogurt ⅔ c instant 2½ oz cheese				11%
⅓ c	←	—	—	—	→	½ c seeds ¾ c meal ¼ c butter			27%
	¼–½ c flour ⅛–¼ c beans/ grits 5–9 oz tofu	1¼ c							32%
	1 c flour ⅔ c beans/grits 19 oz tofu	1 c	1 c w/w flour ¾ c bulgur 6 slices bread						24%
	¼ c flour ⅛ c beans/grits		1 c w/w flour ¾ c bulgur 6 slices bread						32%
	½ c flour ⅓ c beans/grits 9 oz tofu	¾ c	¾ c w/w flour ⅔ cup bulgur 5 slices bread	←	—	→	⅛ c butter ¼ c nuts		15%
	½ c flour ⅓ c beans/grits 9 oz tofu		3 c w/w flour 2½ c bulgur 1 loaf bread	←	→	½ c seeds ⅔ c meal ¼ c butter			42%
	¼ c flour ⅛ c beans/grits 5 oz tofu		3¾ c w/w flour 2¾ c bulgur	←	—	→	½ c butter ¼ c nuts		34%

	½ c flour ⅓ c beans/grits 9 oz tofu	←	—	—	→	⅞ c seeds 1½ c meal ½ c butter	½ c butter ¾ c nuts 1 c ground		25%
	1 c flour ⅔ c beans/grits 19 oz tofu			3 c meal 18–20 tortillas 3 lb canned corn	3½ c milk 1 c instant 4 oz cheese				13%
		¾ c	←	→	1 c milk/yogurt 5 tbsp instant 1¼ oz cheese				29%
		1 c	←	—	→	⅓ c seeds ½ c meal 3 tbsp butter			21%
		1 c	←	—	—	—	→	¼ c yeast	57%
			1 c w/w flour ¾ c bulgur 5 slices bread		⅔ c milk/yogurt 3 tbsp instant ¾ oz cheese				13–25%
			3¾ c w/w flour		1 c milk/yogurt ⅓ c instant 1½ oz cheese		½ c butter ⅞ c nuts		34%
					1½ c milk/yogurt ½ scant c instant		1 c butter 1¾ c nuts		25%
					3 c milk/yogurt 1 scant c instant 1 c grated cheese			2 lb potatoes	7%
					1† c milk/yogurt 5½ tbsp instant	1¼ c seeds 1½ c meal ⅔ c butter			20%
						1 c seeds 1¼ c meal ½ c butter	½ c (scant) butter ¾ c nuts		19%

1 Soy grits = soy granules; soy flour = soy powder.
2 Other grains — rye, oats, millet, barley, etc. — can be substituted for the rice and wheat in these combinations with probably a similar complementary effect.
3 For every cup of whole wheat flour you may substitute 1¼ c macaroni (preferably whole wheat).
4 Instant = Instant non-fat dry milk. If you use non-instant non-fat dry milk, reduce by ⅓, compared to instant.
* Adapted from an idea by Sara Millman.
† Cup, not centimeters.

In fact, you are probably already using many of the possibilities every day anyway! For example, everytime you eat milk on cereal or pea soup with toast you are creating a complementary protein combination. Interestingly, the combination of grains plus beans, peas, or lentils evolved spontaneously, becoming the center of the diet in many different parts of the world—rice and beans in the Caribbean, corn and beans in Mexico, lentils and rice in India, and rice and soy in China. On some level there must have been an awareness in each of these cultures that this combination was better for the body than either food eaten separately.

Only recently has modern science truly understood what must have been known intuitively by the human race for thousands of years. (I remember chuckling, a few years ago, when *The New York Times* reported that a Midwestern university food lab had just discovered that the soybean is edible! Any Chinese would have had an even better laugh, for the Chinese have for 5000 years based an incredibly varied cuisine on the versatile soybean.)

Table VI, "Complementary Protein Proportions," gives you the proportions of food which, in combinations, have been shown to be effective in laboratory tests. The protein usability (or quality) of most of the food combinations presented in the chart is equal to or, in many cases, superior to that of meat, based on the ability to stimulate growth in experimental animals.

Let's return to the example of beans and rice in order to make the importance of protein complementarity very clear, even dramatic. Here is the message in capsule form:

Meat Equivalency Comparison

	Usable protein is equivalent to:
A. *If eaten separately:*	
1½ cups beans (or peas)	6¼ oz steak
4 cups rice	7 oz steak
	13¼ oz steak
B. *If eaten together:* 43% increase	
1½ cups beans (or peas) + 4 cups rice	19 oz steak

This example demonstrates what we now understand scientifically—about this almost universally used combination—that if eaten together in the right proportions, grains plus beans can provide over 40 percent more usable protein than if you ate them separately. Recall that this is true because all the essential amino acids must be present in the correct proportion—simultaneously. The advantage thus gained is shown by first converting the foods, if eaten *separately,* into their protein equivalent as meat and then comparing this amount with the meat equivalent of the foods if eaten *together.* That gain is striking; depending on the combination, it can equal from one to eight ounces of meat! In Appendix D you'll find meat equivalency comparisons for all the other complementary protein combinations (i.e., for all those that appear in Table VI). The increase in usable protein given for each combination on the far right-hand column of Table VI and noted in Appendix D is a very rough estimate based, in most cases, on the improved ability of those food combinations to promote growth in experimental animals (PER* scores), in contrast to the same foods eaten separately. Appendix D also includes, at its end, a

---

* PER is the gain in weight of the growing experimental animal divided by the weight of protein consumed. It is accepted by nutritionists as a good measure of protein quality. PER correlates highly with NPU.

sample calculation as to how I arrived at the estimates. The basic source for much of the data is *Amino Acid Content of Foods and Biological Data on Protein,* Food and Agriculture Organization of the United Nations, Rome, 1970.

Another reason for using the "Meat Equivalency Comparisons" appendix is to help erase the idea that animal protein is basically different from, and cannot therefore be equated with, plant protein.

A Word About Proportions

In the first edition many would-be non-meat cooks were put off by the question of balancing proportions. It all seemed too complicated. Well, don't be; it's not.

First, concentrate on the basic *combinations* given in Chart 11. They are easy to remember and, mostly, quite "natural." Remember that even if you do not follow the proportions exactly, you are probably still much better off for having combined the two foods than if you did not.

Second, with each recipe in the following section, D, I have given some tips on how to add complementary protein when cooking that particular type of dish. Look at these as you experiment with the recipes. You'll discover there a few basic tricks that can easily become second nature to you.

Third, note that it never hurts to put in more milk protein (cheese, non-fat dry milk, cottage cheese, yogurt, etc.) than the proportions call for. The milk protein is so well balanced that it "stands alone," needing no complement. (The proportions given are generally the *minimum* amount necessary to complement the less well-balanced protein in the other food.) This is true to a lesser extent for soy. Soy protein is quite usable even without complementation, so that adding more soy than the proportions indicate will never hurt.

Now, on the eating . . .

D. Complementary Protein Recipes

When I was growing up my brother and I used to say that although our mother was no gourmet cook, she was perhaps the best "short-order" cook in the world. And judging from the reaction to the first edition of this book, I'd say that a lot of other Americans have the same approach to cooking. They like recipes that they can whip up from memory, vary according to what they have on hand, get on the table in a hurry, but that have a flair of originality to them.

This is certainly the way I cook most of the time, except for those special meals for friends when the extra preparation time and care add to the pleasure of the occasion. So in this edition I have divided the recipes into sections that reflect my own cooking habits. The first and largest section is "High-Protein Meatless Meals in a Dish"—with, perhaps, the addition of a salad or vegetable according to your taste. (Suggestions for accompaniments are given too.) If the beans or grain for these dishes can be taken from the refrigerator or freezer already cooked, virtually all of these dishes would appeal to even my "short-order" Mom. Others are quick even starting from scratch.

1. High-Protein Meatless Meals in a Dish

Here are the categories of meals so that you can see at a glance what appeals most to you:

(A) Meals from the Top of the Stove

(B) Bread and Cheese Made Elegant

(C) Super Supper Pancakes

(D) The Universal Flat-Bread Sandwich

(E) Pie-in-the-Sky Suppers

(F) Something from the Oven, but Don't Call It a Casserole!

(G) Pasta Unlimited

(H) A Meal in a Soup Pot

(I) A Meal in a Salad Bowl

The second section, "High-Protein Meatless Menus for Special Occasions," gives complete dinner menus to help in your planning when you have the time for more elaborate dinners.

Following these main sections, you'll find recipes for "All the Extras"—Snacks, Breakfast Foods, Baked Goods, and Desserts. All of these dishes, from the main dish recipes to snacks and desserts, use complementary protein combinations balanced according to the proportions just given (Chart 12), except in cases where a dairy product or seafood provides most of the protein.

(A) *Meals from the Top of the Stove*

These meals are simple to prepare. Many take very little time at all (especially if you have leftover rice and/or beans in the refrigerator or freezer). They underline my advice given earlier: the real trick in saving time (besides using a pressure cooker) is always to cook at least twice the amount of beans that you are going to use for that recipe and freeze what you don't use. Grains will keep for several days in the refrigerator. If, however, you have a pressure cooker, you can cook the rice in the 20 minutes or so that it will take you to sauté the vegetables, set the table, etc.

I'm sure that if you use a pressure cooker or use already cooked grains and legumes, none of these recipes will take more than 30 minutes of your time. Of course the recipes are not intended to be exhaustive. There are infinite possibilities for complementing proteins on top of the stove! I've tried to present a variety of approaches to whet your palate and imagination for your own experimentation.

To guide you in your own creations, here are the easiest ways to get more protein and more usable protein into your "top-of-the-stove dishes":

Tips for grains

1. *Use ⅛ cup soy grits (granules) with every cup of grain.*
   Example: Greek-Style Skillet.
2. *Use a milk product* with grain.*
   Example: Parmesan Rice.
3. *Use ⅓ cup seeds† with every cup of grain.*
   Example: Sesame-Rice Fritters.

Tips for beans**

1. *Use 1⅓ cups grain to every ½ cup beans.* (Often you will want to use more beans per volume of grain. In that case just add some milk product or some seeds.)
   Example: Roman Rice and Beans.
2. *Use a milk product with every dish that is mainly beans.* (You don't have to worry about proportions here.)
   Example: Chili Beans with Cheese Quesadillas.
3. *Use ½ cup seeds to every ⅓ cup beans.*
   Example: Bean Burgers.

Tips for peanuts

1. *Use 1 cup seeds to every ¾ cup peanuts.*
   Example: Confetti Rice.

NOTE: All proportions given in dry measure.

* Milk, non-fat dry milk, yogurt, cheese, etc.
† Sunflower or ground sesame seeds.
** Beans, peas, or lentils.

Recipes:

1. Skillet Vegetable Sauté with Grains:
   Herbed Vegetable Sauté
   Greek-Style Skillet
   Wheat-Soy Varnishkas

2. Skillet Vegetable Sauté with Grains and Beans:
   Roman Rice and Beans
   Savory Rice
   Spanish Bulgur

3. Skillet Fruit-Nut Sauté with Grains:
   Confetti Rice
   Song of India Rice
   Curried Soybeans and Peanuts

4. Fritters and Patties:
   Sesame-Rice Fritters
   Bean Burgers

5. Stews:
   Authentic Chili Beans with Rice or
      Quesadillas
   Spanish Soybeans
   Hearty Latin Stew

6. And Other Delicious Ideas:
   Parmesan Rice
   Creamed Celery Sauté
   Leafy Chinese Tofu
   Sweet-and-Sour Stuffed Cabbage

Herbed Vegetable Sauté

3 servings

average serving = approx. 6 g usable protein
14–17% of daily protein allowance

Have ready:
1 cup raw brown rice,
cooked (3 cups). Why not
cook extra for tomorrow?

Sauté in oil:
1-2 cloves garlic, minced
1-2 celery stalks, chopped
1 onion, chopped
1 green pepper, chopped,
or brocoli, sliced thinly
1-2 carrots (sliced)
¼ lb mushrooms, sliced

Stir in well:
¼ tsp each paprika, sage,
marjoram, and rosemary
½ cup ground, toasted
sesame seed
2 tbsp brewer's yeast*
(optional)
salt, pepper

Serve with:
soy sauce

Add the cooked rice. Stir. Simmer for several minutes
so that the flavors will mix. Add hot stock or water
if needed to prevent sticking, and adjust seasonings to
taste. Serve with soy sauce sprinkled over all (use just
a little).

You can vary the vegetables and the seasonings in
this recipe, using whatever you have available, or any
favorite combination. The rice can be pressure cooked
while the vegetables are being prepared and sautéed,
or it can be cooked ahead. A salad of diced apple/
raisins/nuts or seeds with yogurt-based dressing goes
well with this colorful and zesty pilaf.

Complementary protein: rice + sesame (or yeast)

---

* If your brewer's yeast is too strong to be used in this
quantity, you might like to try the tasteless variety now available.

Greek-Style Skillet

4 servings

average serving = approx. 10 g usable protein
23–28% of daily protein allowance

Have ready:
1 cup raw brown rice,
   cooked with ¼ cup soy
   grits (3 cups)

Sauté until golden:
2 tbsp olive oil
1 medium onion, chopped
1 clove garlic, minced

Add and sauté 5 min more:
1 small or medium eggplant,
   peeled, diced (1 inch
   cubes)
¼ lb green beans or other
   green vegetable (not
   necessary but adds a
   beautiful touch)

Add and sauté 1 min:
½ to 1 tsp mint
½ to 1 tsp dill weed
1 tbsp parsley flakes

Add:
juice of one lemon
   (2 tbsp)
1 cup canned tomatoes
1 8-oz can tomato sauce

Cover and cook 15 min.

*Serve over cooked grain
with yogurt (2 cups)*

This combination of foods and seasonings is typical-
ly Turkish or Greek. For a very special dinner, serve
with a Greek salad combining lettuce, tomatoes, Greek
olives, anchovies, and feta cheese.

Complementary protein: rice + soy

Wheat-Soy Varnishkas

4 servings

average serving = approx. 11 g usable protein
26–31% of daily protein allowance

Have ready:
1 cup dry macaroni sea
  shells or other macaroni,
  cooked and drained

*Sauté and set aside in
another dish:*
¼-½ lb mushrooms, sliced*
1 large onion, chopped

Turn off heat.

*In same skillet, mix until
grain coated:*
¼ cup soy grits
¾ cup bulgur wheat (or
  kasha, i.e. buckwheat
  groats)
1 beaten egg

*Toast grain over medium
heat, stirring constantly
until dry. Pour over grain:*
2 cups stock or water with
  vegetable seasoning

*Cover tightly, lower heat.
Cook 10 min.*

*When grains are fluffy, toss
with:*
sautéed onion and
  mushrooms
cooked macaroni
1 tbsp butter
plenty of salt, pepper (the
  pepper is especially
  important)

Garnish with:
parsley (the color adds a
  lovely touch)

This is a traditional dish in Jewish cuisine when made with kasha (buckwheat groats). I added the protein, and you can make it into a delicious light meal by adding, for example, a grated carrot-and-raisin salad or sweet-and-sour red cabbage (store-bought or homemade).

Complementary protein: wheat + soy

----

* I like this dish even without mushrooms, although it is much better with them. Or substitute or add chopped celery—sautéed just as mushrooms.

Roman Rice and Beans

6 servings

average serving = approx. 8 g usable protein
21–25% of daily protein allowance

Have ready:
¾ cup dried beans (pea, kidney), cooked (about 2 cups)
2 cups raw brown rice, cooked with 2 tsp salt (about 5 cups)

Sauté:
oil as needed (olive is good)
2 cloves garlic, crushed
1 large onion, chopped
1-2 carrots, chopped
1 stalk celery or 1 green pepper, chopped

⅔ cup parsley, chopped
2-3 tsp dried basil
1 tsp oregano

Add:
2-3 large tomatoes, coarsely chopped
2 tsp salt
pepper to taste
2 cups cooked beans (pea, kidney)

Combine:
5 cups cooked brown rice
½ cup or more Parmesan cheese

Add bean mixture to rice mixture. Garnish with more parsley and more grated cheese.

This dish has been one of my family's favorites from the first edition. With a green salad and Italian bread it is a satisfying meal. (It's great for serving to large gatherings too.)

Complementary protein: beans + rice

Savory Rice

4 servings

average serving = approx. 7 g usable protein
16–20% of daily protein allowance

Have ready:
1¼ cups raw brown rice,
  cooked (3 cups)
¼ cup dry soybeans, cooked
  with bay leaf (¾ cup)

2 cloves garlic, crushed
1-2 cups chopped
  vegetables (i.e. carrots,
  celery, mushrooms,
  bamboo shoots, including
  sprouts)

Sauté:
oil as needed (preferably
  peanut)
¾ cup onion, chopped

2 tbsp soy sauce

nuts or seeds (optional)

(Take out already cooked rice. If you forgot last time to cook extra, why not do it this time?)

Oil a wok or large frying pan. Place over a medium to high flame and, starting with the onion, sauté the vegetables quickly, just until they are heated through and coated with oil. Do not overcook, as this oriental way of stir-frying vegetables makes a colorful as well as nutritious dish. The quick cooking retains the nutrients in the vegetables better than any other method. Stir the rice into the vegetables and sprinkle with soy sauce (about 1 tbsp). When the rice is hot, stir in the cooked beans (with bay leaf removed), and serve at once with more soy sauce, with the optional nuts and seeds sprinkled on top.

Complementary protein: rice + beans

Spanish Bulgur

4 servings

average serving = approx. 6 g usable protein
14–17% of daily protein allowance

Have ready:
¼-½ cup dry beans, cooked
　(about 1 cup)

*Sauté until onion golden
and bulgur coated with oil:*
2 tbsp cooking oil
1 clove garlic, minced
½ cup green onions,
　chopped

½ green pepper, diced
1¼ cups raw bulgur

Add:
1 tsp paprika
1 tsp salt
⅛ tsp ground pepper
dash cayenne
1 no. 2 can tomatoes
cooked beans

Cover, bring to boil, then reduce heat and simmer 15 minutes or until liquid is absorbed and bulgúr tender (adding more liquid if necessary).

This dish is lighter than Spanish rice and just as tasty. The beans make it into a whole meal. A good salad with this dish is sliced cucumber and tomato in a vinaigrette dressing.

Complementary protein: wheat + beans

Confetti Rice

4 servings

average serving = approx. 7 g usable protein
16–20% of daily protein allowance

Have ready:
1 cup raw brown rice,
    cooked, (3 cups)

⅔ cup mixed nuts,*
    chopped
½ cup ground sesame seeds

Sauté until onion golden:
oil as needed
1 small onion, chopped
1 cup mixed dried fruits,
    chopped

Stir in:
¼-½ tsp cloves
½ tsp salt
cooked rice
butter (optional)

Pour a little melted butter over all (optional). Serve with fresh steamed green beans for a mouth-watering meal.

Complementary protein: rice + sesame

Sunflower and seeds

---

* If you used peanuts and added sunflower seeds to complement their protein, you would probably have lots more usable protein.

Song of India Rice

4 servings

average serving = approx. 8 g usable protein
19–22% of daily protein allowance

Have ready:
1¼ cups raw brown rice,
  cooked* with 2 tbsp soy
  grits (granules) (3 cups)

Sauté:
1 tbsp butter
1 tbsp curry powder
½ cup cashews and raisins

1 onion, sliced
1 apple, cored and sliced

Add and mix well:
cooked rice and grits
salt and pepper to taste

Serve with:
yogurt

Green peas make a good accompaniment to this dish; or to be traditional serve cooked yellow lentils (dahl).

Variations:
1. Add 1 tsp coriander seeds.
2. Omit curry and add 1 cup shredded cabbage and 1 tsp caraway seed.

Complementary protein: rice + soy

---

* Or, if starting out with uncooked rice, you may want to cook the rice/soy grits with raisins and part of the curry powder so that the raisins are nice and plumb and the rice has absorbed the curry.

Curried Soybeans and Peanuts

4 servings

average serving = approx. 11 g usable protein
26–31% of daily protein allowance

Have ready:
⅓ dry soybeans, cooked
   with bay leaf (about 1
   cup). Why not cook extra
   for tomorrow?
⅔ cup bulgur wheat,
   cooked with
¾ cup brown rice and
   1 tsp tarragon

*Sauté until onion is
transparent:*
oil as needed
1 tbsp curry powder
1 apple, chopped
1 onion, chopped
¼ cup roasted peanuts
¼ cup raisins (optional)

Stir in:
cooked beans
½ tsp ground fresh ginger
paprika (to taste)
soy sauce (to taste—start
   with very little)

*Remove to serving dish and
stir in:*
1-1½ cups yogurt (If you
   stir the yogurt into the hot
   saucepan, it might
   curdle.)

*Serve over the cooked
grain.*

Once the beans and grains are cooked, this dish is really quick to put together, and delicious as well. It is special enough to serve to guests but simple enough to enjoy yourself. For company serve a citrus fruit cup appetizer and Sesame Dream Bars (see page 339) for dessert.

Complementary protein: soybeans + wheat, rice, peanuts.

Sesame-Rice Fritters

3 servings

average serving = approx. 7 g usable protein
16–20% of daily protein allowance

Have ready:
⅔ cup raw brown rice,
  cooked (about 1½ cups)
⅓ cup toasted ground
  sesame seeds*

Mix together:
¼ cup milk + 2 tbsp instant
dry milk

1 egg yolk
2 tbsp whole wheat flour
⅛ tsp pepper
1 tsp salt

Beat until stiff:
1 egg white

oil for frying

Combine rice, ground sesame seeds, and milk mixture; mix well. Fold in stiffly beaten egg white. Drop by tablespoonfuls onto hot, oiled griddle and fry until brown. Drain on absorbent paper.

This is a good way to take rice to a picnic! It's also good served with curry or cream sauce for a light lunch or supper with steamed asparagus, for example, and a fresh tomato salad. It is great as a "finger food" for a party.

Complementary protein: rice + sesame

---

* If you don't already have some toasted ground sesame seeds, why not do up a whole batch now? Simply stir in a dry skillet until golden and blend at high speed until the seeds become a coarse meal. Save the extra for garnishing any type of dish or adding to baked goods and casseroles.

Bean Burgers

4 servings

average serving = approx. 18 g usable protein
42–50% of daily protein allowance

Have ready:
¾ cup peanuts and ⅓ cup
  dry soybeans, cooked
  together and mashed
  (about 2 cups)
½ cup toasted ground
  sesame seeds
½ cup toasted sunflower
  seeds

1 onion, grated
1 carrot, grated
1 stalk celery, chopped
2 cloves garlic, crushed or
  minced

Mix all with:
1 egg, beaten
½ tsp salt
½ tsp dill seed, ground

Sauté:
oil as needed

Shape into patties. Brown on both sides in a little oil. (Or bake in a small loaf pan until dry.) These are tasty with any tomato sauce or even ketchup!

If you have ground sesame seeds and toasted sunflower seeds on hand, the patties are really no trouble to put together. If you want to use soybeans that have been cooked separately, that's OK. Then use roasted peanuts, chopped.

You will find that the cold burgers (or loaf slices) make wonderful sandwiches with cheese, lettuce, and ketchup. For a real feast, serve on a bed of grain with your favorite sauce. Or serve with a steamed or sautéed vegetable for a lighter meal.

Complementary protein: peanuts + soy + sesame/sunflower

Authentic Chili Beans with Rice or Quesadillas

6–8 servings

average serving = approx. 16 g usable protein
37–44% of daily protein allowance

Simmer for 2 hours:
2 cups dried pinto (or kidney) beans (5-6 cups cooked or canned*)
1½ quarts water or stock
½ large onion, chopped
1 clove garlic, minced
1 bay leaf

In separate pan heat:
2 tbsp oil

And add to make roux paste:
2½ tbsp flour
2-3 tsp chili powder
1-2 tsp cumin
1 onion, chopped

Cook roux paste 5 minutes and add to beans while stirring.

Cook for another hour until the beans are soft and the chili is thickened. Adjust seasoning, add salt and pepper to taste, and serve with one of the following:

Rice

Serve over:
2 cups raw rice, cooked (about 4-5 cups)

Top with:
½ lb shredded Monterey jack or cheddar cheese

Quesadillas

1-1½ dozen tortillas

1 lb jack cheese

Slice cheese and lay inside of tortilla, folding it in half like a sandwich. Heat in the oven at 350°F until cheese is thoroughly melted. This is a simple grilled cheese sandwich, and complements the spicy flavor of the chili.

Complementary protein: beans + rice
                            beans + milk product

Spinach, Onion, Garlic, Sesame

---

* If using already cooked beans, heat them in pot with one cup of water or stock and proceed.

Spanish Soybeans over Mixed Grains

8 servings

average serving = approx. 13 g usable protein
30–36% of daily protein allowance

Have ready:
⅔ cup dry soybeans, cooked
   with ½ cup peanuts (1½
   cups). Why not cook extra
   for a future dish?
1⅓ cups raw bulgur and 1½
   cups raw brown rice,
   cooked together (6 cups)

Sauté in large pot:
3 tbsp oil
2 cloves garlic, minced
1 onion, chopped
1 green pepper, chopped
¼ lb mushrooms, sliced
   (optional)

*Add and sauté until coated
with oil:*
cooked soybeans and
   peanuts

*Add, mix well, and simmer
15 min or longer:*
2 cups stewed tomatoes
1 tbsp soy flour
3 tbsp brewer's yeast
1 tsp oregano
1 tsp celery seeds, ground
1 tsp salt
pinch cayenne

Topping:
½ cup grated sharp cheddar
   cheese (optional)

Serve over the mixed grains, with the cheese sprinkled
on top.

This is a very tasty, satisfying dish, though it may
sound ordinary. Serve with a spinach salad, or for a
crowd, add the Easy Mexican Pan Bread (page 224).

Complementary protein: soy + peanuts + wheat
+ rice

Hearty Latin Stew

8 servings

average serving = approx. 7 g usable protein
16–20% of daily protein allowance

Have ready:
1 cup raw brown rice plus
  ¾ cup raw bulgur, cooked
  together (5 cups)
⅔ cup dry soybeans, cooked
  (about 2 cups)

*Sauté lightly in deep skillet
or heavy pot:*
oil as needed
1 small can green chilis,
  diced

½ lb string beans, sliced into
  2-inch pieces
1 tsp chili powder (to taste)
dash hot sauce

Mix in:
1 16-oz can stewed
  tomatoes
1 12-oz can corn
cooked rice
cooked beans
salt
pepper

Simmer for about 15 minutes. This stew will warm the spirit on a cold winter's day.

If you are expecting a crowd, make up some corn bread and a big salad for a hearty buffet.

Complementary protein: soy + wheat + rice

Parmesan Rice

2 servings

average serving = approx. 10 g usable protein
23–28% daily protein allowance

Have ready:
⅔ cup raw brown rice,
cooked with 1 tsp salt
and tossed with 2 tbsp
butter (optional) (2 cups).
Why not cook extra?

Mix together:
1 egg, beaten
¼ cup Parmesan cheese,
grated

juice of 1 lemon
pepper to taste

Add:
cooked rice

Options for extra goodness:
¼ cup chopped parsley
¼ cup toasted ground
sesame seeds

Stir and simmer five minutes. Serve immediately.

Serving ideas:

This goes well with sautéed zucchini or eggplant. These or other vegetables could be sautéed and stirred into the rice.

Or for a more elegant dish, make a mound of the Parmesan rice in the center of a large platter and arrange the sautéed vegetable around the edge. Garnish with parsley.

Or you can use this delightful-tasting recipe as a pie crust. Simply pat it into a pie pan (adding ¼ cup toasted ground sesame seeds for an extra nutty flavor). Bake at 350°F until beginning to get crusty. Fill with your favorite sautéed vegetables, sprinkle with more toasted ground sesame seeds, and add a cream sauce if you wish.

Complementary protein: rice + milk product

Creamed Celery Sauté

4 servings

average serving = approx. 9 g usable protein
21–25% of daily protein allowance

Sauté just until tender:
butter
4 stalks celery, chopped,
    with leaves
1 tbsp dried parsley
    flakes (more if fresh)
1-2 scallions, chopped
1 tsp lemon juice
salt and pepper to taste

*Remove from heat and just
before serving add:*
1½ cups cottage cheese or
    mix of cottage cheese and
    yogurt,* blended smooth

Serve over:
halved baked potatoes or
your favorite pasta

Garnish with:
parsley

This is such a simple idea but so good. Serve with fresh sliced tomatoes and hearty, buttered rye bread. (Try Ellen Ewald's quick "Wheatless Flat Bread" in *Recipes for a Small Planet;* for details, see "Recommended Paperback Cookbooks" at the back of this book.)

Complementary protein: milk product + potato (or wheat)

---

* The combination of part cottage cheese and part yogurt gives a delicious sour cream flavor.

Leafy Chinese Tofu (Soy Curd)

3 servings

average serving = approx. 10 g usable protein
23–28% of daily protein allowance

Have ready:
1 cup raw brown rice,
   cooked (3 cups)

Sauté 5 min in large pan:
oil as needed
2 cups tofu, cut into 1 inch
   squares (⅔ lb)

*Push tofu to center and
around edges put:*
spinach or any leafy green,
   torn

Sprinkle over tofu:
¼ cup toasted ground
   sesame seeds
soy sauce to taste

*Cover and steam to wilt
spinach.*

Be careful not to overcook the spinach. Remove
from heat and drain excess liquid. Sprinkle soy sauce
over the spinach, and serve with rice.

Variation: Spread a mixture of miso (soybean paste)
and sesame butter, blended in equal proportions, on
one side of sliced tofu and sprinkle with wheat germ.
While you brown this side spread the miso-sesame
mixture and sprinkle wheat germ on the second side.
Turn once more to brown the second side.

Complementary protein: soy + rice
                       soy + sesame

Sweet-and-Sour Stuffed Cabbage

4 servings

average serving = approx. 9 g usable protein
21–25% of daily protein allowance

Have ready:
12 whole cabbage leaves,
    steamed until limp
1¼ cups raw brown rice and
    ⅛ cup soy grits, cooked
    together, plus ½ tsp salt

Sauté:
2 tbsp oil
1 onion, chopped

Add and sauté 2 minutes:
½ cup pignolia nuts,
    chopped cashews, or
    toasted sunflower seeds
1 scant tbsp caraway seed
½ cup raisins

Sauce:
1 15-oz can tomato sauce
    with 1 tbsp lemon juice
    and 1 tbsp brown sugar
    (more to taste)

Topping:
1 cup yogurt

Combine rice mixture with sautéed ingredients. Add enough tomato sauce to moisten mixture. Place about 3 tbsp of this filling on each cabbage leaf and roll up, securing with a toothpick if necessary. Place the rolls in a skillet and pour the remaining tomato sauce over them. Cover and cook about 15 minutes or until cabbage is quite tender. The contrast of the green cabbage and the red tomato sauce makes this dish quite beautiful. It is especially good topped with yogurt.

Variations:
1. Moisten mixture with 1 beaten egg instead of the tomato sauce.
2. Instead of removing leaves from the cabbage, cut out the center of the cabbage, boil 10 minutes, and then fill with stuffing.
3. A ½ tsp of cinnamon may be added to mixture before stuffing to give this dish an unusual flavor.

Complementary protein: soy + rice
seed + milk product

(B) *Bread and Cheese Made Elegant*

If you have just bread, cheese, and eggs in the house, you can surprise yourself at the beautiful meals that you can prepare. The complementary protein combination is simple: milk protein + wheat protein.

Recipes:

1. Easy and Elegant Cheese "Soufflé"

2. Crusty Cheddar Bake

3. Monterey Corn Casserole

4. Vegetable Cheese "Soufflé"

5. Instant Pizza Miniatures

6. Gourmet Curried Eggs on Toast (or Rice)

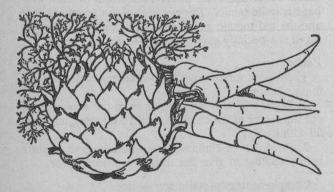

Artichoke, Carrots

Easy and Elegant Cheese "Soufflé"

This simple recipe turned out to be one of the great favorites of the first edition. Here is the same basic recipe, followed by several interesting variations that I have discovered.

5 servings

average serving = approx. 20 g usable protein
46–56% of daily protein allowance

Layer in oiled baking dish:
3 cups grated cheese
4-6 slices bread

Pour over it:
2 cups milk or 1½ cups
   milk and ½ cup liquor
   (wine or vermouth)

*Mix separately and pour
over bread also:*
3 eggs, beaten
½ tsp salt
½ tsp Worcestershire
   sauce
½ tsp thyme
½ tsp dry mustard
pepper

Let stand for 30 minutes. Bake at 350°F 1 hour in a pan of hot water.

This dish sounds so very easy and homey, but is truly elegant. When you take it out of the oven, you yourself won't believe how simply it was made. In a deep dish it has the appearance of a soufflé; in a shallow dish it resembles a quiche.

It is great for supper with soup or you might want to make a hearty supper for friends by serving it with the Tabouli salad recipe found on page 249.

Complementary protein: milk product + wheat

Crusty Cheddar Bake

In the above recipe, use cheddar cheese instead of the Swiss; 1¾ cup milk and ¼ cup sherry for the milk mixture; and ½ tsp ground marjoram instead of the thyme.

Monterey Corn Casserole

In the above recipe, use Monterey jack cheese instead of Swiss; substitute 1 lb canned creamed corn for the milk or milk mixture; and replace the thyme with 4 or 5 drops Tabasco.

Vegetable Cheese Soufflé

Using the cheese and seasoning variation of your choice, layer in ½ cup chopped celery, ¼ cup chopped onion, and ½ lb mushrooms, which have been sautéed together in 3 tbsp butter.

Instant Pizza Miniatures

average serving = approx. 9 g usable protein
21–25% of daily protein allowance

Toast:
bread/English muffins

Spread with:
tomato paste

Top with:
cheese (mozzarella is our
favorite here)

Toast until melted.

Possible garnishes:
Parmesan cheese
chopped scallions
chopped parsley
sliced green pepper
sliced fresh mushroom

What might have been only a melted cheese sandwich
has become a quick supper when you just don't feel like
cooking. Serve with a salad or soup.

Complementary protein: milk + wheat

Rye

Gourmet Curried Eggs on Toast (or Rice)

4–6 servings

average serving = approx. 16 g usable protein
37–44% of daily protein allowance

Have ready:
6-8 large eggs, hard boiled
½ cup shredded Swiss
  cheese
4-6 slices toast or
  1½ cups raw rice, cooked
  (3-4 cups)

*Over low heat melt 2 tbsp
butter and add, stirring
2 min:*
3 tbsp flour
1 tbsp curry powder (more
  or less to taste)

½ tsp beau monde
  seasoning (optional)

*Then add slowly and cook
5 min, stirring:*
¼ cup sherry
2 cups milk
salt and pepper
½ cup shredded Swiss
  cheese (or more)

Garnish with:
chopped parsley

Sauce will seem thin at first, but it thickens in baking.

Place eggs, sliced in half, in an oiled casserole. Cover with curry sauce. Sprinkle with shredded cheese. Bake for 20 minutes at 350°F. Serve over toast (or rice). Sprinkle with chopped parsley.

This simple casserole has a truly "gourmet" flavor. It is especially good served with cooked spinach, asparagus, or broccoli.

Complementary protein: wheat + milk product

(C) Super Supper Pancakes

If you have flour, milk, and eggs in the house, you should never again be at a loss for what to have for supper! Call it a crêpe, a blintze, or a pancake—it certainly will not have the appearance of a "make-do" meal; your results can be quite elegant. The protein complementarity in this section is simple: milk products + wheat and potatoes + milk.

Recipes:

1. Whole Wheat–Sesame Crêpes (Basic Crêpe Recipe) (Don't be put off by the word "crêpe"; they're easy and fun!)

2. Superb Supper Crêpes with Sauce:
   Vegetable-Filled Crêpes with Cheese/Herb Sauce
   Cheese-Filled Crêpes with Sauce

3. Dessert/Brunch or Sweet-Tooth Supper Crêpes:
   Cheese-Fruit Crêpes
   Applesauce-Raisin Crêpes

4. Supper Special Pancakes:
   Herbed Dinner Cakes
   Fruit Pancakes

5. Potato Fritters:
   Potato Latkes
   Potato Corn Cakes

Whole Wheat–Sesame Crêpes (Basic Crêpe Recipe)

4–5 servings (makes approximately 15 crêpes)
3 unfilled crêpes = approx. 7 g usable protein
16–20% of daily protein allowance

Sift together:*
⅔ cup whole wheat flour
½ tsp salt

Beat separately:
2 cups milk

2 eggs
2 tbsp oil

Combine wet and dry and add:
2 tbsp ground sesame seeds
(toasted or raw)

Fry crêpes in a lightly oiled heavy frying pan—a heavy iron omelet pan is best. Make one crêpe at a time, using approximately ¼ cup of batter each. After pouring the batter into a hot pan, tilt the pan to spread the batter into a thin, round layer. Wait until the crêpe is fully solidified and browned on one side before turning it. (With a spatula I loosen all edges before turning.) Cook on the other side until browned. Once you have started frying the crêpes, you may not need to add more oil to the pan. If you do, add only a little, enough to barely cover. Also, the batter will tend to separate, so merely stir and scoop from the bottom each time.

I used to think that crêpes could only be made by great chefs, but then I discovered that they are easy and fun to make. And they have many virtues: they are made from ingredients—wheat, eggs, milk, oil—that we always have; they can become dessert, supper, or brunch; they store well in the refrigerator; and, best of all, *everyone* loves them! It is fun to use ⅔ of the finished crêpes in the main course and to use the rest with a sweet topping for dessert.

Complementary protein: wheat + milk product
sesame + milk product

---

* Sifting is optional.

Vegetable-Filled Crêpes with Cheese/Herb Sauce

4–5 servings

3 crêpes with cheese sauce = approx. 17 g usable protein
39–47% of daily protein allowance

Have ready:
whole wheat–sesame crêpes
    (can be made in advance)
For filling, choose among
fresh vegetables
(3 cups finely chopped):
mushrooms
asparagus
broccoli
cauliflower
onion
green pepper
peas
(any combination)

To basic white sauce made
with:
3 tbsp butter
3 tbsp flour*
3 cups milk
salt and pepper

Add your choice:
2 cups sliced, sautéed
    mushrooms
1½ cup grated cheese
½ cup Parmesan cheese
    (more to taste)
2 cups chopped spinach
    (with 1 tsp lemon juice)
½ cup parsley

Add your choice of herbs:
basil, thyme, rosemary,
    marjoram, etc.
cayenne pepper
Worcestershire sauce

Garnish folded crêpes with
choice of:
parsley
toasted ground sesame
    seeds
Parmesan cheese
sliced olives
paprika

Fill each crêpe with a little sauce and finely chopped cooked vegetables of your choice. Roll up and pour rest of sauce over all. Garnish.

Complementary protein: wheat + milk

* When making white sauce, be sure to cook (almost toast) flour with butter before adding milk.

Cheese-Filled Crêpes with Sauce

4–5 servings

3 cheese-filled crêpes with marinara sauce =
approx. 14 g usable protein
32–39% of daily protein allowance

Have ready:
whole wheat–sesame crêpes
(can be made in
advance)

Filling:
8 oz ricotta cheese (or
cottage cheese, blended)
½ cup Parmesan cheese
½ cup parsley
¼ tsp salt
dash of pepper
dash of nutmeg

Optional:
spinach, just wilted and
chopped fine
mushrooms, sliced and
sautéed

Sauce:
marinara or spaghetti
sauce*
cheese sauce (see preceding
recipe)
mushroom sauce (see
Herbed Dinner Cakes,
page 192)

Possible garnishes:
parsley
toasted ground sesame
seeds
Parmesan cheese
sliced olives
paprika

While sauce is cooking, you can mix the filling ingredients together. Spread several tablespoons of the
filling mixture in the center of each crêpe, then roll up.

Place the rolled crêpes into a large frying pan. Cover
with the sauce and simmer a few minutes, until the
filling is thoroughly heated.

Complementary protein: wheat + milk

---

* For a simple sauce recipe, see Ricotta Lasagne Swirls on
page 229.

Cheese-Fruit Crêpes

4–5 servings

3 filled crêpes = approx. 15 g usable protein
35–42% of daily protein allowance

Have ready:
whole wheat–sesame crêpes
  (can be made in advance)

Filling:
½ cup yogurt
1½ cup cottage cheese
  (or ricotta)
1 tbsp honey
nuts (optional)

Topping:
2 cups your choice of stewed
  or fresh fruit—
    berries
    peaches
    rhubarb, etc.

Mix filling ingredients, then spread several teaspoons of filling in each crêpe. Roll crêpes and place in pan. Cover with topping of your choice. Heat and serve.

Applesauce-Raisin Crêpes

Follow basic crêpe recipe. When you first pour crêpe batter into pan, *sprinkle with:*

a few raisins
dash of cinnamon
¼ tsp honey

Top with a generous tbsp of:
applesauce mixed with
  yogurt

Fry on both sides.

Complementary protein: wheat + milk

Herbed Dinner Cakes*

4 servings

2 pancakes with sauce = approx. 13 g usable protein
30–36% of daily protein allowance

Sift together:
1 cup whole wheat flour
¼ cup soy flour
2 tsp baking powder
½ tsp salt

Beat separately:
1-2 egg yolks (set whites
   aside)†
1 cup milk
3 tbsp oil

*Combine wet and dry
ingredients. Mix.*

Sauté in oil:
1 large onion, chopped
2 green peppers
1 tomato, chopped

Add:
1 tsp oregano
1 tsp basil

Fold sauté mix into batter. Beat egg whites until
stiff and fold into mixture. Fry. Serve with topping of
grated cheddar cheese or with mushroom sauce. Or
stack two cakes for each serving, with cheese in between
and the mushroom sauce on top. A light dinner with a
fresh green salad.

Easy Mushroom Sauce

2 cups mushrooms, sliced
   thinly
2 tbsp butter
1 tbsp flour
1½ cups milk

salt
pepper
dash of Worcestershire
   sauce

Fry mushrooms in butter. When mushrooms are soft,

* For a basic, simple, and good pancake, delete vegetables.
† Pancakes still good, although not quite so light, if you
don't beat whites separately.

add flour to coat the mushrooms. Stir to toast the flour a bit. Add milk and mix thoroughly.

Add salt, pepper, and Worcestershire sauce. Stir over heat until sauce thickens.

Complementary protein: wheat + milk

Green pepper, Scallions, Mushrooms, Garlic

Fruit Pancakes

6 servings
average serving = approx. 8 g usable protein
19–22% of daily protein allowance

Have ready:
¾ cup raw brown rice,
   cooked (about 2 cups)

Mix together:
1 cup whole wheat flour
⅓ cup sesame seed meal
1 tbsp baking powder
1 tbsp brown sugar
½ tsp salt

Blend separately:
2-3 egg yolks
1½ cups milk (or more for
   a thin batter)
¼ cup oil
the cooked rice

Have ready:
3 stiffly beaten egg whites
1 cup fruit chunks (apples,
   pears, peaches, bananas,
   berries, etc.)

Stir the wet ingredients into the dry, using the fewest strokes possible. Just be sure the dry ingredients are wet. Fold in the egg whites, then gently fold in the fruit. Bake on a hot, oiled griddle.

Complementary protein: rice + sesame

Potato Latkes

2–3 servings

average serving = approx. 11 g usable protein
26–31% of daily protein allowance

Combine:
½ onion, grated
1 large potato, peeled,
    grated (liquid drained)
2 tbsp whole wheat flour

2 tbsp chopped parsley
2 eggs, beaten
salt and pepper
5 tbsp instant dry milk
oil for frying

Using this batter, fry like small pancakes in hot oil. Brown both sides well. Top with applesauce and serve with a cottage cheese-and-tomato salad.

Potato Corn Cakes

Add one small can drained whole kernel corn to Potato Latke recipe.

Complementary protein: potato + milk

(D) *The Universal Flatbread Sandwich*

It seems that every culture faced with the same "What's for supper?" dilemma has come up with at least one similar answer: a round flatbread, be it corn or wheat, fried or baked, that can be filled in any number of delicious ways—or eaten plain as bread. In Mexico they call it the "tortilla," in India the "chapati," and in the Middle East the "pita." In my house it's known humbly as a filled sandwich. Since we are lucky enough to live in an area where we can get both tortillas and pita (even delicious whole wheat pita with sesame seeds!), we keep them on hand always for some of our favorite meals.

Here are three filled sandwich recipes that are American takeoffs on traditional cultural dishes. They make great buffet dinners because everyone will enjoy putting his own together. Following these recipes, you'll find other ideas for great filling combinations.

Recipes:

1. Tostadas

2. Middle Eastern Tacos

3. Indian Flavor Fold-Ups: Peas Sautéed/Tomato-Nut Topping

4. American Variations on the Universal Flatbread Sandwich

Tostadas

6 servings of 2

average serving = approx. 17 g usable protein
39–47% of daily protein allowance

Have ready:
2 cups dry pinto beans,
   cooked until quite soft
   (5 cups cooked or
   canned)
1 dozen corn tortillas

Garnishes:
½ lb Monterey Jack or
   cheddar cheese, grated
½ head of lettuce, shredded

1-2 fresh tomatoes,
   chopped
1 onion, finely chopped

Sauce:
1 can El Paso or Ortega
   green chili sauce or
   tacos sauce

Topping:
1 cup yogurt (optional—but
   try it, it's good!)

In a deep, heavy skillet, heat oil very hot. Then
quickly add the beans with a wooden spoon (some
liquid is added this way). The oil should be so hot that
the beans are toasted in the oil. Continue cooking at a
high heat, all the time mashing with the back of the
spoon. Add salt to taste. *Refritoes* is an idiom for "well-
fried," not "refried."

Fry each tortilla briefly in a little bit of oil or heat
them until crisp in the oven. To assemble, spread a tortilla with a sizable amount of beans, then top with the
garnishes, sauce, and yogurt. This dinner makes a festive and delicious community meal.

Complementary protein: beans + corn
                        beans + cheese

---

* If you prefer to make your own sauce, here is an authentic recipe: Peel and remove seeds of 4 ripe tomatoes. Remove
the seeds from 6 green chilies. Chop the tomatoes, chilies, and
1 onion. Mix all three well with 1 clove of garlic, 1 tsp salt,
⅛ tsp pepper, and 1 tsp vinegar.

Middle Eastern Tacos

10 tacos

2 tacos = approx. 10 g usable protein
23–28% of daily protein allowance

Have ready:
10 pieces Middle Eastern
flatbread (pita) or 10
wheat tortillas

Purée together:*
1 cup dry garbanzo beans,
well cooked (3 cups)
½ cup (heaping) toasted

ground sesame seeds or
¼ cup sesame butter
2 cloves garlic
2 tbsp lemon juice
¾ tsp coriander, ground
½ tsp salt
½ tsp cumin, ground
¼-½ tsp cayenne

Increase spices to taste. Let stand at least ½ hour
at room temperature. Cut pieces of Middle Eastern flatbread in half and fill "pockets" with bean mixture. You
may want to heat filled bread in oven before garnishing. Or serve on wheat tortillas, fried until soft but not
crisp. Add the following garnishes and allow everyone
at the table to assemble their own "taco":

shredded lettuce
chopped tomatoes
chopped cucumber

chopped onion
1½ cups yogurt (or cheese)

Wonderfully tasty and satisfying! Be sure to include
yogurt or cheese on each portion to complete the protein complementarity. Of all the recipes that appeared
in the first edition, this is the one we have eaten most
often. The bean-sesame mix makes a great cracker
spread too. And if you already have the beans cooked,
the whole thing can be put together in no time.

Complementary protein: beans + sesame

---

* Add liquid from beans or water if necessary, to make
blending easy.

Indian Flavor Fold-Ups:
Peas Sautéed/Tomato-Nut Topping

4 servings

2 Fold-Ups = approx. 16 g usable protein
37–44% of daily protein allowance

Have ready:
6-8 wheat tortillas or pita
(or, best of all, authentic
Indian chapatis, if you

have an Indian friend to
teach you how to make
them)

(You can easily make both the filling and topping at
the same time in separate skillets).

Filling

Have ready:
1 cup dry split yellow or
green peas, cooked and
mashed (about 3 cups)

Sauté together:
oil as needed

2 cloves garlic, minced or
1 onion, chopped
1 tbsp curry powder
pressed
⅔ cup raw ground sesame
seeds

When the onion-sesame mix is almost done, add the
mashed peas and continue frying over fairly high heat.
Stir constantly until the peas absorb the curry flavor and
have gotten a little toasty, adding more curry and/or
salt to taste.

Topping

Sauté together:
oil as needed
2-3 large tomatoes, sliced
1 large onion
1-2 cloves garlic, minced
or pressed

⅓ cup Spanish (or other)
peanuts
dashes of cumin and
coriander (optional)

Sauce

2 cups yogurt

To assemble: Put the filling, topping, and sauce in separate serving bowls and let each person fill his own tortilla or pita.

Variation: Serve with rice.

Complementary protein: beans + yogurt
sesame + peanuts

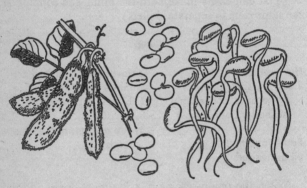

Soy beans   Pods, Beans, Sprouts

American Variations on the Universal Flatbread Sandwich

For a meal that is simple and new each time, fill either pita or tortillas (wheat or corn) with a variety of combinations according to your taste. Here are some of our favorite filling ingredients:

First layer, choose among:
tuna
lentils
sardines
chopped egg
beans, especially pinto, garbanzos (puréed or whole)
shredded cheese

Second layer, choose among:
chopped nuts
chopped red onion
sweet peas
chopped fresh spinach
shredded lettuce, cabbage
chopped cucumber
sliced beets
chopped apple
shredded cheese

toasted sunflower seeds
toasted ground sesame seeds
tomatoes

Seasonings, choose among:
dill
celery seed
curry
chili
curry
cumin
coriander

Dressing, choose among:
French
yogurt
blue cheese
vinaigrette

These sandwiches are good cold; all the ingredients can be placed on the table and everyone can make his or her own favorite combination. Or you can make up the sandwiches and put them in the oven until they are heated through. Try this hot filled sandwich:

Jamie's Hot Filled Pita

tuna	tomatoes, coarsely chopped
yogurt or mayonnaise	cheese, sliced
curry powder	pepper

Put all ingredients in the pocket of a "pita" and warm in the oven until the cheese melts.

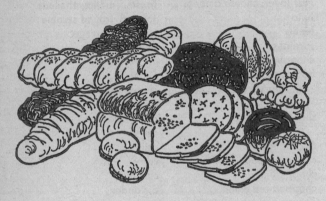

Bread

(E) *Pie-in-the-Sky Suppers*

If you are like me, you hesitate to make pies very often because of the ordeal of making and rolling a pie crust. Here are three ideas for supper pies that do not require rolling out a crust. (And they do not rely on the nutritionally meager store-bought crusts either!) The trick is simply patting the dough ingredients right into the pie plate. It is so simple, in fact, that you will probably wonder why you didn't think of it before. So here are ideas for cheese, bean, and vegetable pies— each with infinite possibilities for delicious variation depending on what you have on hand and your own imagination.

Recipes:

1. "Pat-In" Supper Pie Crusts:
   Easy Whole Wheat Crust
   Rice Crust
   Quick Cornmeal Crust

2. Simple-Elegant Cheese Pie

3. Cornbean Pie

4. Garden Vegetable Pie (With "Pat-In" Crust)

Easy Whole Wheat Crust

Have ready:
6 tbsp butter, softened
  slightly

*Sift into medium-sized
mixing bowl:*
1 cup whole wheat flour
⅛ tsp salt

Cut the butter in very small pieces. Mix ingredients with your fingers until pastry resembles cornmeal. Press over bottom and sides of 9-inch pie plate or cake pan. Bake for 10 minutes if you are using cooked filling, five minutes if you will be baking it with the filling.

This pie crust may be varied as follows:
1. If you are using a filling that does not contain the equivalent of at least ⅔ cup of milk or 1 oz of cheese to complement the whole wheat flour, add ⅛ cup softened soy grits* to the whole wheat flour.
2. If you are using it for a dessert crust, add 3 tbsp brown sugar.

Rice Crust

Use Parmesan Rice recipe, page 178, and add ¼ cup sesame seed meal. Pat into pie shell and bake for 10 minutes at 350°F.

Quick Cornmeal Crust

Mix:

2 cups yellow cornmeal	3 tbsp oil
½ tsp salt	½-¾ cup hot stock (or
2 tbsp brewer's yeast	enough to make stiff batter)

Mix all ingredients and pat into an oiled, deep 9-inch pie or cake dish. This crust is best with a spicy bean filling to complement the protein in the cornmeal.

---

* Soy flour gives it a slightly raw taste that you may not like.

Simple-Elegant Cheese Pie

6 servings

average serving = approx. 12 g usable protein
28–34% of daily protein allowance

Have ready:
whole wheat "pat-in" pie
crust in 8- or 9-inch pie
plate (see page 204).
(There is no need to add
the soy, as this pie has
enough cheese to com-
plement the whole
wheat.)

*Bake for 5-10 minutes at
350°F (until lightly brown)*

*Remove crust from oven and
fill with:*
1 sliced onion, sautéed or
not (optional)
½ cup marinated Italian
sweet peppers (optional,

but it is my *favorite*,
available in most grocery
stores)
¾ lb cheese, sliced (This can
be any cheese you like
that will melt nicely. I
prefer Swiss and Muen-
ster, or Gruyère, but
cheddar, American, etc.,
will work as well.)

Cover the cheese with:
2-3 tomatoes, sliced

*Sprinkle over top of
tomatoes:*
about 2 tbsp oil
2 tbsp oregano (to taste)
pepper (to taste)

Bake at 350°F for about 10 minutes, until cheese is
melted and bubbly and tomatoes are cooked. This
should not brown. Let cool slightly.

Serve as you would a quiche—as an appetizer, or as
the center of a meal with a salad, etc. It is as good as
a traditional quiche, without spending all the time it
takes to roll out a crust and grate the cheese.

Other options:
If you want this as a special dinner pie:

Place about ½ lb sliced and sautéed mushrooms
around the tomatoes. (Just remember to sauté the mush-

rooms in as little oil as possible, or the pie will be greasy.)

Or, if you want it to be more like a regular quiche, you may pour one egg, beaten with a little milk, over the cheese before baking and delete the oil and oregano.

Complementary protein: wheat + milk product

Cheeses

Crusty Cornbean Pie

4–6 servings

average serving = approx. 10 g usable protein
23–28% of daily protein allowance

Have ready:
Quick Cornmeal Crust
   (page 205)
1 cup dry kidney beans,
   cooked (3 cups or 20-oz
   can)

Sauté briefly:
oil as needed
1 onion, chopped
1 carrot, chopped
1 stalk celery, chopped

Add:
cooked beans
pinch cayenne
1 tsp cumin, ground
3 tbsp soy sauce

Topping:
⅓ cup or more of grated
   sharp cheese

Turn into the cornmeal crust. Bake at 350°F about
25 minutes. Remove from oven, sprinkle with cheese,
and bake 5 minutes more.

Complementary protein: beans + corn
                       beans + milk product

Garden Vegetable Pie
(With "Pat-In" Crust)

⅕ of pie = approx. 5 g usable protein
12–14% of daily protein allowance

Have ready:
One whole wheat "pat-in" crust (page 204) or rice crust (page 205). Bake either for 10 minutes.

about 4 cups cooked vegetables of your choice (carrots, cauliflower, broccoli, etc.). Don't let them get mushy!

Cream Sauce

Sauté:
1 tbsp butter
1 tbsp oil
¼ lb mushrooms

parsley
Your choice of herbs:
 tarragon
 thyme
 rosemary, etc.

Add and brown with mushrooms:
3 tbsp whole wheat flour

Optional additions:
¼ lb sliced cheese
1 tsp dried mustard

Gradually add and cook until thickens:
1 cup milk

Possible topping:
2 tbsp toasted ground sesame seeds

Season to taste with:
salt and pepper

Put the cooked vegetables in the pie crust.
Pour the sauce over the vegetables and bake in a 350°F oven, just until vegetables are heated and sauce bubbles. Sprinkle on topping. A beautiful dish that can be different each time.

Complementary protein: wheat + milk product

(F) *Something from the Oven, but Don't Call It a Casserole!*

While the cooking time for these dishes may be longer than for Meals from the Top of the Stove, your actual work time is no greater. Most can be easily adapted to the food you have on hand. Remember, never feel you have to follow the recipe to the letter. Just try to keep the major protein ingredients the same or in the same proportion. And you will see, after trying just a few, that none of them deserve that drab old label, "casserole"!

You can make your favorite oven dish more protein-rich by adding (or substituting for other ingredients):

		Proportions (dry measure)
beans	+ grain*	(1 cup beans to 2⅔ cups grain). If you want to use more beans per volume of grain, add some cheese or sesame seed meal.
beans	+ cheese	(1 cup beans to 2½ oz—or more—cheese)
beans	+ ground sesame seeds or sunflower seeds	(1 cup beans to 2¼ cups ground seeds)
peanuts	+ seeds	(1½ cups peanuts to 2½ cups ground seeds)
seeds	+ cheese	(1 cup seed meal to 1 oz—or more—cheese)
seeds	+ grain	(1 cup seed meal to 2 cups grain)
potatoes	+ milk	(1 lb potatoes to 1½ cups milk or yogurt, or ½ cup instant non-fat dry milk)
grain	+ milk	(¾ cup rice to 1 cup milk or yogurt, or 1¼ oz cheese)

For a complete list of complementary protein combinations, refer back to Table VI, Complementary Protein Proportions.

Remember that if you are unable to follow exactly the proportions given, it still pays to toss in the complementary ingredient—it will help give you more protein.

Recipes:

1. Recipes Using Mainly Vegetables:
   Sue's Famous Vegetable Squares
   Spinach-Rice Pot
   Sesame Eggplant Parmesan
   Crusty Soybean Crowd-Pleaser

2. Recipes Using Mainly Beans:
   Broiled Falafel Patties
   Legumes Continental
   Savory Stuffed Peppers
   Garbanzo Pâté

3. Recipes Using Cottage Cheese:
   Greek Cheese and Spinach Squares
   Noodle-Cheese "Soufflé"

4. Recipes with a Mexican Flavor:
   Enchilada Bake
   Mexican Vegetable Bake
   Easy Mexican Pan Bread

5. Recipes Using Potatoes:
   Golden Parsley Potatoes
   Potato and Mushroom Delight

6. Recipe Using Nuts:
   Nutty Noodles

---

* Rice, wheat, barley, millet, rye, oats, etc.

Sue's Famous Vegetable Squares

5–6 servings

average serving = approx. 13 g of usable protein
30–36% of daily protein allowance

Have ready:
⅓ cup dry soybeans,
cooked with ¼ cup raw
peanuts, then ground in
blender (about 1¼ cups
total). Why not cook
extra?

*Sauté in large saucepan
5 min:*
4 tbsp butter
4 stalks celery, minced
2 carrots, grated

Add for a few more min:
¼ lb mushrooms, chopped

(have more on hand for
optional sauce)
1 onion, minced

Turn off heat and add:
½ cup fresh parsley,
chopped
½ to 1 cup walnuts, coarsely
chopped
½ cup wheat germ
1 egg
cooked and ground beans
and nuts
¼ cup water or stock
(should have consistency
of loose stuffing)
salt and pepper to taste

Pack mixture into a shallow pan so height of mixture
is only ¾ of an inch. Bake at 350° for about 30 minutes, or until loaf is dry. Cool for a few minutes and
serve cut into 2–3-inch squares.

Add a simple mushroom cream sauce* for a truly
elegant dish. The fresh parsley and celery give this a
light taste that is irresistible.

To complete protein complementarity serve with:

¾ cup raw rice and

⅔ cup bulgur, cooked
(about 3 cups)

Complementary protein: soy + peanuts + wheat
+ rice

---

* See Herbed Dinner Cake with Mushroom Sauce, page 192.

Spinach-Rice Pot

4 servings

average serving = approx. 10 g usable protein
23–28% of daily protein allowance

Have ready:
¾ cup raw brown rice,
  cooked (2 cups)

Combine:
2 eggs, beaten
2 tbsp parsley, chopped
½ tsp salt
¼ tsp pepper

Combine:
½ cup grated cheddar
  cheese
cooked rice

Add:
1 lb fresh spinach, chopped

Topping:
2 tbsp wheat germ
1 tbsp melted butter

Take out already cooked rice. (If you forgot last time to cook extra, why not do it this time?)

Combine the cooked rice and cheese. Combine eggs, parsley, salt and pepper. Add the two mixtures to the raw spinach. Pour into an oiled casserole. Top with wheat germ mixed with the melted butter. Bake in a 350°F oven for 35 minutes. Serve this casserole with a contrasting vegetable such as sautéed carrots or yellow squash and hot Pineapple-Corn Muffins (page 327). A light, delicious meal. (I once made this dish on a TV talk show and the stage crew loved it!)

Sesame Eggplant Parmesan

4 servings

average serving = approx. 11 g usable protein
26–31% of daily protein allowance

Sauté over high heat until browned and getting soft:
oil as needed
1 medium eggplant, sliced ½ inch thick

Set eggplant aside and in same skillet combine and simmer 15 min:
1-lb jar of your favorite marinara or spaghetti sauce
with extra herbs: ¼ tsp each

oregano, thyme, rosemary (optional)
½ onion, grated
½ green pepper, grated
1 carrot, grated
¼ cup Parmesan cheese
½ cup toasted ground sesame seeds

Topping:
½ lb mozzarella cheese, sliced

On a large baking platter arrange the eggplant slices. Cover with the sauce and then spread the mozzarella cheese over all. Bake about 15 minutes at 350°F. Or, if you don't have a large enough platter, layer the ingredients in a shallow 2-quart casserole dish.

Even eggplant haters like this dish. It is so easy, but elegant enough for guests. A meal by itself with a fresh green salad, it can become a heartier dinner if you add your favorite pasta or rice as a side dish, or put as a bottom layer under the eggplant.

Complementary protein: sesame + milk product

Crusty Soybean Crowd-Pleaser

6–8 servings

average serving = approx. 10 g usable protein
23–28% of daily protein allowance

Have ready:
2½ cups raw brown rice,
   cooked (about 5¾ cups)
½ cup dry soybeans, cooked
   (about 1 cup)

Combine:
cooked soybeans
2 cups corn, fresh or frozen
2 cups canned tomatoes
1 cup chopped onion
½ cup chopped celery
1 clove garlic, crushed
½ tsp each thyme and
   summer savory

pinch cayenne
2 tsp salt

Combine separately:
¼ cup tomato paste
3 tbsp brewer's yeast
½ cup stock or water

Topping:
⅓ cup or more grated
   cheese
wheat germ
butter

Remove already cooked rice and beans from freezer or refrigerator. (If you forgot last time to cook extra, why not do it this time?)

Place half of the cooked rice on the bottom of an oiled 4–6-quart casserole. Cover with the vegetable mixture. Spread the tomato paste mixture over the vegetables, and cover all with the rest of the rice. Sprinkle with grated cheese and then wheat germ. Dot with butter and bake uncovered for 30 minutes at 350°F.

This is a great dish for a crowd. At an outdoor gathering at a local college, it was served to hundreds.

Complementary protein: rice + soy

Broiled Falafel Patties*

about 10 3-inch patties

average serving = approx. 10 g usable protein
23–28% of daily protein allowance

Purée in blender:
¾ cup dry garbanzos,
cooked (2 cups)
½ cup parsley clusters

Put in mixing bowl with:
¼ cup sesame butter
2 cloves garlic, pressed
¼ cup dry milk

1 egg, beaten with
1 tbsp water
½ tsp dry mustard
1 tsp cumin
½ tsp chili powder
celery salt, to taste
salt and pepper, to taste
1 tsp Worcestershire sauce

Mix well and spoon onto oiled baking pan. Flatten. Brush with oil. Bake for 15 minutes until done, or broil for a few minutes on each side, basting with more oil if needed.

Serve with lettuce and tomato and some tahini (sesame butter). Or put in warm pita bread (or any sandwich bun) that has been slit open, with lettuce on top and a little mayonnaise-ketchup or thousand island dressing. (Or great as hot hors d'oeuvres—just make bite-sized patties.)

Complementary protein: beans + sesame
beans + milk product

---

* Falafels are a traditional Middle Eastern food. We've added the complementary protein (milk) without losing the special original flavor.

Legumes Continental

4 servings

average serving = approx. 10 g usable protein
23–28% of daily protein allowance

Have ready:
1 cup dry garbanzos,
  cooked with extra water
  (save 2 cups stock) or
3 cups cooked or canned
  beans

*Add and continue sautéing
1 min:*
3 tbsp toasted ground
  sesame seed with 1 tbsp
  curry powder or
½ cup walnuts

*Sauté until onions are
transparent:*
oil as needed
2 cups onion, chopped fine

Stir in cooked garbanzos. Place this mixture in a small, oiled casserole.

Sauce

Heat:
¼ cup oil

*Add and stir until toasted
and nutty-smelling:*
¼ cup whole wheat flour

*Blend together and add to
flour:*
⅔ cup instant dry milk
  (½ cup if non-instant)
2 cups stock from beans,
  or water, seasoned

2 tsp salt

Simmer, stirring often, until thickened. Stir in salt. Pour the sauce over the beans in the casserole and bake for 30 minutes in a 350°F oven. Sprinkle chopped parsley on top.

This rich and nutty-tasting dish goes well with any grain. A very special taste for so simple an idea.

Complementary protein: beans + milk product

Savory Stuffed Peppers

6 servings

average serving = approx. 7 g usable protein
16–20% of daily protein allowance

Have ready:
1 cup dry beans, cooked
  and mashed (about 2¼
  cups), pintos are good
6 green peppers, seeds and
  membranes removed
⅔ cup cheese, grated

Sauté:
oil as needed
½ onion, chopped
1 cup celery, chopped

Stir in:
2 cups tomatoes, canned
  (drain, save liquid), or 3
  fresh tomatoes, chopped
1 12-oz can corn
½ tsp basil
1 tbsp parsley, chopped
1 tsp each dill weed and
  cayenne pepper (or less,
  if you prefer)
¼ tsp cumin
salt to taste

liquid from canned tomatoes
  or water, as needed

Add liquid if the mixture is very dry. Salt to taste.
Fill the prepared peppers with the mixture, top with the
cheese, and bake at 400°F in a pan with 1 inch of hot
water in the bottom. Check to be sure the pan doesn't
dry out during the 25 to 30 minutes of baking.

Complementary protein: beans + milk product

Garbanzo Pâté

4 servings

average serving = approx. 11 g usable protein
26–31% of daily protein allowance

Have ready:
⅔ cup dry garbanzos,
  cooked and puréed
  (about 2 cups)

Soak together:
2 cups whole wheat bread
  or bread crumbs
  (stale is all right)
1½ cups hot stock or water,
  seasoned

Sauté:
oil as needed
2 onions, chopped

*Add and sauté until lightly
brown:*
½ cup sesame seed meal
2 tbsp sesame butter

*Combine bread with sauté
mixture and add:*
¼ tsp each thyme,
  coriander, and nutmeg
1 bay leaf
½ tsp salt
¼ cup chopped parsley
3 tbsp soy sauce
puréed beans

Topping:
⅔ cup grated cheese

Put in loaf pan and bake 30 minutes at 325°F. Add cheese on top in last 10 minutes. Good hot or cold (or as a sandwich spread), this rich-tasting loaf goes well with any steamed or sautéed vegetable. For a really hearty meal, serve with your favorite cooked grain also.

Complementary protein: beans + sesame

Greek Cheese and Spinach Squares

6–8 servings

average serving = approx. 16 g usable protein
37–44% of daily protein allowance

Beat in large bowl until
smooth:
2 or 3 eggs
6 tbsp whole wheat flour

1 lb (2 cups) cottage cheese
½ lb (2 cups) grated
    cheddar cheese
½ tsp salt

Add:
1 lb fresh spinach (simply
    tear it up to save time)

Topping:
3 tbsp wheat germ

Pour into well-greased baking pan, approx. 8x12 inches, and sprinkle with wheat germ. Bake uncovered at 350°F for approx. 45 minutes. Cut into squares for serving. This dish goes well with carrots; why not a carrot-and-raisin salad? Or the Carrot-and-Onion Soup, page 238.

This dish would also make a great pie. See the Parmesan Rice recipe on page 178 for "pat-in-rice" crust.

Complementary protein: wheat + milk product

Noodle-Cheese "Soufflé"

6–8 servings

average serving = approx. 14 g usable protein
32–39% of daily protein allowance

Have ready:
½ lb whole wheat or
wheat-soy noodles

Mix together:
3 beaten egg yolks (set
whites aside)
¼ cup butter, melted
(optional)
2 tbsp honey
1 lb cottage cheese (about
2 cups)
1 cup yogurt

Fold in:
½-1 cup raisins (optional)
cooked noodles
3 stiffly beaten egg whites

Choose topping:
whole wheat bread crumbs
wheat germ

Pour into an oiled 2-quart casserole. Choose a topping and dot with butter. Bake at 375°F for 45 minutes. This is a delicious and elegant dish.

Serving suggestion: Accompany with green peas and fresh fruit salad (chopped apples, bananas, oranges, etc.) with a yogurt-and-honey dressing.

Complementary protein: wheat + milk product

Enchilada Bake

4 servings

average serving = approx. 9 g usable protein
21–25% of daily protein allowance

Have ready:
6-8 corn tortillas

½ cup dry beans, cooked
(about 1½ cups)

Sauce

Sauté in oil:
1 onion, chopped
1 clove garlic, minced
5-6 mushrooms, sliced
1 green pepper, chopped

Add and simmer 30 min:
cooked beans
1½ cups stewed tomatoes
1 tbsp chili powder
1 tsp cumin, ground
½ cup red wine
salt to taste

Other layers:

½ to 1 cup grated Monterey
jack (or other) cheese
½ to 1 cup mixture of
ricotta cheese and yogurt
(or blended cottage
cheese and yogurt)

Garnish:
black olives

In an oiled casserole put a layer of tortillas, a layer of sauce, 3 tbsp of grated cheese, 3 tbsp of the cheese-yogurt mix. Repeat until all the ingredients are used, ending with the layer of sauce. Garnish the top with the cheese-yogurt mix and the black olives. Bake at 350°F for 15 to 20 minutes.

This dish goes well with a fruit salad. The Fine Fruit Salad (page 255) is a pleasant taste contrast.

Complementary protein: beans + corn

Mexican Vegetable Bake

4–6 servings

average serving = approx. 7 g usable protein
16–20% of daily protein allowance

Have ready:
½ cup dry garbanzos,
    cooked (1½ cups)

Sauté lightly:
oil as needed
1 small can green chilies,
    diced
½ lb string beans, sliced
    into 2-inch pieces
1 tsp chili powder (to taste)

Add:
dash hot sauce
salt and pepper
1 12-oz can corn
cooked beans

Other layers:
1 16-oz can stewed
    tomatoes or 3 large
    tomatoes, sliced
⅔ cup grated cheese
    (or more)

In a greased casserole dish layer bean mixture, tomatoes, and cheese, ending with cheese. Bake in a
350°F oven for 30 minutes.

For a milder dish you may substitute basil and sage
for the chili seasonings.

Complementary protein: beans + cheese

Easy Mexican Pan Bread

6 servings

average serving = approx. 8 g usable protein
19–22% of daily protein allowance

Have ready:
½ cup dry beans, cooked
with extra water (a dark
bean such as a kidney or
black bean makes the
dish colorful). Reserve
¾ cup stock from beans

*Sauté in oil in ovenproof
skillet:*
1 large onion, chopped
2 cloves garlic, minced

*Leave half of sautéed mix
in unheated skillet and put
other half in medium bowl
with:*
the cooked beans and stock
1 egg, beaten
2 tbsp oil
1 cup cornmeal
2 tsp baking powder

1 tbsp chili powder (or
more to taste)
½ tsp cumin, ground
1 green pepper, diced
(optional)
½ tsp salt

*Mix well and pour into
skillet you left the onion in.
Do not stir, so that onion will
stay on the bottom. Bake
at 350°F for about 15 min.
Just before done sprinkle
with:*
⅓ cup grated cheese
¼ cup sliced black olives

*Before serving garnish with
(optional):*
chopped fresh onion and/or
tomato

I've even gotten letters from people who liked this
recipe! With a fresh salad (try putting in some avocado) it can be a light meal in itself. Or, if you are serving
a crowd, make this along with other dishes with a
Mexican touch.

Complementary protein: beans + corn

Golden Parsley Potatoes

4 servings

average serving = approx. 15 g usable protein
35–42% of daily protein allowance

Layer in a small casserole:
1 lb cooked, sliced potatoes
1 cup grated cheddar

Blend in blender or mix thoroughly:
1-2 eggs
1 cup cottage cheese
1 tbsp parsley flakes
salt and pepper to taste

Pour sauce over potatoes and cheese. Top with additional parsley. Bake at 350°F for 20–30 minutes, until golden. This simple dish is easy to prepare and beautiful to see.

For a light dinner, I served this dish with a spinach salad combining red onion, sliced beets, and other leftover cold vegetables.

Complementary protein: potatoes + milk product

Potato and Mushroom Delight

4–6 servings

average serving = approx. 12 g usable protein
28–34% of daily protein allowance

Have ready:
3 medium potatoes, cooked
   and sliced
1-3 hard-boiled eggs,
   thinly sliced

Sauté 5 min:
2 tbsp butter
¼-½ lb fresh mushrooms,
   sliced

Add and stir 2 min:
2 tbsp flour

Add and stir until thickened:
1 cup milk or buttermilk

Stir in:
Worcestershire sauce to
   taste

1 cup cheese, grated
   (cheddar or other)
1 tsp salt
pepper to taste

Layer in oiled casserole:
half the sliced potatoes
half the eggs
half the cheese sauce

Repeat.

Top with:
toasted ground sesame
   seeds

Bake at 350°F for 20 min.

Serve with broccoli, topped with lemon butter, and a
tomato salad. A very rich-tasting casserole.

Complementary protein: potato + milk product

Nutty Noodles

6 servings

average serving = approx. 10–11 g usable protein
23–31% of daily protein allowance

Have ready:
1/3 cup dry soybeans, cooked
(about 1 cup). Why not
cook extra?
12 oz noodles (whole wheat,
or soy, if possible),
cooked and drained

Sauté until transparent:
1/4 cup butter
2 medium onions, chopped

*Add until all is lightly
browned:*
3/4 cup peanuts
1/2 cup cashews

Add and heat through:
cooked soybeans
cooked noodles

*Mix separately (do not
blend):*
1/3 cup sesame butter
2 cups yogurt (or more)
1 tsp nutmeg (or more)
1 tsp honey
dash cayenne pepper
salt and pepper to taste

Topping:
1/4 cup toasted ground
sesame seeds

Remove to a serving dish or casserole and stir in the
sesame-yogurt mix. Sprinkle the toasted ground sesame
seeds over the top. If the dish is hot enough for your
taste, slip it into a 300°F oven for a few min.

Nutty Noodles are delicious with a lettuce-and-apple
salad, tossed with your favorite yogurt or oil dressing.

Complementary protein: soy + wheat + peanuts
+ sesame

(G) *Pasta Unlimited*

I know of no one (most of all children) who does not enjoy pasta dishes. But many people hesitate to serve them. Pasta meals are considered too rich in calories or too heavily carbohydrate—without enough protein. The pasta recipes in this section have tried to answer both of these objections. First, in place of a lot of cream and olive oil, I have substituted low-fat dairy products and reduced the amount of oil used. Second, all of the dishes include enough protein—in the form of dairy products, nuts, or seafood—to provide between one-quarter and one-third of your body's daily protein need.

Of course the great advantage of most pasta meals is that they are so easily and quickly prepared. Here you'll find practically "instant" meals.

Recipes:

1. Sauce with Cheese:
       Ricotta Lasagne Swirls
       Fettuccine al Marco
       Mushroom Stroganoff
       Pesto Genovese-American

2. Sauces with Nuts:
       Spaghetti with Quick Protein-Rich Sauce
       Spaghetti for Peanuts
       Peanut Sauce with Great Possibilities

3. Sauce with Seafood:
       Clam Sauce with Garlic and Wine

Ricotta Lasagne Swirls

4 servings

average serving = approx. 14 g usable protein
32–39% of daily protein allowance

Have ready:
8 cooked lasagne noodles

Filling:
2 bunches spinach
2 tbsp Parmesan cheese
1 cup ricotta cheese
   (½ lb)
¼ tsp nutmeg
salt and pepper to taste

Use your favorite prepared spaghetti sauce or:
2 cloves garlic, minced
   and sautéed
½ cup onions, chopped and
   sautéed
2 cups tomato sauce
½ tsp basil
½ tsp oregano
salt and pepper to taste

Steam spinach until it is quite limp, but not mushy. You don't need any water to do this. Just put the washed spinach in a pan that has a tight-fitting lid and cook it over low heat about 7 minutes. Chop. Mix the spinach with the cheese, nutmeg, salt and pepper. Coat each noodle with 2–3 tbsp of the mixture along its entire length, roll up, turn on end so that you see the spiral, and place in a shallow baking pan. Mix all of the sauce ingredients together and pour over the rolled-up noodles. Bake at 350°F for 20 minutes.

This is an especially attractive dish and it is much lighter than most Italian-style pasta dishes.

Variation: My mother-in-law uses this recipe to prepare a more traditional lasagne by merely making repeated layers of noodles, filling, and sauce. (For a layered lasagne you'll need more noodles.)

Serving suggestion: Serve with green salad and garlic bread.

Complementary protein: wheat + milk product

Fettuccine al Marco

4 servings

average serving = approx. 14 g usable protein
32–39% of daily protein allowance

Start cooking:
½ lb fettuccine or other
  noodles (spinach
  noodles*)

½ cup parsley
2 cups spinach leaves*
  (optional)
salt and pepper to taste

Blend until very smooth:
1½ cups ricotta or cottage
  cheese
½ cup yogurt
1 egg
¼ cup Parmesan cheese

Garnish (important):
your choice of herbs—for
  instance, basil—and
  sliced black olives (or
  parsley) sprinkled on top

Toss the sauce with the hot, cooked pasta. Garnish. Serve immediately. This dish may not be as rich tasting as Fettuccine al Fredo, but it has a lot fewer calories and a lot more protein—and it is delicious!

Complementary protein: wheat + milk product

* Spinach noodles provide an attractive contrast if you make the white sauce without spinach leaves. But if you put spinach in the sauce, use white pasta for an appealing contrast.

Mushroom Stroganoff

4 servings
average serving = approx. 12 g usable protein
28–34% of daily protein allowance

Start cooking:
½ lb flat egg noodles

Sauté:
1 tbsp butter
1 small onion, finely
  chopped
½ lb mushrooms, halved,
  or if small, leave some
  whole
1-2 cloves garlic, crushed
(Add 2 tbsp fresh or 1
  tbsp dried parsley when
  onion almost done)

Stir in:
3 dashes of Worcestershire
  sauce

*Remove from heat and just
before serving stir in:*
1 cup cottage cheese,
  blended smooth with
½ cup yogurt
salt and fresh ground
  pepper (optional—taste
  first)

Serve immediately over hot egg noodles and garnish
with more parsley. With a favorite green salad and
Italian dressing this may be the most elegant "instant"
dish you've ever made!

Complementary protein: wheat + milk product

Mushrooms

Pesto Genovese-American

6 servings

average serving = approx. 8 g usable protein
19–22% of daily protein allowance

*In covered blender, blend
on high speed until smooth:*
½ cup olive oil
2 cloves garlic
2 tsp crumbled dry basil*

*Let stand 15 min for flavors
to mingle.*

*Gradually add, with blades
spinning, inner cap or
cover removed, and blend
until smooth:*
3 tbsp sunflower seeds (to
be authentic, use pignolia
nuts—if you can afford
them!)
1 tsp salt
¼ tsp pepper

*Add a few at a time until
well blended:*
2 cups firmly packed
parsley* clusters (not
stems)

*Then, stopping blender to
stir down mixture with a
thin scraper, add:*
1 cup freshly grated
Parmesan cheese, or ½
cup commercially grated
Parmesan cheese.

*Cook, following label
directions:*
1 package (1 lb) linguine

Reserve ½ cup of the cooking liquid, then drain off
remaining cooking liquid. Return linguine to kettle and
toss with reserved cooking liquid. Pour onto a large
heated platter, pour pesto sauce over, and toss with two
forks until evenly blended.

Serve with additional grated Parmesan, if you wish.
This dish has a subtle and absolutely unique flavor I
love—especially when served with hot or sweet marinated Italian peppers and garlic bread!

* This dish is more delicious and real Italian if you use
fresh basil. If you can get the fresh basil, delete the dry basil
and replace the parsley with fresh basil.

Spaghetti with Quick Protein-Rich Sauce

4 servings

average serving = approx. 11 g usable protein
26–31% of daily protein allowance

Start cooking:
½ lb spaghetti

Sauce:
oil as needed
1 large onion, chopped
¼ lb mushrooms, chopped
(optional)
⅛ cup soy grits

⅓ cup sunflower seeds
ground in blender with
¼ cup peanuts
1 tsp oregano (optional)
2 tbsp chopped parsley
(optional)
1-lb jar of spaghetti or
marinara sauce
1 tbsp Parmesan cheese
(more to taste)

Sauté onions and mushrooms (optional) in oil in skillet until lightly golden. Add soy grits and ground seeds and nuts, stirring constantly until they are thoroughly toasted (about 5 minutes). Add optional herbs, the spaghetti or marinara sauce, and 1 tbsp Parmesan. Simmer over low heat while you drain the spaghetti. Adjust seasoning to your taste. Serve on spaghetti with more Parmesan.

This is one of my husband's all-time favorite spaghetti dinners, good even without the mushrooms.

Complementary protein: soy + sunflower + peanut

Spaghetti for Peanuts

4 servings

average serving = approx. 16 g usable protein
37–44% of daily protein allowance

Have ready:
2 cups dry broken spaghetti
(whole wheat, if
possible), cooked tender

*In medium saucepan heat
and stir until flour gets
toasty:*
2-4 tbsp butter
3 tbsp whole wheat flour
1 tsp salt
1 tsp dry mustard
¼ tsp pepper

Add and stir until thickened:
2 cups buttermilk (or milk)
½ onion, chopped fine
3 drops hot pepper sauce

*Get ready to layer in oiled
casserole:*
½ cup sliced black olives
1 cup grated cheddar
cheese
1 cup chopped peanuts

Topping:
⅓ cup bread crumbs

Put half the spaghetti in oiled casserole with half the
olives, cheese, and peanuts. Repeat layers. Pour sauce
over the top and put on topping. Bake at 350°F for
25 minutes.

This dish makes a great supper with a tossed green
salad and/or any fresh green vegetable, steamed or
sautéed.

Variation: Turn this spaghetti casserole into a cauliflower casserole by simply substituting cauliflower for
the pasta and adding 1 cup chopped green pepper.

Complementary protein: peanut + milk + wheat

Peanut Sauce with Great Possibilities

about 1 cup

¼ cup = 7 g usable protein
16–20% of daily protein allowance

*Blend in saucepan over
low heat:*
½ cup peanut butter
1 small onion, grated
1 clove garlic, crushed
¼ cup instant dry milk

½ tsp honey
2 tbsp lemon juice
2 tsp soy sauce
(Adjust honey, lemon juice,
  soy sauce to taste.)

Add hot water until the mixture has the consistency of heavy cream. (If you wish a very smooth sauce, blend the mixture in a blender with the hot water.)

This sauce may sound strange, but everyone I know who has tried it finds it superb. Great Possibilities:

1. Over spaghetti (with added sautéed mushrooms—optional).

2. Over rice or bulgur (with added slivered almonds).

3. Over tofu, hot or cold.

4. As a fondue: dip whole wheat bread cubes in it.

5. As a dessert fondue: dip fruit slices—apple is out of this world!

Complementary protein: peanuts + milk

Clam Sauce with Garlic and Wine

4 servings

average serving = approx. 12 g usable protein
28–34% of daily protein allowance

Start cooking:
½ lb spaghetti

Drain juice from 2-3 8-oz cans minced clams and set aside.

Sauté:
¼ cup olive oil
2 cloves garlic, minced

Stir in:
clam juice
¾ cup chopped parsley
2 tbsp white wine
1 tsp basil
½ tsp salt
dash pepper

Now add clams and heat through while you drain the spaghetti. Serve over spaghetti. A special dish that is no trouble at all! For a feast, include garlic bread and Caesar salad.

(H) *A Meal in a Soup Pot*

Out of the world of delicious meatless soups, I have included those that I find myself making most often because they are prepared with ingredients that I almost invariably have on hand—like carrots, potatoes, canned tomatoes, and onions. You will see that I have relied on milk, buttermilk, non-fat dry milk, or cheese for complementing the grain or legume (bean, lentil) protein in most of these soups. Among your favorite soups are probably many from the legume family—black bean soup, navy bean soup, pea-and-carrot soup, for example. When making these from your favorite recipes, just be sure to add a little milk protein in some form—a cheese sandwich served with the soup or cheese stirred in or sprinkled on top.

If, while the soup is on the stove, you put some home-made muffins or bread in the oven, your Meal in a Soup Pot can become a genuine feast.

Recipes:

1. Carrot-and-Onion Soup

2. Lentils, Monastery Style

3. Hearty Tomato Soup

4. Turkish Barley-Buttermilk Soup

5. Turnip-and-Pea Potage

6. Mediterranean Lemon Soup

7. Old-Fashioned Potato Soup

8. Two Cold Summer Soups with Buttermilk
   Cold Zucchini-and-Buttermilk Soup
   Cold Curried Apple-and-Buttermilk Soup

Carrot-and-Onion Soup

4 servings
average serving = approx. 6 g usable protein
14–17% of daily protein allowance

*In heavy pot or pressure
cooker sauté slowly about
5 min:*
3 tbsp butter
4-5 medium carrots, grated*
1 medium onion, minced*
1 tsp salt
1 tbsp sugar

Add and stir until coated:
½ cup dry rice

Add:
4 cups seasoned water **or**
   vegetable stock

Have ready:
1 cup hot milk, or more as
   needed (plus a little extra
   milk powder for protein)
croutons (optional)

Cook until rice is very well done—about 45 minutes (or only 25 with a pressure cooker). You may wish to sieve the soup or blend it into a purée. (I like to purée only half, so that some chewiness is left.) Return it to the pot and add the hot milk to the right thickness for you and a little butter. Do not boil.

This soup is so simple yet has a unique quality that makes it a favorite with my family and with guests. I like it especially because it uses ingredients I almost always have on hand. Any type of homemade bread would make this soup into a special supper.

Complementary protein: rice + milk

---

* I cut the carrots and onion into big chunks and then let my blender reduce them to tiny slivers. If you prefer, however, grate or mince the vegetables.

Lentils, Monastery Style

4–6 servings

average serving = approx. 8 g usable protein
19–22% of daily protein allowance

In a large pot sauté 3-5 min:
¼ cup olive oil
2 large onions, chopped
1 carrot, chopped

Add and sauté 1 min more:
½ tsp each dried thyme and marjoram leaves

Add:
3 cups stock or seasoned water
1 cup dry lentils, washed

salt to taste
¼ cup chopped fresh parsley
1 lb canned tomatoes

Cook in covered pot until lentils are tender (about 45 min)
and add:
¼ cup sherry

Have ready:
⅔ cup grated Swiss cheese

To serve place 2 tbsp of grated cheese in each serving bowl and top with soup. This soup is especially delicious served with corn muffins. Fresh or stewed fruit is a just right finish for the meal if the sweet tooth needs pleasing.

Complementary protein: lentils + milk product

Hearty Tomato Soup
(like Campbell's never dreamed of!)

6 servings

average serving = approx. 5 g usable protein
12–14% of daily protein allowance

*In heavy pot sauté until
onion is golden:*
oil as needed
1 clove garlic, minced
1 onion, chopped
1 stalk celery, chopped
(optional)
1 carrot, chopped

*Add, stir, and sauté until
rice is a little toasty:*
2 tbsp whole wheat flour
¾ cup raw rice
(or 1½ cups cooked rice,
added with the following
ingredients)

Add:
1 28-oz can tomatoes (chop,
mash with spoon)
2 tsp salt
4 white pepper corns or
lots of freshly ground
black pepper
1 tbsp sugar
1 tsp each oregano and
basil

Have ready:
3 cups milk, hot
1 tbsp butter

If starting with raw rice, cook until rice is done—
about 45 minutes. If using precooked rice, cook until all
the flavors mingle—at least 15 minutes. Remove from
heat. For a more elegant soup, purée it in the blender
or through a sieve. Add the milk and butter (the butter
lends a very special flavor!) and more salt and pepper
if needed. Warm but do *not* boil.

The great virtue of this recipe is that something very
special is created from foods that you probably have
on hand most of the time. Serve it with oatmeal bread
for a real hurrah!

Complementary protein: rice + milk

Turkish Barley-Buttermilk Soup

4 servings

average serving = approx. 6 g usable protein
14–17% of daily protein allowance

*Sauté in heavy pot until
golden:*
oil as needed
2 large onions, chopped

*Add and stir until lightly
toasted:*
1 cup barley

*When onion is well
browned, add:*
5 cups seasoned stock

Have ready:
2 cups buttermilk or yogurt
1 tsp dill
butter

Cook until the barley is well done—about 45 minutes–1 hour (or 25 minutes with a pressure cooker). Remove from heat, let cool a bit, and add the buttermilk slowly and more stock if too thick. Sprinkle in dill to taste and butter.

Don't let the simplicity of this soup fool you. Once I was giving a demonstration of nonmeat cooking and the moderator could not stop eating the soup for the entire program!

Complementary protein: barley + milk

Turnip-and-Pea Potage

4 servings

average serving = approx. 5 g usable protein
12–14% of daily protein allowance

*Boil until soft (5 min in
pressure cooker):*
1 lb turnips, peeled, cut in
  chunks
1 large onion, cut in chunks
3 cups seasoned water or
  stock

Then blend in blender with:
1 cup instant dry milk
2 tbsp margarine or butter
2 cups frozen green peas,
  defrosted
salt and fresh ground
  pepper to taste

Return to the soup pot and add salt and pepper. Heat
and serve.

Serve with open-face cheese sandwiches on toasted
rye bread. This practically "instant" soup has a smooth
and subtle taste that is quite satisfying.

Mediterranean Lemon Soup

6 servings
average serving = approx. 6 g usable protein
14–17% of daily protein allowance

*Heat to boiling 1½ qts
seasoned water or leftover
stock and add and cook
until tender:*
½ cup raw brown rice
salt if necessary

Mix separately:
¼ tsp summer savory

2 tbsp brewer's yeast
4 eggs, beaten

Add:
juice and grated rind of
    1-2 lemons (start with
    lesser amount and
    increase to taste at the
    end)

Take 1 cup of the hot stock with rice and slowly add it to the egg mixture. Stir constantly. Remove stock from heat and gradually add egg mixture to it. Serve.

The clean, fresh taste of this soup makes a perfect beginning to many different types of meals. We have enjoyed it with the Middle Eastern Tacos, with fish entrées, and with many vegetable casseroles.

Complementary protein: rice + brewer's yeast

Old-Fashioned Potato Soup

4 servings

average serving = approx. 5 g usable protein
12–14% of daily protein allowance

Sauté in heavy pot:
1 medium onion, chopped
3 stalks celery, finely
  chopped (leaves
  included)

Add and cook until tender:
3 medium-sized potatoes (or
  2 large), peeled and
  diced
3-4 cups water or stock

salt and pepper
1 small bay leaf

*Let cool briefly. Then while
stirring with a wisk, add
slowly:*
1 cup instant dry milk
1-2 tbsp butter

Garnish:
parsley, chives, green onion,
  or dill

Reheat but do not boil. Add salt and pepper to taste.
Garnish with one of the choices above. Serve with
grilled-cheese sandwiches for a quick winter lunch made
with ingredients you almost always have on hand even
though your cupboard may be bare.

Variations: If available, leeks may be used instead of
onions. Add a can of minced clams, diced carrots,
canned asparagus, or cooked cauliflower.

Complementary protein: potato + milk

Cold Zucchini-and-Buttermilk Soup

4 servings

average serving = approx. 5 g usable protein
12–14% of daily protein allowance

Buttermilk, so much cheaper than yogurt, can be the basis for many delightful and practically instant summer soups. Here are just two ideas, but many other vegetables and fruits might be used.

Sauté well:
oil as needed
1 medium zucchini, chopped
   coarsely
1 medium onion, chopped
1 clove minced garlic

Blend all in blender and add:
3 cups buttermilk
salt and pepper to taste

Chill and garnish with dill
   or parsley

Curried Apple-and-Buttermilk Soup

4 servings

average serving = approx. 5 g usable protein
12–14% of daily protein allowance

Sauté well:
oil as needed
1 medium onion, chopped
1 apple,* chopped
2 tsp curry powder
dash of mustard seed
   (optional)

Let cool and add:
3 cups buttermilk

Chill and garnish with dill or parsley.

* A cucumber, with seeds removed, can be substituted.

(I) *A Meal in a Salad Bowl*

I am a salad freak. Especially in the summertime, salads are about the only food that seems appetizing to me. So I have had to learn ways to fill my protein need from the salads I love. And it is not difficult. The recipes here demonstrate some of the many, many possibilities.

Tips, protein-wise, for your usual salad making

To lettuce salads add:
Parmesan cheese
cheese cubes
hard-boiled egg, crumbled
toasted ground sesame
  seeds
toasted sunflower seeds
cooked beans
leftover cooked beans
  and grains

cooked broccoli
green peas
cauliflower

To fruit salads add:
nuts
toasted ground sesame
  seeds
toasted sunflower seeds
yogurt
cottage cheese

Recipes:

1. Exotic Rice Salad

2. Macaroni Salad Ricotta

3. Tabouli

4. Vegetable Salad Carousel

5. Bulgur and Bean Salad

6. Garbanzo-Cheese Salad

7. Lentil Salad

8. Fine Fruit Salad and Other Ideas

9. Tuna Salad Varié

Exotic Rice Salad

4 servings
average serving = approx. 8 g usable protein
19–22% of daily protein allowance

Have ready:
¾ cups dry rice, cooked
and allowed to cool
(about 1½ cups)

Mix together:
prepared rice
½ cup celery, coarsely
chopped
½ cup peanuts, coarsely
chopped

1½ cups yogurt
2 tbsp chutney (or more
to taste)

or

2 tbsp apricot preserves
combined with dash of
lemon juice and ⅛ tsp
ginger

Toss in a salad bowl.

On a summer's eve this tangy salad (served with
sliced beets and cucumber in a vinaigrette dressing)
could be just the meal to refresh the palate.

Complementary protein: rice + milk product
peanuts + milk product

Macaroni Salad Ricotta

4 servings

average serving = approx. 7 g usable protein
16–20% of daily protein allowance

Toss together:
¼ lb whole wheat macaroni,
  cooked tender, drained
  and chilled
1 cup ricotta cheese, mixed
  with 2 tsp mustard and
  thinned with yogurt* so
  that it will mix in the
  salad like mayonnaise
¼ cup sliced or chopped
  ripe olives

1 bell pepper, chopped
  coarsely
2 scallions and tops
  chopped
1 tbsp chopped parsley
red pimentoes, to taste
½ tsp each, dill and basil
salt and pepper, to taste

Serve on a bed of lettuce. Colorful, light, and satisfying.

Complementary protein: wheat + milk product

---

* You can use any combination of ricotta cheese or cottage cheese with yogurt, buttermilk, or milk.

Tabouli

Zesty Lebanese Salad

6 servings
average serving = approx. 4 g usable protein
9–11% of daily protein allowance

Have ready:
¼ cup dry white or
garbanzo beans, cooked,
drained (¾ cup)

Pour 4 cups boiling water over:
1¼ cups bulgur wheat, raw

Let stand covered about 2 hrs until light and fluffy.

To remove excess water, shake in a strainer and squeeze with hands.

Combine:
cooked, squeezed bulgur
cooked beans
1½ cup fresh parsley,*
minced
¾ cup fresh mint, minced
(if not available,
substitute more parsley)
¾ cup scallions, chopped
3 medium tomatoes,
chopped
½ cup (or more) lemon
juice
¼ cup olive oil
1-2 tsp salt
freshly ground pepper to
taste

Chill for at least 1 hour. Serve on raw grape, lettuce, or cabbage leaves.

This recipe is adapted from a traditional Lebanese dish often served on festive occasions. If you want to be truly authentic, let your guests or family scoop it up with lettuce leaves instead of using spoons. For a group I've often served Tabouli with the Middle Eastern Tacos—a great combination.

Complementary protein: wheat + beans

* You can use a blender. A wooden chopstick is good for scraping leaves from the sides of the blender into the blade action.

Vegetable Salad Carousel

4 servings

average serving (using beans) = approx. 13 g
usable protein
30–36% of daily protein allowance

Use any combination you like (be sure to have
vegetables at room temperature):

Potato

1.

6 medium potatoes, cooked,
sliced, and cooled to
room temperature
2 stalks celery, chopped
1-2 green onions, finely
chopped, or ¼ cup
chopped parsley, or both

¼ cup sweet pickles,
chopped
¼-½ lb Swiss cheese, cut in
chunks

Lentil-Mushroom

2.

1 cup dry lentils, cooked
with an onion and bay
leaf until tender *but not
mushy* (remove onion
before using)
2 stalks celery, chopped
1-2 green onions, finely
chopped

¼-½ lb cheese (preferably
Muenster), cut in chunks
¼ cup parsley, finely
chopped
¼ lb raw mushrooms, sliced

Cauliflower-Lima

3.

1 small head cauliflower,
cooked until barely
tender
1 cup dry lima beans,
cooked (2-3 cups)

1 red onion, sliced thinly
¼-½ lb Swiss cheese, cut
in chunks

Dressing:

Combine oil and vinegar to make ½ cup (using 3-4 parts oil to 1 part vinegar, depending on how zesty you like it). Add salt and pepper to taste. Mix well. Pour over vegetables and mix well.

Complementary protein: beans + milk product
potato + milk product

Bulgur and Bean Salad

6 servings

average serving = approx. 4 g usable protein
9–11% of daily protein allowance

*Have ready (Why not cook
extra?):*
¼ cup dry beans (small
  kidneys are good),
  cooked (¾ cup)

Prepare as below:
1¼ cups dry bulgur wheat
2 tbsp oil
2½ cups stock or water

*Add favorite salad
vegetables, including:*
lettuce, torn
spinach, torn
carrots, sliced
radishes, sliced
celery, diced
zucchini, sliced
fresh peas, etc.

Sauté the raw bulgur in the oil, stirring until all of
the grains are coated and the bulgur is golden. Add the
stock, which has been heated to boiling, cover tightly,
and cook until all the liquid is absorbed and the grains
are tender. Refrigerate while you prepare the vegetables
for the salad. When the bulgur is cold, stir in the
cooked beans and toss with the salad vegetables.

Served with Italian dressing, this salad will make a
whole meal with the addition of bread and cheese.

Complementary protein: beans + wheat

Garbanzo-Cheese Salad

4–5 servings

average serving = approx. 8 g usable protein
19–22% of daily protein allowance

Toss together:
½ cup dry garbanzo beans,
  cooked and cooled
  (1½ cups)
⅔ cup cheese, grated

And your favorites, such as:
red leaf lettuce, torn up
spinach, torn
½ cup scallions, sliced

green pepper, chopped
fresh raw shelled peas (or
  defrosted frozen peas)
½ cup raw yellow crook-
  neck squash, diced or
  sliced
½ cup cucumber, chopped
  or sliced
1 cup bean or alfalfa
  sprouts

Toss with favorite dressing.

Naturally you can use any combination of fresh vegetables that are available, just be sure to include the garbanzo beans and cheese.

Complementary protein: beans + cheese

Lentil Salad

4 servings

average serving = approx. 10 g usable protein
23–28% of daily protein allowance

Have ready:
½ cup dry lentils, cooked
with
1 small chopped onion
(about 1 cup)

*Prepare according to
directions below:*
½ cup bulgur with
¼ cup soy grits

Dressing ingredients:
1 cup yogurt

2 tbsp mayonnaise
1 tsp garlic powder
1 tsp mustard (preferably
Dijon)
2 tsp lemon juice (or more
as needed)

Greens:
chopped fresh spinach
scallions
red onions to your taste

(Why not cook 2 cups dry lentils and put the leftover
in the refrigerator for lentil soup later in the week?)
Put a little oil in a heavy skillet over medium heat and
add the bulgur and soy grits. Stirring constantly, toast
the grains for 5–10 minutes. Add 2 cups hot water or
seasoned stock. Cover tightly and cook over low heat
for 10 minutes. The grains should be light and fluffy.
Add the lentils and the dressing ingredients and greens.
Toss thoroughly and chill if desired. Good by itself for
lunch or with some soup for supper.

Complementary protein: beans + wheat
beans + milk products

Fine Fruit Salad and Other Ideas

8 servings

average serving = approx. 5 g usable protein
12–14% of daily protein allowance

*In a large bowl combine
and toss:*
¾ cup peanuts, roasted
1 cup sunflower seeds, raw
   or roasted
1 cup apples, sliced
1 cup bananas, sliced
½ cup tangerine or orange
   sections
1 cup fresh peaches, sliced

1 cup seedless grapes
½ cup raisins
½ cup shredded coconut
2-4 tbsp honey
juice of ½ lemon
½ cup wine

Garnish:
10-15 leaves fresh mint

Garnish with mint leaves. At different times of the year you can substitute any fruit in season. Just be sure to include the peanuts and sunflower seeds for complementarity.

Other delicious salad ideas using peanuts and sunflower seeds:

Peanut-Sunflower-Carrot Salad:
Just combine grated carrots, raisins, peanuts, sunflower seeds, and crushed pineapple (optional) with a dressing of 1 part peanut butter to 2 parts mayonnaise.

Peanut-Sunflower Waldorf Salad:
Sprinkle lemon juice over diced apples (or pineapple chunks) and celery. Add chopped peanuts and sunflower seeds. Moisten with a dressing of blended mayonnaise and peanut butter.

Complementary protein: peanuts + sunflower seeds

Tuna Salad Varié

Here are three of my family's favorite ways to make ordinary tuna fish into an exciting lunch:

Combine:
drained tuna
1 cup cottage cheese
1 small can drained sweet
  peas
pinch of basil or summer
  savory

or

drained tuna
chopped red onion
sliced beets

yogurt
dill

or

drained tuna
chopped apples
chopped celery
dash of apple sauce
  (optional)
yogurt-mayonnaise
  combination to taste
dash of curry (optional)

2. High-Protein Meatless Menus
for Special Occasions

For special occasions, even if it's just having good friends over to share your meal, part of the celebration is putting some extra care and flair into the preparations. Although some of these recipes require no more time than many of the Meals in a Dish, each has a special quality that your guests will appreciate. Here are the types of meals so that you can see what appeals most to you: *

(A) The Indian Feast (Version One)

(B) The Indian Feast (Version Two)

(C) Middle Eastern Specialty

(D) Brazilian Evening

(E) Greek Gala

(F) Mexican Banquet (Version One)

(G) Mexican Banquet (Version Two)

(H) Dinner in Italy

(I)   Oriental Specialty

(J) Soup Supper for Friends

(K) Harvest Dinner

(L) Favorite Soybean Dinner

(M) Pizza Party

---

* Recipes are provided for all those dishes that are italicized in the menus that follow.

(A) *The Indian Feast (Version One)*

Menu:

Fruit-Vegetable Cup

Sweet-and-Pungent Vegetable Curry

Sesame Dream Bars (see page 339)

Fruit-Vegetable Cup

Combine:
pineapple chunks
   (preferably fresh)
apple, diced
mandarin orange slices
carrot, diced
celery, chopped

Dress with:
yogurt and honey, with a
   dash of grated orange
   rind

Honey

Sweet-and-Pungent Vegetable Curry

6 servings

average serving = approx. 11 g usable protein
26–31% of daily protein allowance

Have ready:
⅔ cup dry soybeans (or
    kidneys, limas, or mix of
    the 3), cooked (2 cups;
    save one cup bean liquid),
    or 2 cups canned beans
1 cup raw brown rice,
    cooked with ¾ cup raw
    bulgur (about 3½ cups)

Sauté until golden:
oil as needed
4 carrots, sliced diagonally
2 onions, sliced thinly

Add and sauté 1 min more:
1 tbsp (or more) hot curry
    powder
¼ cup flour

*Add and simmer until carrots
tender, not soft:*
1 cup liquid from beans
    (or water)

Add:
¾ cup raisins
¾ cup cashews (raw or
    roasted)
3 tbsp (or more) mango
    chutney
1 tbsp brown sugar
(more liquid if necessary to
    maintain a thick sauce)

Adjust seasoning. Simmer until raisins are soft and
seasonings mingle. Serve over the cooked grain. A
delightful combination—perfect for the most festive
occasion. It can easily be prepared well in advance.

Complementary protein: soybeans + wheat + rice

(B) *The Indian Feast (Version Two)*

Menu:

   Honeyed Curry Platter

   Fresh Spinach and Mushroom Salad

   Cypress Pt. Carrot Cake (see page 341)

Honeyed Curry Platter

6 servings

average serving = approx. 8 g usable protein
32–39% of daily protein allowance

Have ready:
2 cups raw brown rice,
    cooked (4 cups)
¾ cup kidney beans or
    small red beans, cooked
    and salted (2 cups)
    (optional)*

*In a saucepan make a
cream sauce with:*
2 tbsp butter
1 tbsp arrowroot starch or
    2½ tbsp whole wheat
    flour†
2 cups milk
¾ cup instant non-fat dry
    milk

*When thickened, add to
cream sauce:*
1 tbsp lemon juice
1 tbsp honey
2 tsp curry powder
1 tsp salt

Sauté:
oil as needed
¼ cup sesame meal
1 medium onion, diced
2 cloves garlic, minced
2 medium carrots, diced
2 small zucchini, diced

*Special additions and
garnishes:* (optional)
whole cooked shrimps
sliced fresh nectarines
fresh green grapes

On a large baking platter, place the cooked rice and
beans. Over them arrange the sautéed vegetables and
shrimp (optional). Pour cream sauce over all. Garnish.
The fruit makes this dish an incredible feast for the
eyes and mouth.

Complementary protein: rice + milk
                       sesame + milk
                       rice + beans

---

* Even if you leave out the beans there is enough milk
protein to complement the rice and sesame protein.

† Be sure to toast and stir the flour and butter before adding milk.

(C) *Middle Eastern Specialty*

Menu:

Eggplant spread on crackers (well-cooked
  eggplant blended with sesame butter and
  herbs of your choice)

Cous Cous for Arabian Nights

Tossed Salad

Sesame-Nut Squares (see page 342)

Cous Cous for Arabian Nights (with Garbanzos and Sweet-and-Sour Sauce)

6 servings

average serving = approx. 13 g usable protein
30–36% of daily protein allowance

1. Garbanzos-Vegetable Topping

Have ready:
1½ cups dried garbanzos, cooked (about 4½ cups), or 1 20-oz can garbanzos

Sauté in a deep skillet or Dutch oven:
oil as needed
1 large onion, chopped
3 stalks of celery, chopped
½ lb fresh mushrooms, sliced
4 medium carrots, sliced

Add while sautéing and continue about 10 min:
1-2 tsp dill weed
1 bay leaf
1-2 tsp parsley flakes
1-2 tsp horseradish
salt and pepper to taste
½ tsp dried mustard
1 clove garlic, mashed

Add:
2 cups seasoned stock
½-1 cup white wine

Cover and cook for 10 minutes, then add the cooked garbanzos. Adjust seasoning. Add salt and pepper. Consistency should be like that of a thick soup. Cornstarch may be added for thickening.

2. Sweet-and-Sour Sauce

1 cup milk + ¼ cup instant dry milk
1 egg
1 8-oz can tomato sauce

¼ cup vinegar
½ cup brown sugar
½ tsp dried mustard

In a double boiler beat the egg and the milk together. Then add brown sugar and tomato sauce. Then add vinegar and mustard, all the while stirring with a whisk over low heat.

3. Cous Cous (or Bulgur or Rice)

2 cups raw cous cous
  (bulgur or rice), cooked
  (about 5 cups)

Cous cous is a light, partially refined wheat product that is a basic ingredient in many Middle Eastern dishes. It gives a very special quality to this lovely dish. However, you may also use bulgur (partially cooked cracked wheat) or rice. Cook cous cous according to the directions on the package you purchased, or cook other grains according to the Basic Cooking Instructions.

To serve place a portion of the cooked grain on each plate and top with the garbanzos-vegetable mix and then with the sweet-and-sour sauce. This dish has a flavor unlike any other one you know. It is definitely worth the trouble!

Complementary protein: beans + wheat
                                      beans + milk

(D) *Brazilian Evening*

Menu:

Feijoada (Tangy Black Beans)

Rice with Green Chili Sauce

*Steamed Greens with Sesame Topping and
Orange Slices*

Brazilian Evening

6 servings

average serving = approx. 11 g usable protein
26–31% of daily protein allowance

Feijoada (Tangy Black Beans)

Sauté in heavy, large pot:
oil as needed
1 large onion, chopped
2 cloves garlic, minced

Add:
1 cup dry black beans
3 cups stock or water (or
   substitute wine for up to
   half of the stock)
1 bay leaf
¼ tsp pepper

Bring to boil, then simmer
2 min. Let sit, covered,
unheated, 1 hr.

Add:
1 orange, whole or halved
½ tsp salt
2 stalks celery, chopped
1 tomato, chopped

Simmer, covered with lid ajar, for 2–3 hours or more,
until the beans are tender. Remove a ladleful of beans,
mash them, and return them to the pot to cook until
the mashed beans thicken the mixture. (Or I have done
the whole thing in a pressure cooker—after first
sautéing the onion and garlic. It is much quicker and
still *very* good.)

Rice with Green Chili Sauce

Have ready:
2 cups raw brown rice,
   cooked (about 4⅔ cups)

Sauté:
2 tbsp olive oil

1 onion, chopped
3 cloves garlic, minced

Then add:
2 tomatoes, peeled, seeded,
   coarsely chopped

Simmer a few minutes. Stir in the cooked rice and keep warm over low heat.

Sauce

Blend in blender until smooth:
1 tomato, peeled and seeded
California green chilies, seeded, to taste (start with half of a 2-oz can)
1 tsp salt
2 cloves garlic

Add and blend to chop (not to purée):
juice of 1 lemon
1 onion, cut in chunks
scallions, parsley, to taste
¼ cup vinegar

Just before serving, stir in a little liquid from the bean pot.

Steamed Greens with Sesame Topping and Orange Slices

Steam until barely wilted:
1½ lb trimmed greens, salted (turnip or mustard greens, collards, etc.)

Garnish:
⅓ cup toasted sesame seed meal
1 orange, sliced

Sprinkle 1 heaping tbsp of toasted seed meal on each serving, with orange slices on top or around edges.

Serve the rice with sauce along with the beans and greens for a splendid three-course Brazilian dinner.

Complementary protein: beans + rice

(E) *Greek Gala*

Menu:

Greek Salad (lettuce, anchovies, black olives, onions, feta cheese)

Meatless Moussaka

Easy Apple-Cheese Pie (see page 348)

Meatless Moussaka

6 servings

average serving = approx. 14 g usable protein
32–39% of daily protein allowance

Base Layer

Have ready:
½ cup raw brown rice,
  cooked (1½ cups)
⅓ cup dry soybeans,
  cooked, seasoned, and
  puréed (1 cup)

Sauté and set aside:
oil as needed
1 large eggplant,* peeled
  and sliced
salt and pepper

Sauté:
2 tbsp butter
1 large onion, finely
  chopped

Add to onion and stir:
beans and rice
3 tbsp tomato paste
½ cup red wine
¼ cup chopped parsley
⅛ tsp cinnamon
salt and pepper

*In a casserole layer egg-
plant and then bean-rice
mixture and sprinkle over
all:*

½ cup bread crumbs
½ cup Parmesan cheese,
  grated

Top Custard

4 tbsp butter
3 tbsp whole wheat flour
2 cups milk
2 eggs

1 cup ricotta cheese or
  cottage cheese
  blended smooth
nutmeg

Make a cream sauce by melting 4 tbsp of butter and
blending in the flour, stirring with a wire whisk. Then
stir in the milk gradually, and continue stirring over
low heat until mixture thickens and is smooth. Remove

from heat, cool slightly, and *stir* in the eggs, ricotta, and nutmeg.

Pour the sauce over all and bake about 45 minutes at 375°F, or until top is golden and knife comes out clean from the custard. Remove from oven and cool 20 to 30 minutes before serving. Cut into squares and serve.

NOTE: The flavor of this dish improves on standing one day. Reheat before serving.

Complementary protein: soybeans + rice
soybeans + milk

---

* Or for less oily eggplant, bake the eggplant (peeled and sliced) in a 9x12 casserole dish in enough oil to keep moist at 350°F until quite soft.

(F) *Mexican Banquet (Version One)*

Menu:

Vegetarian Enchiladas

Mexican Fried Rice
(simply sauté precooked rice with sautéed onions, green pepper, garlic, etc.)

Fresh Fruit Salad
(try a dressing with lime juice, yogurt, and honey)

Vegetarian Enchiladas

4 servings

average serving = approx. 7 g usable protein
16–20% of daily protein allowance

Have ready:
8 soft tortillas

Sauce

Sauté:
2 tbsp olive oil
1 cup onions, chopped

Add:
2 cups canned tomatoes
1 8-oz can tomato sauce

1 clove garlic, minced
pinch cayenne
10 drops hot sauce*
½ tbsp chili powder*
1 tbsp honey
½ tsp salt
¼ tsp cumin seed, ground

Simmer, uncovered, for 30 minutes

Filling

Have ready:
½ cup dry pinto beans,
   cooked and mashed or
   ground (about 1½ cup).
   Why not cook extra?

Sauté:
olive oil as needed
1 clove garlic, minced

½ cup onion, chopped
1 small can pitted ripe
   olives (put some aside for
   garnish)

Add:
1 tsp chili powder
¼ tsp salt

Then add mashed or ground beans to the sautéed
mix (and some of the above sauce if the mix seems too
sticky). Stir well.

* This is a very hot sauce. If you prefer something milder,
reduce the amount of hot sauce and chili powder.

Extras

¼ lb cheese, grated   black olive halves

To assemble: Fill eight corn tortillas with 2–3 tbsp of filling and 1 tbsp grated cheese. Place, rolled up, in a shallow baking pan. Cover with sauce, sprinkle with cheese, and garnish with black olive halves. Bake at 350°F for 30 minutes until bubbling hot.

Complementary protein: beans + corn

Celery, Onion, Lemon, Garlic, Kidney Bean, Chick Pea

(G) *Mexican Banquet (Version Two)*

Menu:
    Guacamole (avocado, garlic, lemon juice dip)
      with Toasted Tortillas

    Rice con Queso

    Lettuce-and-Red Cabbage Salad

    Corn Bread (see page 327)

    Lemon Sherbert with *Sesame Crisp Cookies*
      (see page 331)

Rice con Queso

6 servings

average serving = approx. 17 g usable protein
39–47% of daily protein allowance

Have ready:
1½ cups raw brown rice, cooked, with salt and pepper (about 3 cups)
½ cup dry black beans (or black-eyed peas, pinto beans, etc.), cooked (about 1⅓ cups)

1. rice-beans mix
2. ricotta cheese, thinned slightly with milk or yogurt until spreadable (use ½ lb all together)
3. shredded jack cheese (use about ¾ lb all together)

Mix together:
prepared rice and beans
3 cloves garlic, minced, pressed
1 large onion, chopped
1 small can chilies

Topping:
½ cup shredded cheddar cheese

Assemble:
In casserole repeat layers of:

Optional garnishes:
chopped black olives, chopped fresh onions, parsley

End with a layer of the rice-beans mix. Bake at 350°F for 30 minutes. During last few minutes of baking, sprinkle grated cheese over the top. Garnish.

This is an ideal dish for a buffet dinner. My guests always ask for this recipe!

Complementary protein: rice + beans
rice + milk product

(H) *Dinner in Italy*

Menu:

Minestrone con Crema

Spaghetti with Clam Sauce with Garlic and Wine (see page 236)

Tossed Green Salad with Caesar Dressing

Poppy Seed Cake (see page 337)

Minestrone con Crema

6–8 servings

average serving = approx. 10 g usable protein
23–28% of daily protein allowance

Have ready:
½ cup dry garbanzos,

cooked until almost done
(1½ cups)

Pesto

Mash in mortar or blend in blender to make smooth paste:
½ cup fresh basil, spinach, or parsley leaves (dry leaves won't work)

1 clove garlic, minced
1 cup grated Parmesan cheese
olive oil as needed

Set aside.

Soup

Put in large pot with beans, bean liquid, and water to cover:
5 kohlrabi or turnips with leaves chopped (about 2 cups) and bulbs diced
1 head cabbage, finely chopped or grated
2 cups beet greens or

spinach, without stems, chopped
¼ cup parsley
salt to taste

Have ready:
3 cups milk
sherry to taste (optional)

(Seem like a lot of vegetables? Believe me, it works!)
Bring to a boil, then simmer about 1 hour. Add the milk and simmer (do *not* boil) the soup 15 minutes more. Stir in the pesto (and sherry, optional) and heat 5 minutes more. Serve at once. This soup is truly delicious. (A friend who swears that he dislikes both greens and turnips ate this soup with gusto!)

Complementary protein: beans + milk

(I) *Oriental Specialty*

Menu:

Sweet-and-Sour Vegetables with Tempura

Fried Rice with Sesame
   (stir fry precooked rice with ¼ cup
   toasted ground sesame seeds)

Peanut Dessert Fondue with Fresh Fruit (see
page 350)

Sweet-and-Sour Vegetables with Tempura

6 servings

average serving (using tofu) = approx. 16 g
usable protein
37–44% of daily protein allowance

Have ready:
2 cups raw brown rice,
cooked with ¼ cup soy
grits (about 5-6 cups).

Stir fry at last minute, as
menu suggests, if you
wish.

1. Tempura (Oriental breaded, deep-fried vegetables)

Have ready:
1 batch of pancake batter
made from the "Comple-
mentary Protein Quick
Mix" found on page 307.
Use 2 eggs; beat the
egg whites until stiff and
fold them in just before
using.*
6 cups sliced raw vegetables
and tofu (optional). Use
mix of carrots, broccoli,
onion, cauliflower,
zucchini etc. Use *half*

the vegetables for
tempura and half for
stir-fried vegetables (see
below).
Deep skillet or pot with at
least 2 inches of hot oil
(350°F)
2 sets of chopsticks or tongs,
or your fingers plus a
slated spoon
Bed of shredded cabbage
or clean towel for
draining the tempura

To make: Using one set of chopsticks or tongs, or
your fingers, pick up a vegetable slice and dip it into
the batter. Drop the coated vegetable into the hot oil.
Cook, turning once or twice, until golden brown. Cook
several slices at a time, but do not crowd. Remove from

---

* So that the egg white will not "wilt" before you are ready
to use it, you can beat only one egg white and add it to half
the batter. When ready for the second half, beat the second
egg white, fold in, and finish the tempura.

hot oil with another set of chopsticks, tongs, or a slated spoon. Place to drain on shredded cabbage (beautiful for serving) or a clean towel.

While you are frying the tempura, make the:

2. Stir-Fried Vegetables

Sauté in another large pan:
2 tbsp peanut oil
the other 3 cups of mixed
  vegetables
more tofu (optional)

*Add and sauté for a minute
while you prepare the
sauce:*
some sliced onion
1-lb can of pineapple
  chunks, drained (save
  liquid)

3. Sweet-and-Sour Sauce

Mix well:
juice from the canned
  pineapple
2½ tbsp cornstarch

¼ cup brown sugar
¼ cup vinegar
1 tbsp tamari or soy sauce

Add this to the vegetables and stir until the sauce becomes clear and glutinous.

To serve: Spoon the cooked rice onto a large platter (or you may need two). Spread the tempura vegetables on shredded cabbage (optional) around the edges. Spoon the stir-fried vegetables in sauce over the rice. And, if you like, sprinkle some finely chopped scallions over all. A beautiful dinner.

Complementary protein: wheat + soy
                       rice + soy

(J) *Soup Supper for Friends*

Menu:

Hearty Vegetable Soup

No-Wait Wheat-Oat Bread (see page 319)

Green Salad

Chocolate Chip Cookies (see page 333)

Hearty Vegetable Soup

about 3 quarts

1 cup = approx. 3 g usable protein
7–8% of daily protein allowance

Have ready:
⅓ cup dry soybeans, cooked with bay leaf (about 1 cup)

Sauté:
2 tbsp olive oil
1 cup onions, chopped
2 cups vegetables, chopped (carrots, mushrooms, celery, etc.)

Add:
1 cup canned tomatoes (drain and reserve liquid)
2-3 peppercorns
pinch cayenne
2 tbsp nutritional yeast
½ tsp each basil, tarragon, oregano, celery seed, summer savory
¼ tsp each thyme, rosemary, marjoram, sage
2 tbsp soy sauce
½ cup raw brown rice
⅓-½ cup raw bulgur wheat, or ⅓ cup raw whole wheat kernels
cooked beans
6-8 cups vegetable stock, including liquid from tomatoes

Bring to boil. Remove 1 cup to small bowl and mix to smooth consistency with:
1 heaping tbsp miso (soy paste)

Add the paste back to the soup. Simmer for 1–2 hours until the grains are tender *or* pressure cook 10–15 minutes. Add more liquid if necessary.

This soup gets heartier each time you reheat it. It makes a full meal with bread and cheese.

Complementary protein: rice + wheat + soy

(K) *Harvest Dinner.*

Menu:

> *Walnut Cheddar Loaf*
>
> Steamed Broccoli with Hollandaise Sauce
>
> Fried Sliced Apples
>
> *Indian Pudding* or *Soybean Pie* (see. pages 346 and 349)

Walnut-Cheddar Loaf

5–6 servings

average serving = approx. 9 g usable protein
21–25% of daily protein allowance

Have ready:
½ cup raw brown rice,
  cooked (about 1¼ cups).
  Why not cook extra?

Combine:
1 cup black walnuts,
  coarsely ground
  (can use blender)

1 cup cheese, grated
2 tbsp lemon juice
2 cups chopped onions,
  sautéed
2 eggs, beaten
¼ tsp salt
2 tbsp nutritional yeast
1 tsp caraway seeds
cooked rice

Mix well. Place in oiled loaf pan. Bake at 350°F for 30 minutes.

Especially nice if served with a cheese sauce with whole walnuts sprinkled on top.

Complementary protein: rice + milk product

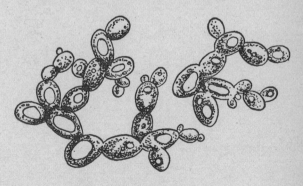

Yeast patterns

(L)　*Favorite Soybean Dinner*

Menu:

Soybean Croquette Platter

Green Peas

Cole Slaw

Cottage Cheese Cake (see page 336)

Soybean Croquette Platter

4 servings
average serving = approx. 13 g usable protein
30–36% of daily protein allowance

Have cooking:*
¾ cup raw brown rice,
  cooked with ⅔ cup
  bulgur wheat + 1 tsp salt
  (about 3-4 cups)

Have ready:
⅓ cup dry soybeans, cooked
  with 1 chopped onion,
  1 bay leaf, and 1 tsp
  salt, then drained and
  mashed (about 1 cup)

Croquettes

*Blend in blender with 2 tsp
butter, or chop finely with
food chopper and add to
mashed beans:*
¼ cup peanuts
¾ cup walnuts
3 tbsp tomato paste
1 onion, cut in chunks for
  blender
½ cup bread crumbs

*(Mixture should be quite
moist; if not, add more
tomato paste.) Form into
balls and dip into:*
1 well-beaten egg

Roll in:
wheat germ or bread
  crumbs

*Bake at 400°F for 30
minutes until brown.*

Sauce

your favorite marinara
  sauce
or
cheese sauce (simple white
  sauce plus grated cheese)

or
mushroom sauce (white
  sauce plus mushrooms)

To serve: Arrange cooked grains on a serving platter, placing croquettes on top. Pour sauce over cro-

quettes. Garnish with parsley. This platter would even be more lovely if you had a fresh steamed or sautéed green vegetable arranged about the outer edge.

If the soybeans have been cooked ahead, the croquettes can be prepared for the oven in minutes. I prefer this carefree method of baking croquettes to top-of-the-stove cooking, which requires more tending. Also, baking gives the croquettes an all-over crispness. (Incidentally, these croquettes are also delicious with that old standby of the quick meal, tomato ketchup.)

Complementary protein: rice + wheat + soy + peanuts

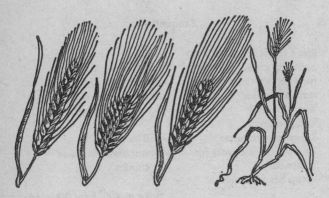

Barley

---

* These grains are especially good in this recipe if they are sautéed first. See Appendix A, "Basic Cooking Instructions."

(M) *Pizza Party*

Menu:

Complementary Pizza

Caesar Salad

"Complementary" Pizza

four 10-inch pizzas

half of 1 pizza = approx. 16 g usable protein
37–44% of daily protein allowance

Dough

2 tbsp dry baking yeast	1 tsp salt
1¼ cups warm water	2½ cups whole wheat flour
1 tsp honey	1 cup soy flour
¼ cup olive oil	garnishes

Dissolve the yeast in the water with the honey. Mix with oil, salt, and flours in a large bowl. Blend well and knead until smooth and elastic on a floured board. Let rise in the bowl in a warm place until doubled in volume (about 1½ hours). Punch down and knead again for a few minutes to make dough easy to handle.

Sauce

Sauté in large pot until onions are soft:	4 cups canned tomatoes, chopped
3 tbsp olive oil	1 small can tomato paste
1 cup onions, finely chopped	1 tbsp dried oregano
1 tbsp minced garlic	1 tbsp fresh basil or
	1 tsp dried basil
	1 bay leaf
Add, boil, lower heat, cook 1 hr, stirring occasionally:	2 tsp honey
	1 tbsp salt
	pepper to taste

Remove bay leaf and, if a smoother sauce is desired, you may purée or sieve it.

Assembly

cornmeal as needed
1 lb. mozzarella cheese,
    grated
½ cup Parmesan cheese,
    freshly grated

Possible garnishes:
sliced garlic, sliced onion,
    sliced mushrooms, sliced
    green pepper

To make 4 10-inch pizzas, divide the dough into quarters, stretch each quarter to a 5-inch circle while you hold it in your hands, then roll it out to 10 inches and about ⅛ inch thick. Dust pans with cornmeal, place the pizzas on top, and pinch a small rim around the edge. For each pizza use ½ cup tomato sauce, ½ cup mozzarella cheese, and 2 tbsp Parmesan. Top with your choice of garnishes.

Bake 10 to 15 minutes at 500°F.

The pizza looks like work, but it makes a wonderful supper dish—high protein in content *and* quality.

Complementary protein: wheat + soy

3. And All the Extras

The recipes in this section prove that a snack, a baked food, or a sweet doesn't have to be considered just an energy food, a filler, or a mere self-indulgence! They can also contribute substantially to meeting your body's need for protein. If, as I have pointed out earlier, much of what you eat throughout the day has some protein in it, then it will all easily add up to enough— without that big piece of meat!

Don't think that in order to make complementary protein combinations you have to use one of my recipes: You can convert any bread, breakfast, or dessert recipe on your "family favorites" list into one with more protein, and more usable protein, by simply adopting a few new and easy habits.

Here are the extras:

(A) Snacks, Appetizers, and Candies—That Count

(B) Start-Right Breakfasts

(C) Baked-In Protein

(D) Protein for Dessert

(A) *Snacks, Appetizers, and Candies—That Count*

As long as you are not overweight, there's nothing necessarily wrong with snacking. It all depends on what you choose! And, there's no reason why pretzels, potato chips, and sour-cream dip have to be the universal party fare when high-protein dips and spreads are so easy to prepare.

Recipes:

1. Snacks That Count:
   Instant Puddings: Cottage Cheese Pudding, Buttermilk Pudding
   Peanut Butter Protein Sandwich
   Spreads: Vegetable-Sesame Spreads (Avocado and Tomato), Low-Calorie Cheese Spread, Soy-Sesame-Peanut Spread

2. Appetizers That Count:
   Cold Gallentine
   Sesame Crisp Crackers
   Dips: Bean Dip Arab Style, Bean Dip Mexican Style, Cottage Cheese–Seafood Dip
   Party Snacks

Suggestions for Hot Hors d'oeuvres

3. Candies That Count:
   Peanut Butter Log
   Sesame Seed Delight
   Tiger's Candy

Instant Cottage Cheese Pudding

To cottage cheese add: toasted sunflower seeds
chopped nuts   dried fruit
apple sauce   dash of cinnamon

Choose your favorite ingredients and mix together to your taste for a great snack.

Snacks That Count

Instant Buttermilk Pudding

To leftover rice add: nuts or seeds
buttermilk   raisins
brown sugar

This "pudding" has the greatest sweet-sour taste that is addicting. If you think you don't like buttermilk, try it this way.

Peanut Butter Protein Sandwich

Peanut butter + instant non-fat dry milk + banana (optional)
honey (optional)

Remember that when you eat peanut butter by itself your body can only use about 40 percent of the protein in it. The rest is wasted because the amino acids are unbalanced. This is why advertising peanut butter as a good source of protein is misleading *unless* one knows how to combine it with other protein sources to create an amino acid balance that the body can use more fully.

So, go get your jar of peanut butter. If it is partly eaten, there'll be room to add some non-fat dry milk powder. The exact proportion is 2 parts peanut butter to slightly less than 1 part milk powder (or slightly less than ½ cup milk powder for every cup of peanut butter). However, this much powder will make the peanut butter too stiff. So either add less powder (any you add is helpful, protein-wise) or add honey to soften it up. Or, if the peanut butter-milk mix is stiff, I like to add a quarter of a mashed banana when I am making a sandwich for my little girl. She loves it that way.

Make your peanut protein count!

Complementary protein: peanut + milk

Vegetable-Sesame Spreads

1. *Avocado Spread:* Mash a ripe avocado with toasted ground sesame seeds. Spread on herbed bread like the Triti-Casserole Bread (see page 322).

2. *Tomato Spread:* Stir toasted ground sesame seeds into tomato paste, adding a sprinkle of basil and oregano. Spread on lightly toasted English muffin and cover with a slice of mozzarella or other cheese. Place under broiler until cheese melts. Garnish with scallions or parsley. To serve as an appetizer, cut in quarters.

Low-Calorie Cheese Spread

Ricotta cheese or cottage cheese, plain	Or add: chopped dried fruit chopped nuts

Try either cheese on toast, English muffins, or a bagel. Add just a touch of marmalade. Delicious!

If you want more protein and fewer calories, riccota is a great substitute for cream cheese. It has one third the calories and 75 percent more protein.

Soy-Sesame-Peanut Spread

about 2 cups

⅛ cup serving = approx. 3 g usable protein
7–8% of daily protein allowance

In dry skillet roast slowly
until light brown, stirring
constantly:
½ cup soy flour

Blend with:
heaping ⅓ cup peanut
butter
1⅛ cup toasted ground
sesame seed or ½ cup
sesame butter

salt, if necessary
Add enough water or other
liquid to make smooth
consistency.

Add to taste (optional):
garlic powder
onion powder
grated onion
herbs, fresh or soaked

To give the flavors a chance to mingle, be sure to let the herbed mixture stand at room temperature at least 1 hour before serving. I love this spread on pumpernickel bread with tomato. It can also be sweetened (deleting onion and herbs, of course) with fruit juice or honey; or it can be thinned with your favorite salad dressing to use as a vegetable sauce or salad dressing. Or use it to bind together your leftover grain (rice or bulgur wheat) to make skillet patties.

Complementary protein: soy + sesame + peanut

Appetizers That Count

Cold Gallentine

6 servings

average serving = approx. 6 g usable protein
14–17% of daily protein allowance

Have ready:
½ cup raw brown rice,
cooked (about 1¼ cups)

1 tsp salt
pepper to taste
pinch nutmeg

Sauté:
2 tbsp butter
1 medium onion, chopped
¼ pound mushrooms,
coarsely chopped

Add to egg mixture:
the cooked rice
2 tbsp brewer's yeast
¾ cup bread crumbs
¼ cup nuts or toasted
ground seeds

Mix separately:
2 eggs, beaten

Then add sautéed vegetables. Place the mixture in an oiled casserole. Bake at 375°F for 30 minutes. Serve cold with an optional spread:

Mix:
2 tbsp ricotta cheese

2 tbsp yogurt
2 tbsp mayonnaise

Makes a fine hors d'oeuvre or lunchtime dish.

Variation: 2 or 3 whole or halved hard-boiled eggs can be placed in center of mixture before baking.

Complementary protein: rice + yeast

Sesame Crisp Crackers

3–4 dozen crackers

⅛ of recipe = approx. 4 g usable protein
9–11% of daily protein allowance

Stir together:
1½ cups whole wheat flour
¼ cup soy flour
¼ cup sesame seeds,
   ground
¾ tsp salt

Blend in well:
⅓ cup oil

Then add:
½ cup water (as needed)

Add enough water to the dough to make it soft enough to roll out very easily into a thin sheet. Gather the dough into a ball, then roll it to ⅛ inch thick. Cut it in cracker shapes or sticks and place on an unoiled baking sheet. Bake at 350°F until the crackers are crisp and golden.

These crackers go well with soups as well as sweets. Be sure to serve them with your favorite dips, spreads, and cheeses.

Complementary protein: rice + sesame

Bean Dip Arab Style

See recipe for the filling in the "Middle Eastern Tacos," page 198. It combines garbanzo beans (chickpeas) and sesame butter with an incredible assortment of spices. Serve on wheat crackers.

Complementary protein: beans + sesame

Bean Dip Mexican Style

Cook pinto beans until very soft. Purée, adding a little oil to improve the texture if you wish. For extra goodness, add chili powder, garlic, and cumin to taste. Fry as in the recipe for Tostados on page 197. Stir in lots of grated cheddar or jack cheese. Use as a dip with corn chips or quartered and toasted tortillas.

Complementary protein: beans + milk product

Cottage Cheese—Seafood Dip

Blend cottage cheese with chopped onion and drained, canned minced clams. Add herbs if you like. Great as a light dip with fresh vegetables.

Party Snacks

4½ cups, 18 servings

average serving = approx. 3 g usable protein
7–8% of daily protein allowance

Combine:
¾ cup peanuts, roasted
1 cup sunflower seeds,
  roasted
1 cup cashews, roasted

1 cup raisins
1 cup coconut shreds,
  toasted
salt (optional)

Serve as a party snack. This also makes a simple dessert after a big meal. You can vary the recipe by leaving all of the ingredients raw. Try substituting sliced dates for the raisins and walnuts for the cashews. This makes a richer snack.

Complementary protein: peanuts + sunflower seeds

Nuts and Seeds

Candies That Count

Peanut Butter Log

one 10-inch log

1-inch slice = approx. 3 g usable protein

7–8% of daily protein allowance

½ cup peanut butter
2½ tbsp non-fat dry milk
(3½ instant)—more as
needed

½ cup raisins
2 tbsp honey
shredded coconut (optional)

Blend peanut butter (and honey), then work in as much powdered milk as you need to make the mixture easy to handle and fairly stiff. Pick up the mixture and knead in the raisins, distributing them evenly. Roll into a 1-inch-thick and 10-inch-long log. Then roll in coconut for eye-appeal. Chill and slice or pull apart.

This mixture can be molded into balls or any shape and even pressed into cookie molds to make an exciting snack for small children (and big ones too). Many mothers have told me that when their children ask for sweets, they give them a piece of this log—with a clear conscience. And I know of a nursery school that let the children make their own; and the kids loved it.

Complementary protein: peanuts + milk

Sesame Seed Delight

18 pieces

1 piece = approx. 3 g usable protein
7–8% of daily protein allowance

Cream together:
¼ cup each butter and
  sesame butter

Blend with:
1 cup ground sesame seeds
⅓ cup instant dry milk
½ cup wheat germ

½ cup grated coconut
  (optional)
¼ cup ground nuts
  (optional)
¼ cup honey
¼ cup raisins
2 tsp vanilla or almond
  extract

Squeeze into 1-inch balls. Chill several hours.

Variations: Add ¾ tsp mace, cinnamon, or cardamom.

Complementary protein: sesame + milk

Tiger's Candy

2 dozen balls

2 balls = approx. 3 g usable protein
7–8% of daily protein allowance

Blend together:
½ cup peanut butter*
⅔ cup ground sunflower
    seeds

Stir in:
1 tbsp brewer's yeast
    (optional)
¼ cup instant dry milk

1-2 tbsp honey
¼ cup raisins, chopped fine
¼ cup dates, chopped fine
    (or substitute other dried
    fruit or more raisins)

Have ready:
carob powder or shredded
    coconut

Probably the easiest way to blend all of the ingredients is by using your hands. If the mixture is too dry, add liquid milk; if too wet, add more powdered milk. Roll into balls and roll in coconut or carob powder. Chill.

Complementary protein: peanuts + sunflower seeds

---

* The peanut butter in excess of the proportions given is complemented by the dry milk.

(B) *Start-Right Breakfasts*

There is no more important meal than breakfast to which to apply your newly learned protein "wizardry"! And no easier one. Most breakfast foods lend themselves easily to "spiking" with protein.

1. To make instant cold, protein-rich breakfast cereal, add to leftover grain (rice, bulgur):

Your choice of:	buttermilk
toasted sunflower seeds	milk
toasted ground sesame	cottage cheese
seeds	ricotta cheese
wheat germ	
peanuts	*Choose 1 for sweet taste:*
	honey
With (choose 1)	dried fruit
yogurt	fresh fruit

2. To make your hot cereal into a protein-rich breakfast, *while cooking* add your choice of:
   soy grits (1 tbsp for each serving—they cook in just a few minutes)
   wheat germ (to taste)
   extra non-fat dry milk powder (1 tbsp for each serving)
   toasted ground sesame seeds (to taste)

3. And for the many who like just toast in the morning, you too can have a healthy breakfast if you:
   a. Make your own bread and include extra non-fat dry milk, wheat germ, soy flour or grits, ground sesame or sunflower seeds. The Whole Wheat Quick Bread (see page 318) is a terrific breakfast bread.
   b. Or spread your toast with ricotta cheese or cottage cheese. My favorite breakfast is a toasted pumpernickel bagel with a thick coat of cottage cheese and a little orange marmalade!

4. To make waffles or pancakes give you protein as well as energy, add:

soy flour (¼ cup soy flour to 1 cup whole wheat flour)

extra non-fat dry milk (at least 3 tbsp non-fat dry milk to 1 cup whole wheat flour)

wheat germ

or top your pancakes with ricotta cheese or cottage cheese and fruit

For additional pancake recipes and topping ideas see "Super Supper Pancakes," page 187. Many are also perfect for a special breakfast or brunch.

Recipes:

1. Complementary Protein Quick Mix
    (for making pancakes, waffles, biscuits,
        muffins, coffee cake, or tempura etc.)

2. Pancakes:
        Oatmeal-Buttermilk Pancake
        Johnnycakes

3. Waffles
        Wheat-Soy Waffles
        Cornmeal-Soy Waffles

4. Cereal
        Easy Crunchy Granola
        Rice-Cream-and-Sesame Cereal

Complementary Protein Quick Mix
(for making pancakes, waffles, biscuits, muffins, coffeecake, or tempura)

½ cup of basic mix = 8 g usable protein
18–22% of daily protein allowance
(NOTE: recipes using egg and milk provide
even more protein)

Basic Quick Mix

Combine and mix
thoroughly:
6½ cups whole wheat or
  whole-wheat pastry flour
1½ cups soy flour

1 tbsp salt, or to taste
1 cup instant dry milk
⅓ cup baking powder
2½ cups wheat germ

Store in a tightly covered jar in the refrigerator ready to make any of the following options or your own experiments.

Complementary protein: wheat + soy

Pancakes

Combine:
1 egg, beaten*
1 cup milk, buttermilk, or
  yogurt

3 tbsp oil

Add to:
1½ cups Quick Mix

---

* To make lighter pancakes, use 2 eggs and fold in stiffly beaten egg whites just before baking.

Waffles

Combine:
2 eggs, beaten*
1½ cups milk
3 tbsp melted butter or oil

2 tbsp honey

Add to:
1¼ cups Quick Mix

Biscuits

Combine:
⅓ cup oil or melted butter
⅔ cup milk, buttermilk, or
  yogurt

2¼ cups Quick Mix

Turn out on floured board, knead lightly. Pat or roll 1 inch thick; cut with biscuit cutter and place on greased baking sheet. Or cut in triangles, fill with brown sugar and cinnamon, and roll up. Bake at 450°F for 12 to 15 minutes.

Muffins

Combine:
2 eggs, beaten†
1 cup milk, buttermilk, or
  yogurt
2 tbsp oil
2 tbsp honey or molasses
2½ cups Quick Mix

Add (optional):
chopped dried fruit (dates,
  apricots, raisins, etc.) or
chopped nuts or
fresh berries or
canned, drained fruit,
  chopped

Bake at 400°F for 15 minutes.

---

* To make lighter waffles, beat egg whites until stiff and fold in just before baking.
† For lighter muffins, add whites stiffly beaten.

Coffeecake

Combine:
1 egg, beaten
¼ cup oil
¾ cup milk, buttermilk, or
    yogurt
½ cup brown sugar
1½ cups Quick Mix

Add (optional)
any of the options above
    for muffins

For topping combine:
1½ tsp cinnamon
¼ cup tightly packed brown
    sugar
1 tbsp oil
½ cup nuts

Sprinkle crumbly mixture over batter. Bake at 375°F for 30 minutes.

Tempura (Oriental breaded, deep-fried vegetables)

See Sweet-and-Sour Vegetables with Tempura on page 280.

Cauliflower, Asparagus, Potatoes

Oatmeal-Buttermilk Pancakes

6 servings (18–24 4-inch pancakes)

average serving of 3–4 pancakes = approx.
10 g usable protein
23–28% of daily protein allowance

Mix:
½ cup water
½ cup instant dry powdered milk
1 tbsp honey

Add:
2 cups buttermilk
1½ cups rolled oats

If using unrefined rolled oats, refrigerate this mixture over night for the oats to soften.

Beat in:
1 cup whole wheat flour
1 tsp baking soda

½ tsp salt
2 eggs, beaten

Either fry on a hot griddle immediately or, for an even better result, let stand for from 1 to 24 hours. These pancakes are moist and deliciously chewy.

Complementary protein: wheat + milk

Johnnycakes

6 servings (makes about 24 4-inch cakes)

average serving of 4 cakes = approx. 6 g usable protein
14–17% of daily protein allowance

Mix:
1 cup water
½ cup instant dry milk
    powder

Add and mix:
1 egg, beaten
1 tbsp honey
2 tbsp oil

Combine separately:
1 cup freshly ground
    cornmeal
⅓ cup soy flour
¼ cup whole wheat flour
    (or more as needed)

Stir the dry ingredients with the liquid ingredients.
Add more whole wheat flour to achieve the consistency
you prefer. Pour like pancakes onto a hot, oiled grill
or skillet. Serve with honey and butter or other favorite
topping.

These cakes have a different flavor and texture from
pancakes; a welcome change.

Complementary protein: corn + soy + milk

Wheat-Soy Waffles

about 5 waffles

1 waffle = approx. 8 g usable protein
19–22% of daily protein allowance

Mix together:
1 cup whole wheat flour
1 tsp salt
¼ cup soy flour
2 tsp baking powder

Mix separately and beat well:
2 eggs*
1½ cups milk
3 tbsp melted butter or oil
2 tbsp honey

Stir wet ingredients into dry ingredients. Lumps are Ok. Bake on hot, oiled waffle iron.

These are delicious, light waffles. They are especially good with the addition of about ½ cup chopped nuts. Make a lot and keep leftovers for toasting. On toasted leftover waffles try:

cream tuna
sliced tomato and melted cheese
whipped cottage cheese with fruit topping

Complementary protein: wheat + soy

---

* Separating eggs, beating the whites stiff and folding in as the last step, makes an even lighter waffle.

Cornmeal-Soy Waffles

6 waffles

2 waffles = approx. 13 g usable protein
30–36% of daily protein allowance

Beat in medium bowl:
2 eggs

Add and blend well:
1 cup milk + 1 tbsp
  non-fat dry milk
3 tbsp oil
3 tbsp molasses

Stir together separately:
1 cup cornmeal
⅓ cup soy flour
½ tsp salt
2 tsp baking powder

Add dry to wet ingredients. Bake in hot oiled waffle iron using about ½ cup batter per waffle.

These are surprisingly delicious waffles, golden and crunchy, easy to make. Make lots and freeze leftovers. They are just as delicious popping out of a toaster. I love them with cottage cheese and honey on top.

Complementary protein: corn + soy + milk

Easy Crunchy Granola

about 12 cups

1 cup = approx. 9 g usable protein
21–25% of daily protein allowance

Preheat oven to 400°F.

In a large baking pan, or dutch oven, toast in oven until nicely browned:
7 cups rolled oats
1 cup rolled wheat (or substitute more oats)

Shake every few minutes.

When oats and wheat are done, add:
1 cup wheat germ
1¼ cups ground sesame seeds

⅓ cup instant dry milk (¼ cup non-instant dry milk)
2 tbsp brewer's yeast
½ to 2 cups coconut shreds

Toast complete mixture for about 5 min.

Stir in and toast for about 5 min more:
½ cup vegetable oil
½ to 1 cup honey
1 tbsp vanilla

Remove from oven and store in a loosely covered jar or casserole.
Optional: When adding wheat germ, etc., stir in about a cup each of any or all of the following:
1. peanuts, whole or ground
2. walnuts, whole or ground
3. sunflower seeds, whole or ground

Complementary protein: sesame + milk

Rice-Cream-and-Sesame Cereal

4 servings

average serving = approx. 10 g usable protein
23–28% of daily protein allowance

If you like Cream of Wheat or Cream of Rice cereal and would like the same good taste but with the food value of whole grains, try this simple technique.

Rice Cream Powder

Roast in dry skillet over medium heat, stirring until browned:
¾ cup washed raw brown rice

Grind in blender until fine. Roast again in dry pan.
(Store cooled powder in tightly covered container.)

Cereal

Bring to boiling point:
4 cups milk
2 tsp salt

Lower heat and simmer, covered, about 10 min until thick.

Add and stir constantly:
1 cup rice cream powder

Stir in:
1 tbsp brewer's yeast
2 tbsp ground sesame seeds (raw or toasted)

Serve with more toasted ground sesame seeds, milk, butter, honey, or molasses. Try making the cereal with wheat, rye, or corn flour.

Complementary protein: rice + milk

(C) *Baked-In Protein*

Bread and other baked items can be a good source of protein with only minor (and taste-improving) changes in the way they are usually made. Only two slices of most of the breads in this section will provide at least one-fifth of your daily protein allowance— about twice what you would get from the best commercial bread. And that is before you put anything on it! Making the protein in baked goods count will become second nature once you become acquainted with the simple ways any recipe can be adapted.

Tips for sound protein baking habits

When one of your favorite recipes calls for flour:

    for every cup add ¼ cup soy flour or powder or
    ⅛ cup soy grits (adds a nice crunchy texture)

        or

    delete some and substitute your choice of:

wheat germ	ground sesame or sunflower seed
wheat bran	instant non-fat dry milk
brewer's yeast	

When the recipe calls for cornmeal:

    for every cup add ⅓ cup soy flour or (¼ cup soy grits)

        +

    ⅓ cup instant non-fat dry milk

        or

    ¾ cup cooked beans (ever try beans in cornbread?)

When the recipe calls for nuts:

    for every ½ cup substitute ¼ cup sunflower seeds

When the recipe calls for milk:
> add extra non-fat dry milk (or throw it in even if recipe doesn't call for milk!)
> > *or substitute*
> cottage cheese (more protein)

---

*Recipes:**

1. Non-Yeast Bread:
   > Whole Wheat Quick Bread
   > (Use Corn Muffin Recipe for Corn Bread.)

2. Yeast Bread:
   > Quick: "No-Wait" Wheat-Oat Bread, Quick-and-Easy Pumpernickel
   > Regular: Wheat-Soy-Sesame Bread, Triti-Casserole Bread, "Marjorie will be sage in time" Bread

3. Steamed Bread:
   > Boston Brown Bread

4. Muffins and Sticks:
   > Nebraska Bran Muffins
   > Orange Sesame Muffins
   > Corn Muffins and Corn Bread with Variations
   > Peanut Butter Corn Sticks

---

* See Complementary Protein Quick Mix, page 307, for biscuits, muffins, and coffeecake.

Whole Wheat Quick Bread

1 loaf of 15 thick slices

1 slice = approx. 4 g usable protein
9–11% of daily protein allowance

Preheat oven to 350°F.

Sift into a bowl:
2 cups whole wheat flour
1 tsp baking soda
2 tsp baking powder
1 tsp salt

Add:
½ cup soy flour

6 tbsp corn oil
1½ cups sour milk (or 1½
   cups milk with 2 tsp
   vinegar)
½ cup molasses (or honey,
   if you prefer)
¼ cup wheat germ
¼ cup instant dry milk

Stir well. Spoon into buttered 9x5-inch loaf pan. Let stand for 20 minutes. Bake for about 35 minutes, or until the bread is nicely browned and tests dry with a toothpick.

A lovely bread, especially for breakfast.

Complementary protein: wheat + soy

No-Wait Wheat-Oat Bread

2 loaves of 15 slices each

1 slice = approx. 5 g usable protein
12–14% of daily protein allowance

First, warm 1½ cups oatmeal
in oven.

1 tbsp salt
¼ cup oil

In a large bowl dissolve:
2-3 pkge yeast in:
    4 cups warm water with
    2 tbsp honey
Let stand 10 min in warm
place till foamy.
Let stand 10 min.

Add:
¼ cup honey (or part
    molasses)

Add:
warm oatmeal
Let stand a few min.

Add:
¼ cup wheat germ
1 cup soy grits
6 cups whole wheat flour
    (save 1 cup for kneading)

Knead well until elastic. Place in 2 large loaf pans or 3 small ones. Bake for 15 minutes at 275°F; then bake for 30–40 minutes more at 350°F.

This earthy, substantial bread is fantastic with soup. It can be made in an hour and needs no rising. It is best warmed fully.

Variations: You may delete the oats and use your favorite combination of flours, to total about 9 cups, including 1½–2 cups soy to complement the grain.

Complementary protein: wheat + soy

Quick-and-Easy Pumpernickel

1 large loaf of 15–20 slices

1 slice = approx. 5 g usable protein
12–14% of daily protein allowance

Combine:

1 cake (or pkge or tbsp)
  yeast
¼ cup warm water
1½ cups stock

¼ cup molasses
2 tbsp oil
2 tsp salt
2½ cups rye flour

Beat about 3 minutes, preferably with an electric beater. Continue beating, but stop to add the following one at a time, beating after each addition:

⅓ cup powdered milk
2 eggs
2 tbsp caraway seeds
⅓ cup soy grits
2 tbsp brewer's yeast (adds
  extra nutrition, but bread
  can be made without it)

2½ cups whole wheat flour,
  added gradually and
  mixed with the hands
  between additions

Let mixture stand 10 minutes.

Knead dough about 5 minutes—you must use extra flour during kneading as this batter is very sticky.

Shape into 1 long or 2 small loaves.

Put loaf pan(s) in a large pot or roaster and pour about 1 inch of boiling water into the pot. Cover tightly. Set on top of a radiator, in the sun, or in any warm place. Let rise 30 minutes, or a little longer if you think it will rise more. Remove pan from water.

Bake 10 minutes in a 200°F oven.

Bake 30 minutes longer in a 350°F oven.

A delightful pumpernickel, a rich, smooth taste with good cutting quality.

Complementary protein: rye + milk
                       wheat + soy

Wheat-Soy-Sesame Bread

1 loaf of 12 slices

1 slice = approx. 8 g usable protein
19–22% of daily protein allowance

In large bowl dissolve:
2 pkge or 3 tbsp dry baking
yeast in
2 cups warm stock or water

Add:
¼ cup oil
¼ cup honey

1 tsp salt
¾ cup ground sesame seeds
½ cup soy flour
2 tbsp soy grits
4-5 cups whole wheat flour
(enough to make stiff
dough)

Knead until smooth and elastic, then set in a warm place to rise until doubled in volume (about 1½ hours). Punch down and knead a few minutes, adding whole wheat flour as needed. Shape into 1 loaf, and place in oiled pan. Let rise for about 1 more hour, or until nearly doubled, and bake at 350°F about 30 minutes.

This bread is excellent. Many people have told me it is their favorite yeast bread.

Complementary protein: wheat + soy + sesame

Triti-Casserole Bread

1 loaf of 12 wedges

1 wedge = approx. 5 g usable protein
12–14% of daily protein allowance

*In a large bowl dissolve
together until foamy:*
1 pkge dry yeast
2 tbsp sugar
¼ cup lukewarm water

*In a small saucepan
combine and warm until
onion softens:*
1 tbsp butter
1 tbsp minced onion
1 cup cottage cheese
2 tbsp dill seed or caraway
seed, or 1 tbsp dill weed

Add to yeast mix.

Add:
1 tsp salt
¼ tsp soda
1 egg, unbeaten
1½ cups tritiflour* (substitute
wheat or rye)
½ to 1 cup whole wheat
flour (enough to make
stiff dough)

Brush when done with:
soft butter
salt

Cover, let rise until doubled. Stir down and put in a greased 8x1½-inch casserole dish. Let rise. Bake at 350°F for about 45 minutes, until bread is browned and sounds hollow when tapped. When bread is removed from oven, brush with warm butter and sprinkle with salt.

This is a low but rich bread that goes beautifully with a spread, such as avocado or nut, or warm with butter for dinner.

Complementary protein: grain + milk product

* Triticale flour is from a new hybrid plant, a cross of rye and wheat. It has more protein than the best wheat and is reported to have a better amino acid balance also. This recipe comes from the Triticale Foods Corporation, Suite 101 Park Place, Lubbock, Texas 79408.

"Marjorie will be sage in time" Bread

4 loaves of 12 slices each

1 slice = approx. 4 g usable protein
9–11% of daily protein allowance

In a large bowl dissolve:
2 pkge (or tbsp or cakes)
  yeast in
½ cup lukewarm water

*Combine, adding one at a
time and stirring well after
each addition:*
3½ cups stock or seasoned
  water
½ cup oil
½ cup honey or molasses, or
  a mixture of the 2
1 cup powdered milk
2 eggs

2 tbsp brewer's yeast
  (optional)
4 tbsp soy grits
⅔ cup soy powder
1 cup sesame seeds, ground
⅓ cup wheat germ
⅓ cup crude bran (optional)

Add, 1 cup at a time:
8-10 cups whole wheat flour
  with
2 tsp sage
1 tsp marjoram
1 tsp thyme

Let stand in covered bowl 10–15 minutes. Knead about 10 minutes until glossy and elastic. Cover with a damp towel and let rise in warm place until almost double. Bread made with whole wheat flour rises *very* slowly. This may take 4–5 hours before it is double. Punch down and knead about 5 minutes. Put in 4 oiled loaf pans. Bake 30 minutes in a 350°F oven.

This is the most fragrant, best herb bread ever.

Complementary protein: milk + wheat
                        soy + wheat
                        milk + sesame

Boston Brown Bread

one 2-quart loaf of 15 slices

1 slice = approx. 3 g usable protein
7–8% of daily protein allowance

Stir together:
1¾ cups whole wheat flour
1 cup yellow cornmeal,
    finely ground
⅓ cup soy flour
1 tsp baking soda
1 tsp baking powder
1 tsp salt

Blend separately:
¾ cup molasses
2 cups milk

Add:
1 cup raisins

Stir dry ingredients into wet. Grease the insides and lids of molds or cans having tightly fitting lids (one 2-quart mold or 2 smaller ones). Tin foil may be used instead of lids. Fill three-fourths full, cover, and place on a trivet in a heavy kettle over 1 inch of boiling water. Cover the kettle closely. Turn heat high until steam begins to escape and then lower heat for rest of cooking. Steam 3 hours, replenishing with hot water as needed.

Try this bread with ricotta or cream cheese mixed with chopped dates and nuts. It is dark and rich but is not at all heavy.

Complementary protein: cornmeal + soy + milk

Nebraska Bran Muffins

about 30 muffins

2 muffins = approx. 6 g usable protein
14–17% of daily protein allowance

In a large bowl mix and let stand:

3 cups bran flakes (can subsitute part All-Bran cereal)

1 cup boiling water

Beat in medium bowl and add to bran:

2 eggs

1¼ cups sugar or 1 cup honey

2 cups buttermilk
½ cup corn or other oil

Sift together and fold into bran:

2 cups whole wheat flour
½ cup soy flour
2½ tsp soda
½ tsp salt

Bake at 375°F for 15 minutes in a greased muffin tin.

A variation of these muffins was developed for the Nebraska centennial. The addition of soy is quite fitting and increases the protein content and usability. The batter may be refrigerated in covered jars several weeks. These are my very favorite breakfast muffins—delicious with ricotta cheese and honey!

Complementary protein: wheat + soy

Orange-Sesame Muffins

about 12 muffins
1 muffin = approx. 4 g usable protein
9–11% of daily protein allowance

Mix together:
1½ cups whole wheat flour
½ cup soy flour
1 tsp salt
¼ cup sesame seeds, ground
2 tsp baking powder

In another bowl beat with an electric mixer:
1-2* eggs
½ cup yogurt or buttermilk
¼ cup oil
½ cup honey
1 tbsp grated orange peel
juice from 2 oranges

Pour the wet mixture into the dry ingredients and stir just enough to moisten them. Fill muffin tins two-thirds full and bake at 375°F about 20 minutes or until muffins are golden.

This fairly sweet muffin goes well with a light meal.

Complementary protein: wheat + soy + sesame

---

* Two eggs make a much lighter muffin.

Corn Muffins and Corn Bread with Variations

12 muffins or one 8-inch-square pan

2 muffins = approx. 6 g usable protein
14–17% daily protein allowance

Preheat oven to 375°F.

In a large bowl mix:
mix:
1 cup whole ground
cornmeal
⅓ cup soy flour
¼ cup whole wheat flour
2 tsp baking powder
1 tsp salt

In a small bowl, mix:
1 egg

1 cup milk + ¼ cup instant
dry milk (2½ tbsp non-
instant dry milk)
3 tbsp honey
3 tbsp oil

Plus options:
1 cup grated carrots or
1 cup chopped dates or
prunes or
1 8-oz can crushed, drained
pineapple

Add the liquid mixture to dry mixture and beat until smooth (preferably with an electric mixer). Pour into a well-oiled muffin tin or cake pan and bake about 20 minutes (about 30 for bread) until a toothpick comes out clean. Try any one of the options and you'll be delighted at what can happen to simple muffins and corn bread!

Complementary protein: cornmeal + soy + milk

Peanut Butter Corn Sticks

12 sticks

1 stick = approx. 3 g usable protein
7–8% of daily protein allowance

Stir together:
1 cup whole wheat flour
1 tbsp baking powder
½ tsp salt
½ cup yellow cornmeal

Blend separately:
¼ cup peanut butter
2 tbsp honey
1 egg, beaten
⅔ cup milk

Stir the liquid into the dry ingredients, fill oiled corn stick, gem, or shallow muffin pans two-thirds full. Bake at 425°F 12 to 15 minutes.

These corn sticks are not too sweet. They accompany vegetable soups or stews very nicely.

Complementary protein: peanuts + milk + wheat

Cashew nuts

(D) *Protein for Dessert*

Your dessert can contribute just as much protein to your dinner as your main dish. These cookies, cakes, puddings, and pies hopefully will give you some sense of the range of possibilities for making complementary protein desserts. Make up your own with favorite recipes by simply following these rules of thumb:

---

1. *For Baking*
   Refer to "Tips for sound protein baking habits" on page 316.

2. *For Dessert Fillings*
   When a recipe calls for:
   sour cream or cream cheese substitute any combination* of:

cottage cheese	ricotta
yogurt	buttermilk

3. In addition to the recipes that follow, here are common but often neglected desserts that are *not* empty calories:

egg custards	fruit cup with toasted nuts
bread pudding	or seeds
rice pudding	pumpkin pie

---

* Sometimes it is better to mix ingredients gently with a fork. Blending can make them thinner than you would want for some recipes.

Recipes:

1. Cookies:
    Sesame Crisp Cookies
    Peanut Butter Cookies with a Difference
    Chocolate Chip Cookies

2. Cakes:
    Chameleon Spice Cake (Apple, Banana, or
        Carob)
    Cottage Cheese Cake
    Poppy Seed Cake
    Corn-Spice Coffeecake
    Sesame Dream Bars
    Applesauce-Ginger Squares (or Banana
        Bread)
    Cypress Pt. Carrot Cake
    Sesame-Nut Squares

3. Puddings:
    Sweet Rice Delight
    Wheat-Soy Pudding
    Tangy Rice-Sesame Pudding
    Indian Pudding

4. Pies:
    Easy "Pat-In" Dessert Pie Crust
    Easy Apple-Cheese Pie
    Soybean Pie

5. Dessert Fondue:
    Peanut Dessert Fondue with Fresh Fruit

Sesame Crisp Cookies

30 cookies
1 cookie = approx. 2 g usable protein
5–6% of daily protein allowance

Blend:
½ cup sugar
½ cup oil or margarine
1 egg, beaten

Add:
¼ cup milk
½ cup instant dry milk
(⅓ cup non-instant)

Sift together in separate bowl:
1 cup whole wheat flour
1 tsp ground cinnamon
½ tsp baking powder*
¼ tsp baking soda*
¼ tsp salt

Add:
1¼ cups oatmeal
¾ cup ground sesame seeds
½ cup raisins, chopped

Combine wet and dry ingredients. Drop batter by teaspoonfuls onto oiled cookie sheet; flatten with the bottom of a glass, which is dipped into cold water each time. Bake at 375°F for 10 minutes.

The amount of milk powder called for fills the sesame-milk proportions, with still enough left over to improve the protein quality of the flours.

This recipe has become my mother's favorite and a great success at her office and church parties.

Complementary protein: sesame + milk

---

* Optional, for a lighter cookie.

Peanut Butter Cookies with a Difference

about 30 cookies
1 cookie = approx. 2 g usable protein
5–6% of daily protein allowance

In large bowl beat with electric mixer until creamy and light:
½ cup oil
1 cup honey

Add and continue beating:
¾ cup peanut butter

Beat in:
2 eggs, beaten

½ cup instant dry milk
  (⅓ cup non-instant)
2 tsp baking powder
½ tsp salt
1 tsp cinnamon
½ tsp mace
¼ tsp cloves

Stir in by hand:
½ cup rolled oats
½ cup raisins
¾ cup whole wheat flour

Make sure everything is well blended. Drop by teaspoonfuls on an unoiled cookie sheet. Bake 10 to 12 minutes at 325°F.

Complementary protein: peanuts + milk
wheat + milk

Chocolate Chip Cookies

about 60 cookies

1 cookie = approx. 1.5 g usable protein
3–4% of daily protein allowance

In a large bowl cream:
½ cup soft butter
1½ cups brown sugar,
 packed

Add and beat until fluffy:
3 eggs, beaten
1 tsp vanilla
⅓ cup instant dry milk
 (¼ cup non-instant)
1 tbsp water

*In a medium-sized bowl
stir together:*
2¼ cups whole wheat flour
1 tsp soda
½ tsp salt

*Add to wet ingredients and
stir in:*
12 oz semisweet chocolate
 chips
¾ cup peanuts, chopped
1 cup sunflower seeds

Drop by teaspoonfuls onto greased cookie sheet. Bake at 375°F for 10–15 minutes or until browned.

I took these cookies to my husband's office party and everyone thought they were so good they could not believe that they could also be nutritious.

Remember you can add complementary protein ingredients to any cake or cookie recipe that calls for nuts. Just add peanuts and sunflower seeds in the proper proportions in place of the nuts or seeds called for in the recipe.

Complementary protein: peanuts + sunflower seeds

Chameleon Spice Cake
(Apple, Banana, or Carob)

12 servings

average serving with frosting = approx. 7 g
usable protein
16–20% of daily protein allowance

Preheat oven to 350°F.

*In a large bowl cream
together:*
1 cup honey
½ cup oil

Add:
3 eggs, one at a time,
   beating well after each
   one
2 tsp vanilla
½ cup milk or buttermilk

*In a medium-sized bowl
stir together:*
2 cups whole wheat pastry
   flour
½ cup soy flour
½ cup instant dry milk
   powder
½ cup wheat germ
4 tsp baking powder
1 tsp salt

*For apple or banana cake
only, add along with the
flour mixture:*
1 tsp cinnamon
½ tsp nutmeg
½ tsp allspice

Add dry ingredients to wet and beat well. If mixture
is too dry (it should be like normal cake batter), add
some buttermilk or milk.

Stir in:
for apple cake:
2-3 cups finely chopped
   apples (unpeeled)

for banana cake:
1½ cups mashed bananas
   (about 3 medium
   bananas)

for carob cake
Don't use spices, but add:
½ cup carob powder + 1
   tsp instant coffee, mixed
   with ⅓ cup water

Beat well again.

Fold in ⅔ cup ground sunflower seeds or chopped nuts. Then pour into an oiled 9x13-inch pan and bake about 45 minutes or until a toothpick comes out clean.

Optional: Add ½ cup coconut to banana cake or carob cake when adding flour.

Frosting

Cream together:
2 tbsp soft butter
¼ cup honey
1 tsp vanilla

For carob frosting beat in:
2-3 tbsp milk or buttermilk
¼ cup carob powder
⅔ cup instant powdered
milk

For spice frosting beat in:
2-3 tbsp milk or buttermilk
1 cup instant powdered milk

Dash with:
cinnamon, nutmeg, and
allspice to taste

Whip until smooth, adding more liquid or more powder to create desired consistency. For a fruit frosting, try substituting fruit juice for milk and adding grated orange rind instead of spices. If your child sneaks a fingerful of this frosting off the cake, you don't have to worry. It's good for him.

Complementary protein: wheat + soy

Cottage Cheese Cake

8 servings

average serving = approx. 9 g usable protein
21–25% of daily protein allowance

Have ready:
9-inch graham cracker
crust in spring-form pan

Blend until smooth:
1 lb cottage cheese
1 cup lemon or plain
yogurt

3 egg yolks (set whites
aside)
1 tsp vanilla
1 tbsp lemon juice and the
rind of one lemon
½ cup honey
¼ tsp salt
¼ cup whole wheat flour

Fold in stiffly beaten egg whites (3). Pour into crust.
Bake in a medium oven until the center is firm. Loosen
cake from sides of pan but let it cool before removing.
(A spring-form pan is by far the easiest to use.)

Serve with fresh berries.

Poppy Seed Cake

10 servings

average serving = approx. 4 g usable protein
9–11% of daily protein allowance

Soak together 1 hour in
large bowl:
1 box poppy seeds (2½ oz)
1 cup milk

Add and beat together:
2 eggs
¾ cup oil
1½ cups sugar
½ tsp vanilla or almond
   extract

Mix separately:
2 cups whole wheat flour
¼ cup instant milk
   powder
dash of cinnamon and/or
   nutmeg
2½ tsp baking powder

Add dry ingredients to wet. Mix. Bake in a greased
and floured cake pan at 350°F for 45 minutes.

This cake can be whipped together in 10 minutes. It
originates with a very close friend, who always de-
lights her guests (especially me) and her children
when she makes it!

It is delicious plain but can be made more special
by adding a lemon frosting. Use the frosting recipe
for Chameleon Spice Cake, page 335, omitting the
spices, substituting 2–3 tbsp lemon juice for the milk,
and adding the grated peel of one lemon. If you frost
the cake while it is hot, the frosting will drip down the
sides.

Complementary protein: wheat + milk

Corn-Spice Coffeecake

6–8 servings

average serving = approx. 4 g usable protein
9–11% of daily protein allowance

Have ready:
buttermilk and applesauce
for topping

Mix together:
1 cup fine cornmeal
1/3 cup soy flour
4 tbsp non-fat dry milk
(5½ tbsp instant)
½ cup whole wheat flour
1 cup brown sugar

Mix in a saucepan:
1½ tsp baking powder
½ tsp cinnamon
½ tsp nutmeg
pinch salt
1 cup raisins
¼ cup vegetable oil
1¼ cups water

Simmer mixture in saucepan a few minutes. When cool add to dry ingredients. Mix well. Pour into a well-greased loaf pan or cake pan and bake 1 hour at 375°F.

Top with a thick sauce made by combining applesauce and buttermilk. Delicious as a breakfast dish or dessert.

Complementary protein: cornmeal + soy + milk

Sesame Dream Bars

2 dozen

1 bar = approx. 2 g usable protein
5–6% of daily protein allowance

Cookie Base

Cream together until light and fluffy:
½ cup butter, softened
½ cup honey

Add and blend well:
1¼ cups whole wheat flour
¼ cup soy flour

Spread the mixture in an oiled 13x9x2-inch pan (a smaller pan will give you a cakey bar) and bake at 350°F for 15 to 20 minutes, or until firm and just beginning to brown. Cool 5 minutes before adding top layer.

Top Layer

Beat until light:
2 eggs

¼ tsp salt
½ tsp baking powder

Beat in:
¾ cup honey or brown sugar
1 tsp vanilla

Stir in:
½ cup shredded coconut, unsweetened
¼-½ cup ground sesame seeds

Blend in:
¼ cup whole wheat flour

Spread in an even layer over hot cookie base. Return to oven and bake 20 more minutes. Allow the cake to cool for about 30 minutes before cutting into squares. A heavenly taste combination.

Complementary protein: wheat + soy + sesame

Applesauce-Ginger Squares
(or Banana Bread)

sixteen 2-inch squares

1 square = approx. 3 g* usable protein
7–8% of daily protein allowance

*In a large bowl mix
together:*
1 cup applesauce
¾ cup honey
⅓ cup oil or melted butter

Mix separately:
1¼ cups whole wheat flour

⅓ cup soy flour
1 tsp baking soda
½ tsp each salt, cinnamon,
    ginger, cloves
⅓-⅔ cup roasted peanuts,
    ground or chopped†
½-1 cup sunflower seeds,
    ground or whole†

Blend dry ingredients into liquid. Bake in an 8-inch-square pan for 30 minutes at 350°F. The pan should be oiled and floured.

Variation: Substitute 2 mashed ripe bananas, 1 tsp vanilla, and 1 egg for the applesauce. Reduce honey to ½ cup. Bake at 350°F in a small oiled bread pan for about 1 hour. Banana and peanut is an especially good-tasting combination.

Complementary protein: peanuts + sunflower seeds

---

* Based on lesser amounts of nuts and seeds.

† The larger amount of nuts and seeds makes a very nutty cake, but will increase the amount of protein.

Cypress Pt. Carrot Cake

12 servings
1 hearty slice = 6 g usable protein
14–17% of daily protein allowance

Combine:
1½ cups whole wheat flour
½ cup soy flour
2 tsp cinnamon
2 tsp soda
½ tsp salt

Mix separately:
2 cups grated carrots
1 cup crushed pineapple
  (drained)
½ cup chopped nuts
½ cup ground sesame seeds
3½ oz coconut

Beat in a large bowl:
3 eggs
¾ cup oil
¾ cup buttermilk
2 cups sugar

Sauce (optional):
½ cup buttermilk
1 cup sugar
½ tsp soda
1 tsp corn syrup
½-1 stick butter

Add the carrot mixture to the egg mixture, then add the flour and spices. Bake at 350°F for 1 hour in an angel-food-cake or flouted-edge pan. Cook sauce almost boiling for 5 minutes. Remove cake from mold, punch tiny holes in top, and pour sauce over the cake.

Obviously this is an incredibly rich treat! Save it for New Year's or other celebrations.

Complementary protein: wheat + soy
                       sesame + milk

Sesame-Nut Squares

12 squares

1 square = approx. 4 g usable protein
9–11% of daily protein allowance

In a large bowl beat until thick:
2 egg yolks (set whites aside for beating)

Blend in:
⅔ cup honey

Stir together separately:
¼ cup whole wheat flour

¼ cup instant dry milk
½ tsp each cinnamon and nutmeg
1 cup ground sesame seeds
2 tsp baking powder
¼ tsp salt
1 cup black walnuts, chopped

Add dry ingredients to honey-yolk mixture. Mix well. Beat the egg whites stiff and fold in. Turn into oiled, medium-sized baking pan. Bake 30 minutes at 375°F. Served when still warm, these squares are light and delicate. Cooled, they are a little chewy but just as good.

Complementary protein: sesame + milk

Sweet Rice Delight

4 servings

average serving = approx. 5 g usable protein
12–14% of daily protein allowance

Have ready:
½ cup raw brown rice,
   cooked (1½ cups)

Combine:
½ cup toasted
   sesame seed meal
¼ cup honey
½ cup coconut

1 cup canned pineapple
   chunks, drained
1 banana, sliced
½-1 cup other fruit, fresh,
   or drained if canned
1 cup yogurt

Have ready:
chopped nuts (optional)

Mix together gently all of the ingredients except the nuts. Just before serving stir again and sprinkle the chopped nuts on the top, or stir them in if desired.

This dessert is best made several hours ahead of time and refrigerated until the flavors blend. It is a good way to use up any leftover brown rice and makes a nice substitute for rice pudding lovers.

Complementary protein: rice + sesame
                              sesame + milk product

Wheat-Soy Pudding

about 4 servings
average serving = approx. 8 g usable protein
19–22% of daily protein allowance

In medium saucepan heat:
2 cups milk
dash of salt

Stir in and cook over low heat, continuing to stir until thick:
½ cup whole wheat flour

Remove from heat and stir in:
2 tbsp honey
¼ cup raisins
2 tbsp soy flour

In separate bowl beat:
1 egg yolk

Add some hot mixture to it, then return all to saucepan.

Beat until stiff and fold in:
1 egg white

Put in 8x8-inch pan and sprinkle on top:
2 tbsp ground sesame seeds
2 tbsp honey

Bake for 25–30 minutes at 375°F.

Served hot or cold, this pudding is delicious with yogurt, buttermilk, or milk. It makes a great breakfast pudding too.

Complementary protein: wheat + soy

Tangy Rice-Sesame Pudding

6 servings

average serving = approx. 6 g usable protein
14–17% of daily protein allowance

Combine well:
¾ cup raw brown rice,
   cooked (about 1¾ cups)
2-2½ cups orange juice
6 tbsp ground sesame seeds
⅔ cup brown sugar,
   packed
grated rind of 1 orange
4 eggs, well beaten

½ tsp each cinnamon and
   ginger
¼ tsp nutmeg
1 tsp vanilla extract
½ cup raisins (optional)

Garnish:
2 fresh oranges, peeled,
   sectioned

Combine all the ingredients well. Place in oiled baking dish and bake at 350°F for 1 hour, or until firm.
Especially good served warm. Arrange fresh orange
slices on each dessert bowl for an elegant ending to
your meal.

Complementary protein: rice + sesame

Indian Pudding

4–6 servings

average serving = approx. 12 g usable protein
28–34% of daily protein allowance

Bring to a boil:
4 cups milk

Add gradually:
1 cup yellow cornmeal
¼ cup soy grits, soaked in
  ½ cup water

*Lower heat, beat with whisk
until mixture begins to
thicken. Remove from heat.*

Add:
⅓ cup butter*
½ cup brown sugar
⅔ cup light molasses
¾ tsp salt
½ tsp cinnamon, ground
¼ tsp each cloves and
  ginger, ground
⅛ tsp each allspice and
  nutmeg, ground

Let cool slightly. Add:
2 eggs, beaten

Pour into a buttered baking dish and bake 45–60
minutes in a 325°F oven, or until pudding is firm.

This pudding is delicious both hot and cold, especially with yogurt, sour cream, or ice cream. For variation you may add ½ cup dried fruit and omit the
sugar.

Complementary protein: corn + soy + milk

---

* An unmessy way to measure butter: fill a cup ⅔ full of
water, then add butter until cup is brimming. Drain off water.

Easy "Pat-In" Dessert Pie Crust

Combine in medium-sized
mixing bowl:
1 cup whole wheat flour

3 tbsp brown sugar
6-8 tbsp soft butter, cut in
very small pieces

Mix with your fingers until pastry resembles corn-meal. Press over bottom and sides of a 9-inch pie pan (round). Bake 5 minutes at 350°F.

Fill with your favorite filling and bake according to pie instructions.

Complementary protein: use milk product or soy in filling to complement wheat in crust.

Easy Apple-Cheese Pie

6 servings

average serving = approx. 6 g usable protein
14–17% of daily protein allowance

Have ready:	*In a medium bowl*
Easy "Pat-In" Dessert Pie Crust	*beat with a fork (not with an electric mixer):*
	8 oz ricotta cheese
Heat oven to 350°F.	½ cup brown sugar (or less to taste)
Peel, core, and cut into slices:	1 egg
	½ cup yogurt
4 eating apples	1 tsp vanilla
and place on crust in circles, overlapping slices slightly.	

Pour this mixture over the apples and bake for about 30 minutes, until pie is lightly browned and a knife comes out clean.

Cool and chill in refrigerator for at least 1 hour.

This simple-to-make pie is very special and it goes well with many different types of dinners—from the traditional to the exotic.

Complementary protein: wheat + milk product

Soybean Pie

6 servings

average serving = approx. 9 g usable protein
21–25% of daily protein allowance

Have ready:
Easy "Pat-In" Dessert Pie
  Crust

Combine:
1½ cups soybean purée
¾ cup honey

¼ tsp salt
1 tsp cinnamon
½ tsp ginger
¾ tsp nutmeg
2 eggs, slightly beaten
¾ cup milk
4 tbsp instant dry milk

(Make bean purée by grinding 2 heaping cups very well-cooked soybeans through the fine blade of a food grinder or in a blender.) Pour combined ingredients into crust. Bake at 450°F for 15 minutes; reduce heat to 350°F and bake 30 minutes longer, or until a knife comes out clean.

It tastes incredibly like pumpkin!

Complementary protein: wheat + soy
                            soy + milk

Peanut Dessert Fondue with Fresh Fruit

4 servings

average serving = approx. 7 g usable protein
16–20% of daily protein allowance

Have ready:
1 cup Peanut Sauce with
  Great Possibilities, warm
  or cool (see page 235)

3 cups sliced fruit (apples,
  bananas, pears are
  especially good

Put sauce in middle of table and let every one dip.
It's fantastic!

Complementary protein: peanuts + milk

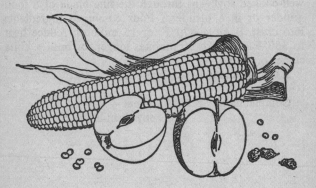

Corn, Apple, Raisins, Soy

Appendices

Wheat

Appendix A

Basic Cooking Instructions for
Beans, Grains, Nuts, and Seeds

Definitions

Soy grits (or soy granules) = partially cooked cracked soybeans.

Soy powder = soybean flour.

Bulgur wheat = partially cooked (parboiled) wheat, usually cracked.

Ground sesame seed = sesame meal. (Can be easily made at home; see cooking instruction C-2 below).

Stock = any leftover liquid from cooking beans, vegetables, etc.

Seasoned water = water with a small amount of powdered vegetable seasoning. (Available without additives in health food stores; can be substituted for stock in any recipe.)

In order to avoid repetition among the recipes in Part IV, section D, here are instructions for preparing the basic ingredients often called for.

A. Cooking Beans

1. Regular Cooking: wash beans in cold water, and soak overnight in three times the volume of water; *or* bring the beans and water to a boil, cover tightly, and let sit for 2 hours. Simmer the beans, partially covered, adding water if necessary, for about 2 hours, depending on the type of bean and the consistency you want. If you want to mash or puree the beans, you will want to cook them until they are quite soft.

2. Pressure Cooking: a pressure cooker is a real advantage in cooking beans as well as grains. Since the foods cook so much more quickly, a meal doesn't require as much forethought! Pressure cooking also gives you a more tender bean. Soaking or precooking, as in method 1, saves a little time but with pressure cooking it really is not necessary. Bring the washed beans, and three to four times their volume in water, to a boil in the cooker. Cover and bring to 15 pounds pressure. Cook beans for 25–45 minutes. Cool immediately. Don't attempt to cook split peas, or any bean that tends to foam, in a pressure cooker or you may find yourself with a clogged cooker and a big mess.

3. Roasting: cook beans by one of the above methods for a firm bean. Spread the beans on a lightly oiled baking sheet. Sprinkle with salt, if desired, and bake at 200°F for about 1 hour, until they are well browned. When they are hot, they will be crunchy outside and tender inside. When they are cool, they will be hard and crunchy throughout. You can also roast the beans in a lightly oiled frypan over medium heat on top of the stove. Stir constantly. Soybeans, when roasted, or when chopped or ground in a blender, can be eaten alone. They make a garnish to be sprinkled on a variety of dishes; or use them when nuts or nutmeal are called for.

4. Making Soybean Curd (Tofu): soy curd can be purchased in many parts of the country. If it is not available to you, you might wish to try making it. *The Natural Foods Cookbook* (see "Recommended Paperback Cookbooks" at the end of this book) has several recipes. I am not including a recipe here because my single attempt failed. However, the "failure" served as a base for delicious salad dressing made by blending spices, herbs, onions, garlic, and avocado.

B. Cooking Grains

1. Regular Cooking: wash the grains in cold water. Bring stock or water, equal to twice the volume of the grains, to a boil (for millet or buckwheat, use three times the volume). Put in the grains, bring to a boil again, lower heat and simmer (covered) for 30–45 minutes, until all of the liquid is absorbed.

2. Pressure Cooking: in the pressure cooker follow the same method, but instead of simmering the grain bring to 15 pounds pressure and cook for about 20 minutes. Cool under cold water when cooking time is up. You may wish to vary the amount of water in order to create the texture of grain you prefer. If you have trouble with sticking, here's the trick I use: place about 1 inch of water in the bottom of the pressure cooker. Put the grain into a stainless-steel bowl that will fit easily into the pressure cooker (with plenty of room between the top of the bowl and the lid of the pressure cooker). Add water to the level of about ¾ inch above the level of the grain. Put the bowl inside the pressure cooker, cover, and begin cooking. This method is also handy when I need to cook both grains and beans at the same time, but separately. I merely put the small stainless-steel bowl inside the pressure cooker. I then place the beans with adequate water around the outside of the bowl, and the grains inside the bowl.

3. *Sautéing:* this method is most frequently used in cooking bulgur wheat and buckwheat groats, but can be used with any grain to achieve a "nuttier" flavor. Wash the grains and put in a dry saucepan or pressure cooker over low heat. Stir until dry. Add just enough oil to coat each kernel. Sauté the grains, stirring constantly, until all of the grains are golden. Stir in boiling water or stock (amounts given in B-1 above) and bring the mixture to a boil. Cover and simmer 30–45 minutes; or, if using a pressure cooker, bring to 15 pounds pressure and cook 20 minutes. Cool cooker immediately.

C. Cooking Nuts and Seeds

1. *To Roast Whole Seeds or Nuts:* place in a dry pan and roast over medium flame until they have desired brownness; or spread them on a baking sheet and toast them in a 200°F oven. Use the seeds whole, or grind them in a blender, a few at a time, or with a mortar and pestle. Add salt if desired.

2. *To Roast or Toast Ground Seeds or Nuts:* buy the meal or, to make it yourself, grind the seeds or nuts in a blender. Then roast the meal in a dry pan, stirring constantly, adding salt if desired. Or spread the meal on a baking sheet and bake at 200°F, stirring often. (You can also grind small quantities of whole grains in your blender.)

3. *Nut and Seed Butters:* it is easy to make your own fresh nut and seed butters if you have a blender. From whole roasted or raw seeds or nuts: grind as for meal, adding a little oil to "start" the butter; continue adding as many nuts or seeds as your blender can handle. From roasted or raw ground nuts or seeds: stir a little oil, and honey if desired, into the meal, and you will have creamy nut or seed butter.

Appendix B

Calorie/Protein Comparisons

Listed here are the number of calories you have to consume in order to get *one gram of usable protein* from selected foods. Foods having more than 60 calories per gram of protein are excluded. See text for explanation.

Sources of Protein Listed in Increasing Order of Calories	No. of Calories per Gram of Usable Protein	Sources of Protein Listed in Increasing Order of Calories	No. of Calories per Gram of Usable Protein
1. Seafood*		Herring, Pacific, canned in oil	14
Haddock	5	Sardines, Atlantic, canned in oil	22
Cod	5		
Halibut	6		
Shrimp	6	**2. Nutritional Additives**	
Squid	6	Egg white, dried	9
Lobster	6	"Tiger's Milk"	8
Rockfish	6	Brewer's yeast (nutritional yeast)	12
Flounder or sole	6	Baker's yeast	15
Herring	8	Wheat germ	19
Clams	8		
Carp	8		
Swordfish	8	**3. Dairy Products**	
Tuna, bluefin	8	Dried egg white	6
Salmon, humpback	8	Cottage cheese, uncreamed	7
Bass, striped	8		
Mackerel, Pacific	9	Cottage cheese, creamed	10
Tuna, canned in oil	9		
Shad	11	Non-fat milk and buttermilk	12
Oysters	11		
Perch	13		

* Raw unless otherwise indicated.

Sources of Protein Listed in Increasing Order of Calories	No. of Calories per Gram of Usable Protein
Dried non-fat milk solids	12
Whole egg	14
Ricotta cheese	14
Parmesan cheese	16
Edam cheese	16
Plain yogurt from skim milk	18
Swiss cheese	19
Cheddar cheese	23
Whole milk	23
Camembert cheese	24
Blue mold cheese	24
Roquefort cheese	26
Plain yogurt from whole milk	27
Yogurt, sweetened, w/fruit	30
4. Fresh Vegetables	
Soybean sprouts	12
Mushrooms	14
Broccoli	16
Brussels sprouts	16
Kale	17
Spinach	18
Asparagus	18
Cauliflower	18
Green limas	19
Turnip greens	20
Chard	20
Mustard greens	22
Collards	24
Mung bean sprouts	25
Peas	25
Okra	27
Artichokes	28
Corn	37
Potato, white	60

Sources of Protein Listed in Increasing Order of Calories	No. of Calories per Gram of Usable Protein
5. Legumes (Dry Seed)	
Tofu (soybean curd)	15
Soybeans	20
Mung beans	25
Broad beans	28
Split or whole peas	30
Cowpeas (black-eyed peas)	33
Limas	33
Kidney beans (red)	39
Common white beans	39
Garbanzos (chick-peas)	40
Lentils	47
6. Flours	
Soybean flour, defatted	11
Soybean flour, low fat	12
Soybean flour, full fat	18
Gluten flour	23
Rye flour, dark	34
Whole wheat flour	41
Buckwheat flour, dark	43
Barley flour	58
Cornmeal, whole ground	80*
7. Grains, Cereals, and Their Products	
Wheat germ	19
Wheat bran	24
Wheat, whole grain (hard red spring variety, w/most protein)	40

* Notice that brown rice and cornmeal exceed the 60-calorie limit.

Sources of Protein Listed in Increasing Order of Calories	No. of Calories per Gram of Usable Protein	Sources of Protein Listed in Increasing Order of Calories	No. of Calories per Gram of Usable Protein
Oatmeal	41	Pignolia nuts	36
Whole wheat bread	43	Sunflower seeds	40
Buckwheat pancake	46	Peanuts	49
Pumpernickel	47	Peanut butter	51
Rye bread and whole-grain rye	48	Cashews, roasted	55
Egg noodles, macaroni, and spaghetti	50	Whole sesame seeds	57
		Black walnuts	60
Cracked wheat cereal	52	Pistachio nuts	60
Bulgur, from hard red winter wheat	53	Brazil nuts	88†
Corn bread with whole ground meal	55	**9. For Comparison: Meat and Poultry**	
Millet	60	Chicken fryer, breast	7
Barley	60	Turkey, roasted	9
Brown rice	69*	Lamb, lean only	10
		Porterhouse steak, lean and marbled	14
8. Nuts and Seeds		Hamburger	15
Pumpkin and squash seeds	32	Pork loin chop, lean and fat	18
		Lamb rib chop, lean, marbled, and fat	32

---

† Brazil nuts also exceed the calorie limit, but are included because of their very high content of sulfur-containing amino acids, a rare virtue among plant foods.

Appendix C

Protein Cost Comparisons

Protein Sources Listed in Increasing Order of Cost	Cost per 43.1 g Usable Protein*
1. Dairy Products	
Dried non-fat milk solids (@ $1.00 ℔)	26¢
Cottage cheese from skim milk (@ 59¢ ℔)	36¢
Buttermilk (@ 34¢ qt)	52¢
Whole egg (@ 78¢ doz)	41¢
Whole milk, non-fat milk (@ 35¢ qt)	59¢
Dried egg white (@ Swiss cheese (@ $1.67 ℔)	84¢
Cheddar cheese (@ $1.33 ℔)	73¢
Ricotta cheese (@ $1.09 ℔)	$1.28
Blue mold cheese (@ $1.69 ℔)	$1.08
Parmesan cheese (@ $2.60 ℔)	$1.00
Yogurt from skim milk (@ 44¢ ℔)	$2.28
Camembert cheese (@ $3.00 ℔)	$2.36

Protein Sources Listed in Increasing Order of Cost	Cost per 43.1 g Usable Protein*
2. Legumes (Dry Seed)	
Soybeans, soy grits, and flour (@ 60¢ ℔)	27¢
Cowpeas (black-eyed peas) (@ 28¢ ℔)	28¢
Split peas (@ 34¢ ℔)	34¢
Lima beans (@ 31¢ ℔)	27¢
Common white beans (@ 43¢ ℔)	49¢
Chick-peas (garbanzos) (@ 50¢ ℔)	54¢
Lentils (@ 35¢ ℔)	49¢
Kidney beans (@ 44¢ ℔)	49¢
Mung beans (@ 93¢ ℔)	67¢
Black beans (@ 90¢ ℔)	92¢
3. Grains, Cereals, and Their Products	
Whole wheat flour (@ 25¢ ℔)	28¢
Rye flour, dark (@ 43¢ ℔)	43¢

* A reminder: 43.1 grams of usable protein is the daily allowance for the "average" American male weighing 154 pounds. "Usable protein" means that the protein has been reduced by the NPU score to the level that the body can actually use.

Protein Sources Listed in Increasing Order of Cost	Cost per 43.1 g Usable Protein*
"Roman Meal" (@ 49¢ ℔)	53¢
Whole-grain wheat, hard red spring (@ 35¢ ℔)	35¢
Oatmeal (@ 44¢ ℔)	44¢
Spaghetti (@ 52¢ ℔)	77¢
"Protein Plus" (@	
Bulgur, red (@ 51¢ ℔)	66¢
Barley, pot or Scotch (@ 54¢ ℔)	91¢
Macaroni (@ 51¢ ℔)	75¢
Brown rice (@ 38¢ ℔)	69¢
Gluten flour (@ 91¢ ℔)	55¢
Wheat bran (@ 49¢ ℔)	54¢
Barley flour (@ 49¢ ℔)	81¢
Buckwheat flour, dark (@ 70¢ ℔)	87¢
Egg noodles (@ 69¢ ℔)	88¢
Millet (@ 44¢ ℔)	75¢
Cornmeal, whole ground (@ 50¢ ℔)	98¢
Whole wheat bread (@ 59¢ ℔)	$1.02
Rye bread (@ 56¢ ℔)	99¢

4. Seafood

Turbot (@ 89¢ ℔)	42¢
Squid (@ 90¢ ℔)	65¢
Herring (@ 60¢ ℔)	42¢
Cod (@ $1.59 ℔)	70¢
Perch (@ $1.19 ℔)	75¢
Tuna, canned in oil (@ $1.60 ℔)	80¢
Catfish (@ $1.59 ℔)	$1.09

Protein Sources Listed in Increasing Order of Cost	Cost per 43.1 g Usable Protein*
Sardines, Atlantic, canned in oil (@ $2.25 ℔)	$1.46
Salmon (@ $2.39 ℔)	$1.66
Oysters (@ $2.79 ℔)	$3.07
Crab in shell (@ $1.35 ℔)	$1.92
Clams, soft, in shell (@ 98¢ ℔)	$2.33
Shrimp, canned wet pack (@ $4.30 ℔)	$3.44

5. Nutritional Additives

Wheat germ (@ 69¢ ℔)	40¢
"Tiger's Milk" (@ $2.64 ℔)	$1.13
Brewer's yeast (nutritional yeast) (@ $1.88 ℔)	85¢

6. Nuts and Seeds

Peanut butter (@ 82¢ ℔)	73¢
Raw peanuts (@ 69¢ ℔)	60¢
Sunflower seeds or meal (@ $1.52 ℔)	$1.28
Sesame seeds or meal (@ $1.50 ℔)	$1.46
Peanuts (@ $1.09 ℔)	90¢
Pumpkin and squash kernels (@ $2.62 ℔)	$1.46
Raw cashews (@ Brazil nuts (@ $1.10 ℔)	$1.46
Black walnuts (@ $4.63 ℔)	$4.30

Protein Sources Listed in Increasing Order of Cost	Cost per 43.1 g Usable Protein*	Protein Sources Listed in Increasing Order of Cost	Cost per 43.1 g Usable Protein*
Cashews (@ $2.52 ℔)	$2.29	Chicken breast, w/bone (@ 85¢ ℔)	76¢
Pignolia nuts (@ $6.00 ℔)	$3.76	Pork loin chop, med. fat w/bone (@ $1.45 ℔)	$1.53
Pistachio nuts, in shell (@ $2.73 ℔)	$5.44	Porterhouse steak, choice grade, w/bone (@ $2.05 ℔)	$2.17
7. Meats and Poultry Hamburger, reg grade (@ 79¢ ℔)	64¢	Lamb rib chop, choice grade, w/bone (@ $2.19 ℔)	$2.66

Appendix D

Meat Equivalency Comparisons and Sample Calculation

The following meat equivalency comparisons graphically illustrate the advantage of combining complementary proteins. For each of the 22 combinations already given in the Table VI, I have, in the following pages, converted the foods, if eaten *separately*, into their protein equivalents as meat and then compared this amount with the meat equivalent of these foods if they are eaten *together*. The differences, as you will see, are quite striking.

Of course, the calculations are rough estimates. To show you how the estimates were arrived at, I have included a sample calculation following the last of the 22 meat equivalency comparisons.

1. Beans/Peas + Rice

Meat Equivalency Comparison

	Usable protein is equivalent to:
A. *If eaten separately:*	
1½ cups beans	6¼ oz steak
4 cups rice	7 oz steak
	13¼ oz steak
B. *If eaten together:* 43% increase	19 oz steak
1½ cups beans + 4 cups rice	

---

2. Beans/Peas + Wheat

Meat Equivalency Comparison

	Usable protein is equivalent to:
A. *If eaten separately:*	
½ cup beans	2 oz steak
3 cups whole wheat flour	5 oz steak
	―
	7 oz steak
B. *If eaten together:* 33% increase	
½ cup beans + 3 cups whole wheat flour	9⅓ oz steak

---

3. Beans/Peas + Corn

Meat Equivalency Comparison

	Usable protein is equivalent to:
A. *If eaten separately:*	
½ cup beans	2 oz steak
2 cups cornmeal	1½ oz steak
	3½ oz steak
B. *If eaten together:* 50% increase	
½ cup beans + 2 cups cornmeal	5¼ oz steak

---

4. Beans/Peas + Milk*

Meat Equivalency Comparison

	Usable protein is equivalent to:
A. If eaten separately:	
1 cup beans	4¼ oz steak
½ cup (scant) non-fat dry milk	3⅓ oz steak
	7½ oz steak
B. If eaten together: 11% increase	
1 cup beans + ½ cup (scant) non-fat dry milk	8⅓ oz steak

5. Beans/Peas + Sesame/Sunflower Seeds

Meat Equivalency Comparison

	Usable protein is equivalent to:
A. If eaten separately:	
1 cup garbanzo beans	4¼ oz steak
1½ cups sesame seeds	4 oz steak
	8¼ oz steak
B. If eaten together: 27% increase	
1 cup garbanzo beans + 1½ cups sesame seeds	10½ oz steak

* Milk includes other milk products, such as yogurt and cheese.

6. Soybeans + Rice

Meat Equivalency Comparison

	Usable protein is equivalent to:
A. If eaten separately:	
½ cup soybeans	5 oz steak
5 cups rice	9 oz steak
	—
	14 oz steak
B. If eaten together: 32% increase	
½ cup soybeans + 5 cups rice	18½ oz steak

---

7. Soybeans + Rice + Wheat

Meat Equivalency Comparison

	Usable protein is equivalent to:
A. If eaten separately:	
⅔ cup soybeans	6½ oz steak
1 cup rice	1¾ oz steak
¾ cup bulgur wheat (or 1 cup wheat flour)	1¼ oz steak
	9½ oz steak
B. If eaten together: 24% increase	
⅔ cup soybeans + 1 cup rice + ¾ cup bulgur wheat	11¾ oz steak

---

8. Soybeans + Wheat

Meat Equivalency Comparison

	Usable protein is equivalent to:
A. *If eaten separately:*	
2 cups soy flour (or 1⅛ cups soy grits)	12 oz steak
8 cups whole wheat flour	13¾ oz steak
	25¾ oz steak
B. *If eaten together:* **32% increase**	
2 cups soy flour (or 1⅛ cups soy grits) + 8 cups whole wheat flour	34 oz steak

---

9. Soybeans + Rice + Wheat + Peanuts

Meat Equivalency Comparison

	Usable protein is equivalent to:
A. *If eaten separately:*	
⅓ cup soybeans	3¼ oz steak
¾ cup rice	1⅓ oz steak
⅔ cup bulgur	1 oz steak
¼ cup peanuts	1 oz steak
	6½ oz steak
B. *If eaten together:* **15% increase**	
⅓ cup soybeans + ¾ cup rice + ⅔ cup bulgur + ¼ cup peanuts	7½ oz steak

---

10. Soybeans + Wheat + Sesame/Sunflower Seeds

Meat Equivalency Comparison

	Usable protein is equivalent to:
A. *If eaten separately:*	
1 cup soy flour	6 oz steak
6½ cups whole wheat flour	11 oz steak
1 cup sesame seed	2¾ oz steak
	19¾ oz steak
B. *If eaten together:* 42% increase	
1 cup soy flour + 6½ cups whole wheat flour + 1 cup sesame seed	28 oz steak

---

11. Milk* (or Soybeans) + Wheat + Peanuts

Meat Equivalency Comparison

	Usable protein is equivalent to:
A. *If eaten separately:*	
½ cup non-fat dry milk or soy flour	3 oz steak
7½ cups whole wheat flour	12¾ oz steak
1 cup peanut butter	7 oz steak
	22¾ oz steak
B. *If eaten together:* 34% increase	
½ cup non-fat dry milk or soy flour + 7½ cups whole wheat flour + 1 cup peanut butter	30½ oz steak

---

* Milk includes other milk products, such as yogurt and cheese.

12. Soybeans + Sesame/Sunflower Seeds + Peanuts

Meat Equivalency Comparison

	Usable protein is equivalent to:
A. *If eaten separately:*	
⅔ cup soybeans	6 oz steak
1¾ cups sesame seeds	4¾ oz steak
1½ cups peanuts	6½ oz steak
	17¼ oz steak
B. *If eaten together:* 25% increase	
⅔ cup soybeans + 1¾ cups sesame seeds + 1½ cups peanuts	21½ oz steak

13. Soybeans + Corn + Milk*

Meat Equivalency Comparison

	Usable protein is equivalent to:
A. *If eaten separately:*	
1 cup defatted soy flour (or ¾ cup soy grits)	9¼ oz steak
3 cups cornmeal	2 oz steak
¾ cup non-fat dry milk	5¾ oz steak
	17 oz steak
B. *If eaten together:* 13% increase	
1 cup defatted soy flour + 3 cups cornmeal + ¾ cup non-fat dry milk	19¼ oz steak

---

* Milk includes other milk products, such as yogurt and cheese.

14. Rice + Milk*

Meat Equivalency Comparison

	Usable protein is equivalent to:
A. *If eaten separately:*	
1½ cups rice	2⅔ oz steak
2 cups skim milk	3⅓ oz steak
	6 oz steak
B. *If eaten together:* 29% increase	
1½ cups rice + 2 cups skim milk	7¾ oz steak

15. Rice + Sesame/Sunflower Seeds

Meat Equivalency Comparison

	Usable protein is equivalent to:
A. *If eaten separately:*	
3 cups rice	5¼ oz steak
1 cup sesame seeds (or 1½ cups seed meal)	3 oz steak
	8¼ oz steak
B. *If eaten together:* 21% increase	
3 cups rice + 1 cup sesame seeds	10 oz steak

* Milk includes other milk products, such as yogurt and cheese.

16. Rice + Yeast

Meat Equivalency Comparison

	Usable protein is equivalent to:
A. If eaten separately:	
2 cups rice	3½ oz steak
½ cup brewer's yeast	3½ oz steak
	7 oz steak
B. If eaten together: 57% increase	
2 cups rice + ½ cup brewer's yeast	11 oz steak

---

17. Wheat + Milk*

Meat Equivalency Comparison

	Usable protein is equivalent to:
(With Milk)	
3 cups whole wheat flour	5 oz steak
6 tbsp non-fat dry milk (slightly more than ⅓ cup)	3 oz steak
	8 oz steak
B. If eaten together: 13% increase	
3 cups whole wheat flour + 6 tbsp non-fat dry milk	9 oz steak

---

* Milk includes other milk products, such as yogurt and cheese.

(With Cheese)

A. *If eaten separately:*	Usable protein is equivalent to:
4 slices whole wheat bread (or ¾ cup dry macaroni)	1 oz steak
1 oz cheese	1 oz steak
	—
	2 oz steak
B. *If eaten together:* 25% increase	
4 slices whole wheat bread + 1 oz cheese	2½ oz steak

---

18. Wheat + Milk* + Peanuts

Meat Equivalency Comparison

A. *If eaten separately:*	Usable protein is equivalent to:
7½ cups whole wheat flour	12¾ oz steak
½ cup non-fat dry milk or soy flour	3 oz steak
1 cup peanut butter	7 oz steak
	—
	22¾ oz steak
B. *If eaten together:* 34% increase	
7½ cups whole wheat flour + ½ cup non-fat dry milk or soy flour + 1 cup peanut butter	30½ oz steak

---

* Milk includes other milk products, such as yogurt and cheese.

19. Milk* + Peanuts

Meat Equivalency Comparison

	Usable protein is equivalent to:
A. *If eaten separately:*	
5 tbsp non-fat dry milk	2⅓ oz steak
1 cup peanut butter	7 oz steak
	9⅓ oz steak
B. *If eaten together:* 25% increase	
5 tbsp non-fat dry milk + 1 cup peanut butter	11⅔ oz steak

---

20. Milk* + Potatoes

Meat Equivalency Comparison

	Usable protein is equivalent to:
A. *If eaten separately:*	
⅔ cup non-fat dry milk	5 oz steak
3 large potatoes (about 2 lb)	1⅓ oz steak
	6⅓ oz steak
B. *If eaten together:* 7% increase	
⅔ cup non-fat dry milk + 3 large potatoes	6¾ oz steak

---

* Milk includes other milk products, such as yogurt and cheese.

21. Milk* + Sesame/Sunflower Seeds

Meat Equivalency Comparison

	Usable protein is equivalent to:
A. *If eaten separately:*	
¼ cup non-fat dry milk	2 oz steak
1½ cups sesame seed meal	3 oz steak
	⎯
	5 oz steak
B. *If eaten together:* 20% increase	
¼ cup non-fat dry milk + 1½ cups sesame seed meal	6 oz steak

22. Sesame/Sunflower Seeds + Peanuts

Meat Equivalency Comparison

	Usable protein is equivalent to:
A. *If eaten separately:*	
1 cup sunflower seeds	3¾ oz steak
¾ cup peanuts	3 oz steak
	⎯
	6¾ oz steak
B. *If eaten together:* 19% increase	
1 cup sunflower seeds + ¾ cup peanuts	8 oz steak

* Milk includes other milk products, such as yogurt and cheese.

Sample Calculation: Conversion of Non-Meat Protein into Beef Equivalent

Legumes and Rice

I. Eaten separately—no complementarity of protein quality
  A. Legumes
    1. 1½ cups legumes = 61.5 grams protein
    2. Adjusting for protein quality:
       Protein Efficiency Ratio (PER*) = 1.65
         (for legumes eaten alone)
       Protein Efficiency Ratio = 2.30
         (for beef)
       1.65/2.30 × 100 = 72%, i.e., the approx.
         amount of protein available to the body from
         legumes is only 72% of that available
         from beef
       Thus, 72% of 61.5 grams = 43.7 grams
         of protein equivalent to beef
    3. Converting protein equivalent to meat equivalent:
       only 25% of beef is protein; therefore, 4 × 43.7
       grams = 174.8 grams, or about 6¼ oz of beef
  B. Rice
    1. 4 cups of rice = 59.2 grams protein
    2. Adjusting for protein quality:
       Protein Efficiency Ratio = 1.91
         (for rice eaten alone)
       Protein Efficiency Ratio = 2.30
         (for beef)
       1.91/2.30 × 100 = 83%; 83% of 59.2 grams =
         49 grams of protein equivalent to beef
    3. Converting to meat equivalent: 4 × 49 =
       196 grams, or about 7 oz of beef

---

* PER is the gain in weight of the growing experimental animal divided by the weight of protein consumed. It is accepted by nutritionists as a good measure of protein quality. PER correlates highly with NPU, a term which is explained in the text.

II. Eaten together—complementarity increases protein
  A. 1½ cups legumes = 61.5 grams ⎫
                    +   ⎬ = 120.7 grams
     4 cups rice = 59.2 grams   ⎭
  B. Adjusting for protein quality:
       2.52 = approx. PER of legumes and rice
         eaten together (in proportions given)
       2.30 = PER of beef
       2.52/2.30 × 100 = 110%
       110% of 120.7 grams = 132.2 grams protein
         equivalent to beef
  C. Converting protein equivalent to meat equivalent:
       132.2 × 4 = 529 grams, or about 19 oz beef

Appendix E
Pesticide Residues in the American Diet, 1964–1970

Item	Percent of Diet*	Percent of Chlorinated Pesticides Item Contributes to Diet	Average Content DDT, DDE, and TDE, ppm†		Percent Change 1964-1970
			1964-1968	1968-1970	
1. Dairy products (8-13% fat)	31	18	0.112	0.067	−40%
2. Meat, fish, and poultry (17-23% fat)	10	27	0.281	0.216	−23%
3. Grains and cereals	16	11	0.008	0.005	−38%
4. Potatoes	7	4	0.003	0.002	−33%
			(DDT & DDE only)		
5. Leafy vegetables	3	13	0.036	0.005	−86%
6. Legumes	3	2	0.026	0.005	−81%
7. Root vegetables	3	—	0.007	0.004	−43%
8. Fruits (all)	21	25	0.027	0.024	−12%
9. Oils, fats, shortening	3	2	0.041	0.008	−80%
10. Sugar and adjuncts	3	1			

* Excludes beverages, which are generally pesticide-free; based on typical diet of 16- to 19-year-old males.

† Based on averages of data presented for five cities—Boston, Kansas City, Los Angeles, Baltimore, and Minneapolis —these chlorinated pesticides comprise two-thirds of the total; they are the only ones for which data are sufficiently complete to permit tabulation.

Source for pesticides in diet: R. E. Duggan and G. Q. Lipscomb, "Dietary Intake of Pesticide Chemicals in the U.S. (II)," June 1966–April 1968," and "(III)," June 1968–April 1970." "(III)," June 1968–April 1970," Pesticides Monitoring Journal, 2:153–62, 1969; and Ibid., 4:331–35, 1972.

Source for DDT, DDE, TDE levels: P. E. Cornelliussen, "Residues in Food and Feed: Pesticide Residues in Total Diet Samples (IV)," Pesticides Monitoring Journal, 2:140–52, 1969; and "(VI)," Ibid., 5:313–30, 1972.

Appendix F
Whole Wheat Flour Compared to White Flour

	Composition of Whole Wheat Flour (per 100 g, or 3½ oz)		Composition of All-Purpose White Flour Compared to Whole Wheat Flour			
			White Flour		Enriched White Flour	
1. Protein	13.3	g	10.5 g	79%	10.5 g	79%
2. Minerals						
Calcium	41	mg	16 mg	39%	16 mg	39%
Phosphorous	372	gm	87. mg	23%	87 mg	23%
Iron	3.3	mg	0.8 mg	24%	2.9 mg	88%
Potassium	370	mg	95 mg	26%	95 mg	26%
Sodium	3	mg	2 mg	67%	2 mg	67%
3. Vitamins						
Thiamin	0.55	mg	0.06 mg	11%	0.44 mg	80%
Riboflavin	0.12	mg	0.05 mg	42%	0.26 mg	216%
Niacin	4.3	mg	0.9 mg	21%	3.5 mg	81%

Appendix G
Brown Rice Compared to Other Types of Rice

	Composition of Brown Rice (per 100 g, or 3½ oz)		Composition of Other Types of Rice						
			White Rice		Enriched White Rice		Converted Rice (Enriched)		
1. Protein	7.5	g	6.7	g	90%	6.7	g	90%	7.4	g	99%

	Brown Rice		White Rice			Enriched White Rice			Converted Rice (Enriched)		
1. Protein	7.5	g	6.7	g	90%	6.7	g	90%	7.4	g	99%
2. Minerals											
Calcium	32	mg	24	mg	75%	24	mg	75%	60	mg	190%
Phosphorous	221	mg	94	mg	43%	94	mg	43%	200	mg	90%
Iron	1.6	mg	0.8	mg	50%	2.9	mg	180%	2.9	mg	180%
Potassium	214	mg	92	mg	43%	92	mg	43%	150	mg	70%
Sodium	9	mg	5	mg	56%	5	mg	56%	9	mg	100%
3. Vitamins											
Thiamin	0.34	mg	0.07	mg	21%	0.44	mg	130%	0.44	mg	130%
Riboflavin	0.05	mg	0.03	mg	60%	0.03	mg	60%	0.03	mg	60%
Niacin	4.7	mg	1.6	mg	34%	3.5	mg	74%	3.5	mg	74%

Appendix H
Sugars, Honey, and Molasses Compared
Composition (per 100 g, or 3½ oz)

	White Sugar (Granulated)	Brown Sugar (Beet or Cane)	Molasses (Third Extraction or Blackstrap)	Honey (Strained or Extracted)	Maple Sugar
1. Minerals	mg	mg	mg	mg	mg
Calcium	0	85	684	5	143
Phosphorus	0	19	84	6	11
Iron	0.1	3.4	16.1	0.5	1.4
Potassium	3.0	344	2927	51	242
Sodium	1.0	30	96	5	14
2. Vitamins					
Thiamin	0	0.01	0.11	trace	—
Riboflavin	0	0.03	0.19	0.04	—
Niacin	0	0.2	2.0	0.3	—

Source: "Composition of Foods," Agriculture Handbook, No. 8, USDA. Values given vary in other sources.

Sesame seed, flower and pod

Notes According to Part and Section

PART I
EARTH'S LABOR LOST

A. Diet for a Small Planet Revisited

1. *Washington Newsletter,* National Farmers Union, Vol. 21, No. 34, October 25, 1974, p. 3.
2. *Ibid.*
3. *Economic Report of the President,* GPO, p. 169.
4. *The State of Food and Agriculture, 1972,* The Food and Agriculture Organization of the United Nations, Rome.
5. *Business Week,* November 2, 1974.
6. Brown, Lester, and Eckholm, Erick, "The Empty Breadbasket," *Ceres,* March–April 1974, p. 60.
7. UNDP, *Commitment,* No. 3, 1974, service bulletin.
8. Brown, Lester, "Rising Food Prices: Who's Responsible?" *Science,* Vol. 180, No. 4084, April 27, 1973, p. 1.
9. *Bread for the World Newsletter,* January 1975, from a USDA source.
10. William Robbins, *The New York Times,* February 2, 1975, p. 1.

B. A Protein Factory in Reverse

1. "Agricultural Production Efficiency", a report of the National Academy of Sciences, *The New York Times,* January 13, 1975, p. 1. For discussion, see: Borgstrom, Georg, *Focal Points,* Macmillan, 1971, pp. 173–4.
2. *Washington Newsletter,* National Farmers Union, Vol. 21, No. 34, October 25, 1974, p. 3.

3. *Feed Situation,* USDA Economic Research Service, November 1974.

4. Wilcox, Walter W., *et al., Economics of American Agriculture,* Prentice-Hall, 1974, p. 318.

5. *The New York Times,* October 11, 1974, p. 41.

6. How many pounds of grain and soy are consumed by the American steer to get one pound of edible meat?

   (a) The total forage (hay, silage, grass) consumed: *12,000* pounds (10,000 pre-feedlot and 2,000 in feedlot). The total grain- and soy-type concentrate consumed: about *2850 pounds* (300 pounds grain and 50 pounds soy before feedlot, plus 2200 pounds grain and 300 pounds soy in feedlot). Therefore, the actual percent of total feed units from grain and soy is about 25 percent.

   (b) *But* experts estimate that the grain and soy contribute more to weight gain (and, therefore, to ultimate meat produced) than their actual proportion in the diet. They estimate that grain and soy contribute (instead of 25 percent) about 40 percent of weight put on over the life of the steer.

   (c) To estimate what percent of edible meat is due to the grain and soy consumed, multiply that 40 percent (weight gain due to grain and soy) times the edible meat produced at slaughter, or 432 pounds: $.40 \times 432 = 172.9$ pounds of edible portion contributed by grain and soy. (Those who state a 7:1 ratio use the entire 432 pounds edible meat in their computation.)

   (d) To determine how many pounds of grain and soy it took to get this 172.9 pounds of edible meat, divide total grain and soy consumed, 2850 pounds, by 172.9 pounds of edible meat: 2850/172.9 = *16–17 pounds.* (I have taken the lower figure, since the amount of grain being fed may be going down a small amount.)

   These estimates are based on several consultations with the USDA Economic Research Service and the USDA Agricultural Research Service, Northeastern Division, plus current newspaper reports of actual grain and soy currently being fed.

7. Monfort, Kenneth, in *Milling and Baking News,* July 30, 1974, p. 22.

8. USDA, Economic Research Service and Agricultural Research Service, Northeastern Division, consultations with experts.

9. F. Wokes, "Proteins," *Plant Foods for Human Nutrition*, Vol. 1, No. 1, 1968, p. 32.

10. See note 6 above.

11. Zwerdling, Daniel, "Beefed Up: Drugs in the Meat Industry," *Ramparts*, June 1973, p. 37.

12. Hodgson, Harlow J., "We Won't Need to Eliminate Beef Cattle," *Crops and Soils Magazine*, November 1974, p. 9.

13. *Ibid.*

14. Patton, Donald, *The United States and World Resources*, Van Nostrand, 1968, p. 112.

15. *Major Statistical Series of the U.S. Department of Agriculture, How They are Constructed and Used,* Vol. 5: Consumption and Utilization of Agricultural Products, Handbook #365, June 1972, p. 6.

16. *Fisheries of the United States, 1973,* Current Fishery Statistics, Department of Commerce, No. 6400, March 1974, p. 49. Gives import of fishmeal, virtually all of which goes to feed.

17. Calculated from *Livestock-Feed Relationships,* National and State Statistical Bulletin #530, June 1974, pp. 175–77. Last data given is for 1971. Calculated thus: "carry-in" + production — "carry-out" — exports = domestic consumption.

18. *Fats and Oils Situation,* USDA Economic Research Service, November 1974. Estimates of humanly consumed soy are so small they are not readily picked out of these statistics. One expert estimate was that only 3 percent of domestically used soy crop goes to humans.

19. Borgstrom, Georg, *The Food and People Dilemma,* Duxbury Press, N. Scituate, Mass., 1973, p. 50.

20. Calculated from *Livestock-Feed Relationships* (see note 17 above). I have excluded dairy cows, sheep, mules, horses, and the category called "unallocated," so my estimates of actual grain "loss" are conservative.

21. Calculated as follows: 120 million tons of grain "lost" annually in the United States × 2000 pounds in a ton = 240 billion pounds "lost" ÷ 3.9 billion people on earth = 61.5 pounds per capita ÷ 365 days in a

year = .168 pounds per capita per day × 16 ounces in a pound = 2.7 ounces per capita per day = more than ⅓ cup of dry grain, or one cup cooked volume.

22. One-half pound of meat required 8 pounds of grain and soy fed to a steer (i.e., half of the 16 required to produce one whole pound), and 8 pounds of grain is equivalent to about 16 cups of dry grain, or 48 cups of *cooked* grain.

23. Schertz, Lyle P., in *War on Hunger,* Agency for International Development, June 1971.

24. Each American consumes 1850 pounds of grain directly in the form of cereal products and indirectly through grain-fed livestock products. There are roughly 3.9 billion people in the world.

> 1850 pounds × 3.9 billion people = 3.3 billion metric tons
> Total world production = 1.2 billion metric tons

25. "The Nature of the Crisis," *War on Hunger,* Agency for International Development, October 1974, p. 31.

26. Aronowitz, Stanley, *Food, Shelter and the American Dream,* Seabury Press, 1974, p. 35.

27. Anderson, Harry, B., "The Food Crisis, Hunger Persists in U.S. Despite Progress Made in the Past Five Years," *The Wall Street Journal,* December 3, 1974.

28. "The Fate of U.S. Protein Sources" is a compilation of estimates from these sources:

    (a) Corn, barley, oats, and sorghum: see note 17 above.

    (b) Soybeans: see note 18 above.

    (c) Wheat: *Wheat Situation,* USDA Economic Research Service, November 1974, p. 2.

    (d) Milk: see note 15 above.

    (e) Total harvested acreage: see note 2, Chapter K.

C. The Fatted Calf

1. Kottman, Roy M., "Animal Agriculture Meeting Its Critical Issues Head-On," in *Proceedings: Sixteenth National Institute of Animal Agriculture, 1966,* p. 34.

2. Barkdale, William E., President of the American

Forage and Grassland Council, "Let Them Eat Grass," Op-Ed, *The New York Times*, January 2, 1975, p. 33.

3. Margolius, Sidney, "Beef Grades Obsolete, Need Change," *Fort Worth Star-Telegram*, January 3, 1974, B-3.
4. *Ibid.*
5. "New Beef Gradings," *The New York Times*, September 11, 1974, p. 21.
6. See note 3 above.
7. News release, U.S. Department of Agriculture, USDA 2584-74.

D. The Hidden Talent of Livestock

1. "Major Uses of Land and Water in the U.S., Summary for 1959," Agricultural Economic Report No. 13, Farm Economics Division, Economic Research Service, USDA, p. 2.
2. Oltjen, Robert R., "Tomorrow's Diets for Beef Cattle," *The Science Teacher*, Vol. 38, No. 3, March 1970.
3. Virtanen, A. I., "Milk Production of Cows on Protein-Free Feed," *Science*, 153:1603–14, 1966.
4. See note 2 above.
5. Borgstrom, Georg, *Too Many*, Macmillan (London), 1969, p. 244.
6. *Ceres*, Vol. 6, No. 2, March–April 1973, p. 62.
7. *Ibid.*, May–June 1973, p. 56.
8. See note 6 above; p. 60.
9. See note 2 above.
10. Rensberger, Boyce, in *The New York Times*, November 28, 1974, p. 44.
11. Barksdale, William E., "Let Them Eat Grass," *The New York Times*, January 2, 1975, p. 33.
12. Hodgson, Harlow J., "We Won't Need to Eliminate Beef Cattle," *Crops and Soils Magazine*, November 1974, pp. 9–11.
13. Seth King, *The New York Times*, February 8, 1975; report of research by Dr. Harlow Hodgson, W. F. Wedin, and N. L. Jacobsen.
14. Fischer, Norman H., "Hybrid Beefalo Is Seen Playing Big Role in Filling Meat Needs More Economically," *The Wall Street Journal*, 1974.

E. Wasting the Waste

1. *Environmental Science and Technology,* Vol. 4, No. 12, 1970, p. 1098.
2. Borgstrom, Georg, *The Food and People Dilemma,* Duxbury Press, 1973, p. 103.
3. Commoner, Barry, *The Closing Circle,* Alfred A. Knopf, 1971, p. 148.
4. *The New York Times,* June 24, 1974, p. 46.
5. Inglett, George (ed.), "Nutritive Evaluations of Animal Manures," by L. W. Smith, in *Symposium: Processing Agricultural and Municipal Wastes, 1973,* Avi Publishing Co., Box 831, Westport, Conn.
6. Calvert, C. C., "Animal Wastes as Substrates for Protein Production," in *Federation Proceedings,* Vol. 33, No. 8, August 1974. Biological Waste Management Lab., Agricultural Research Service, USDA, Beltsville, Maryland.
7. Bohn, Heinrich L., "A Clean New Gas," *Environment,* Vol. 13, No. 10, December 1971, p. 6.
8. See note 4 above; p. 43.
9. Calculated with these assumptions: (1) that each one of the 100,000 cattle in feedlot consumed about 2500 pounds of grain and soy; (2) that a person needs about 500 pounds of grain a year to sustain him.

F. The Protein Sink

1. Borgstrom, Georg, *The Food and People Dilemma,* Duxbury Press, 1973, p. 64.
2. Borgstrom, Georg, *Too Many,* Macmillan, 1969, p. 328.
3. Milnes, Max, "General Outlook for Seed Protein Concentrates," *World Protein Resources,* A. M. Altschul (ed.), Advances in Chemistry Series 57, Washington, D.C., 1966, p. 53.
4. Calculated from: Trezise, Philip, "Disengagement," *Ceres,* March–April 1974, p. 40.
5. See note 1 above; p. 62.
6. *Ibid.*
7. *Ibid.,* p. 128.
8. *Foreign Agriculture Circular, Livestock and Meat,* USDA, March 1974.

9. Unpublished Bureau of Census Data for 1973, Suzanne Early.

10. Quoted in: Barnet, Richard, and Muller, Ronald, "A Reporter at Large: The Multinational Corporations," *The New Yorker*, December 2, 1974.

11. *Feed Situation*, USDA Economic Research Service, November 1974.

12. *State of Food and Agriculture*, Food and Agriculture Organization of the U.N., 1972, pp. 182–86.

13. *Fisheries of the U.S., 1973*, Current Fishery Statistics, Department of Commerce, No. 6400, March 1974, p. 47.

14. See note 1 above; p. 65.

15. "The Fate of the World's Protein Resources" is a compilation of estimates from these sources:
    (a) Grain: Brown, Lester R., *By Bread Alone*, Praeger, 1974, p. 44. Also see the United Nations document "Assessment of the World Food Situation: Present and Future," Table 15, paragraph. During 1969–1971 1200 million metric tons of grain were consumed annually in the world; 420 million of these were consumed as animal feed.
    (b) Oilseeds: see note 1 above.
    (c) Fish: Holt, S. J., "The Food Resources of the Ocean," *Scientific American*, 221:178–94, 1969, and see note 1 above.
    (d) Milk products: see note 1 above and Borgstrom, Georg, *Focal Points*, Macmillan, 1971, p. 242.

G. Land That Grows Money Can't Grow Food

1. Revelle, Roger, "Food and Population," *Scientific American*, Vol. 231, No. 3, September 1974, p. 167.

2. Borgstrom, Georg, *The Food and People Dilemma*, Duxbury Press, 1973, Table 16, p. 123.

3. *The State of Food and Agriculture, 1965*, The Food and Agriculture Organization of the United Nations, Rome.

4. See note 2 above; p. 65.

5. *Ibid.*, p. 66.

6. *Ibid.*

7. McNamara, Robert, "Development in the Developing World," *Vital Speeches of the Day*, Vol. 38, No. 16, June 1, 1972.

8. Howe, James, "Protectionism, American Jobs and the Poor Countries," Overseas Development Council, Communiqué No. 17, October 1972.

9. Barnet, Richard, and Muller, Ronald, "A Reporter at Large: The Multinational Corporations," *The New Yorker*, December 2, 1974, p. 114.

10. "World Report," *Ceres*, Vol. 6, No. 1, January–February, 1973, p. 13.

11. *International Monetary Fund Survey*, September 2, 1974, p. 286.

12. Fenton, Thomas, *Coffee, the Rules of the Game and You* (pamphlet), p. 8. The Christophers, 12 E. 48th St., New York, N.Y. 10017.

13. The history of the International Coffee Agreement and the reasons for its demise can be found in the newsletters of the World Coffee Information Center, 1100 17th St. N.W., Washington, D.C. 20036.

H. Mining the Soil

1. Albrecht, William A., "Physical, Chemical, and Bio-Chemical Changes in the Soil Community," in *Man's Role in Changing the Face of the Earth*, William L. Thomas, Jr. (ed.), University of Chicago Press, 1956, p. 671.

2. Rensberger, Boyce, "Danger of Soil Erosion Arises in Food Shortage," *The New York Times*, January 11, 1975, p. 58.

I. Eating Low on the Food Chain

1. Duggan, R. E., and Lipscomb, G. Q., "Dietary Intake of Pesticide Chemicals in the United States (II), June 1966–April 1968," *Pesticides Monitoring Journal*, 2:162, 1969; and "(III), June 1968–April 1970," *ibid.*, 5:335, 1972.

2. Harrison, H. L., Loucks, O. L., Mitchell, J. W., Parkhurst, D. F., Tracy, C. R., Watts, D. G., and Yannacone, V. J., Jr., "Systems Studies of DDT Transport," *Science*, 170:503–8, 1970.

3. Corneliussen, P. E., "Residues in Food and Feed: Pesticide Residues in Total Diet Samples (IV)," *Pesticides Monitoring Journal*, 2:140–52, 1969.

4. Henderson, C., Inglis, A., and Johnson, W. L., "Mer-

cury Levels in Fish, 1969–1970," *Pesticides Monitoring Journal,* 6:144–50, 1972.

5. Novick, Sheldon, "A New Pollution Problem: Federal Officials Comment," *Environment,* 11:8, 1969.

J. The Great American Steak Religion

1. The average per capita protein consumption is about 100 grams, but our actual need is near 50 grams. For information on the nutritive value of the U.S. food supply, see the *National Food Situation,* a USDA Economic Research Service quarterly for the discussion of protein need, and see "How Much Is Enough?", Part II, section D, of this book.

2. *The World Almanac, 1972.* Our beef consumption increased 32 pounds and chicken 15 pounds in the last ten years.

3. Rensberger, Boyce, "Curb on U.S. Waste Urged to Help World's Hunger," *The New York Times,* October 25, 1974, p. 2 and p. 20.

4. Per capita we consume 250 pounds of meat and poultry or ⅔ pound per day. Reduced by one-quarter, this amount becomes ½ pound of meat or poultry per day.

5. According to USDA estimates, the average American gets 42 percent of his protein from meat, poultry, and fish. See "National Food Situation," *U.S.D.A. Economic Research Service Quarterly,* 1971 figures. That means that 58 percent comes from non-meat sources. Fifty-eight percent of our total protein intake of 100 grams is 58 grams of protein from non-meat sources. For protein need, see section D, "How Much Is Enough?", in Part II of this book.

6. Oltjen, Robert, in *The Science Teacher,* Vol. 37, No. 3, March 1970.

K. Meatless, Guiltless?

1. King, Seth, "Five Grain Dealers Dominate in a Hungry World," *The New York Times,* November 10, 1974, p. 2 (Business section).

2. Presently our harvested acreage is approximately 350 million acres. Of that, about 122 million acres are

planted with the major feed grains and about 55 million acres are planted with soybeans. In addition, consider the relatively small acreage of wheat fed to livestock and the large acreage devoted to hay (over 50 million acres).

3. Wilcox, Walter, *et al., Economics of American Agriculture,* Prentice-Hall, 1974, 436 pp.

4. Trezise, Philip, "Disengagement," *Ceres,* March–April, 1974, p. 40.

5. See discussion in Part I, section B, of this book: "A Protein Factory in Reverse."

6. Norum, Prof. Kaare A., University of Oslo, School of Medicine, in a news conference at the World Food Conference, November 13, 1974, Rome; "Fact Sheet on Food Assistance."

7. Newsletter, January 1975, of Bread for the World, 235 East Forty-Ninth Street, New York, N.Y. 10017.

8. Bowie, Robert (of Harvard Center for International Affairs), "Food Strategy," *The Christian Science Monitor,* 1974.

9. See note 6 above.

10. *Time,* special hunger story by the editors, November 11, 1974, p. 76.

11. *1971 Handbook of Agricultural Charts,* USDA, Agriculture Handbook #423, p. 42.

12. Hedges, Irwin R., "When Food Is Aid," *War on Hunger,* Agency for International Development, 1973, p. 5.

13. See note 6 above.

14. See note 4 above.

15. *Ibid.*

16. Borgstrom, Georg, *The Food and People Dilemma,* Duxbury Press, 1973, p. 129.

17. McNamara, Robert, "Development in the Developing World," *Vital Speeches of the Day,* Vol. 38, No. 16, June 1972.

18. Cotter, William, "'How Africa Is Short-Changed,'" *Africa Report,* November–December 1974, p. 6.

19. *Ibid.*

20. Chenery, Hollis, "Restructuring the World Economy," *Foreign Affairs,* January 1975, p. 246.

21. "Why Foreign Aid," *War on Hunger,* Agency for International Development, December 1974, p. 3.

22. See note 18 above.
23. Ward, Barbara, "A People's Strategy of Development," Overseas Development Council, Communiqué No. 23, May 1974.
24. *The Defense Monitor,* The Center for Defense Information, Vol. 3, No. 6, May 1974, p. 5, and Parker, Daniel, "AID and the World Food Conference, *War on Hunger,* Agency for International Development, October 1974, p. 7.
25. *The New York Times,* October 29, 1974, p. 51.
26. *The Defense Monitor,* The Center for Defense Information, Vol. 1, No. 4, September 8, 1972.
27. Brown, Lester R., *In the Human Interest,* W. W. Norton, 1974, pp. 159, 163, 165.
28. See note 10 above; p. 79.
29. See note 18 above; p. 54.
30. Howe, James, "Protectionism, American Jobs and the Poor Countries, Overseas Development Council, Communiqué No. 17, October 1972.
31. Erb, Guy, "U.S. Trade Goals and the Poor Countries," Overseas Development Council, Communiqué No. 20, July 1973, and see note 17 above.
32. Bogdanov, Oleg, "Monetary Crisis and Development," *Development Forum,* April 1974, p. 1.
33. McCarthy, Colman, "U.S. Hunger to Fast," *Herald Statesman,* Yonkers, N.Y., January 3, 1975.

PART II
BRINGING PROTEIN THEORY DOWN TO EARTH

C. Quality Makes the Product

1. Guthrie, Helen A., *Introductory Nutrition,* C. V. Mosby Co., St. Louis, 1967, p. 53.
2. *Protein Requirements,* report of a Joint FAO/WHO Expert Group, Food and Agriculture Organization, Rome, 1965, p. 43. Also see *Energy and Protein Requirements,* report of Joint FAO/WHO Ad Hoc Expert Committee, WHO Technical Report Series No. 522, Rome, 1973.

D. How Much Is Enough?

1. *Evaluation of Protein Nutrition,* National Academy of Sciences, National Research Council, Washington, D.C., Pamphlet No. 711, p. 16.
2. *Canadian Bulletin on Nutrition,* Dietary Standard for Canada, 1964, p. 24c.
3. *Protein Requirements,* report of a Joint FAO/WHO Expert Group, Food and Agriculture Organization, Rome, 1965, p. 22.
4. *Recommended Dietary Allowances, Food and Nutrition Board,* National Academy of Sciences, National Research Council, Washington, D.C., 8th Revised Edition, 1974, pp. 47–48.
5. Personal correspondence from Dr. Scrimshaw, December 27, 1974.
6. *Energy and Protein Requirements,* report of Joint FAO/WHO Ad Hoc Expert Committee, WHO Technical Report Series No. 522, Rome, 1973, p. 66–69.

E. Protein Individuality

1. Williams, R. J., "We Abnormal Normals," *Nutrition Today,* 2:19–23, 1967.
2. *Protein Requirements,* report of a Joing FAO/WHO Expert Group, Food and Agriculture Organization, Rome, 1965, p. 32.

F. Is Meat Necessary?

1. *Amino Acid Content of Foods and Biological Data on Proteins, Food and Agriculture Organizations,* Rome, 1970. Most NPU scores used are taken from this publication.

G. Complementing Your Proteins

1. Altschul, A. M., *Proteins, Their Chemistry and Politics,* Basic Books, 1965, p. 115.

H. Protein Isn't Everything

1. "National Food Situation," *U.S.D.A. Economic Re-*

search Service Quarterly. Current and updated estimates of the nutritive value of the U.S. food supply are published in each fall issue. These figures are for 1971. Note that these statistics are based on quantity available for consumption, and do not take into account losses after food leaves the retail outlet.

2. Guthrie, Helen A., *Introductory Nutrition,* C. V. Mosby Co., 1967, pp. 122, 123, 130.

3. Erbe, Richard, "Mass Screening and Genetic Counseling in Mandelian Disorders," *Ethical, Social and Legal Dimensions of Screening for Human Genetic Disease,* Marc Lappé, Richard Roblin, and James Gustafson (co-eds.), Birth Defects: Original Articles Series, The National Foundation, March of Dimes, Vol. 10, No. 6, 1974, pp. 85–97.

4. Personal correspondence, December 17, 1974.

5. *Composition of Foods,* Agriculture Handbook No. 8, USDA Agricultural Research Service, Table 4, p. 146.

PART III
EATING FROM THE EARTH

C. Protein Tables and Tips for Complementing Protein

1. Liu, Ellen H., and Ritchey, S. J., "Nutritional Value of Turkey Protein," *Journal of the American Dietetic Association,* 57:39–41, 1970.

E. Getting the Most Protein for the Least Calories

1. Mayer, Jean, "Nutritional Aspects of Preventative Medicine," in *Preventative Medicine,* D. W. Clark and B. MacMahon (eds.), Little, Brown, 1967, p. 200.

Turkeys

Sources for the Tables

Several sources were used to estimate NPU scores:
1. Altschul, A. M., *Proteins, Their Chemistry and Politics,* Basic Books, 1965, p. 118.
2. *Amino-Acid Content of Food and Biological Data on Protein,* Food and Agriculture Organization of the United Nations, Rome, 1970.
3. *The State of Food and Agriculture 1964,* Food and Agriculture Organization of the United Nations, p. 105.

Recommendations for Further Reading

BOOKS

1. Aronowitz, Stanley, *Food, Shelter and the American Dream,* Seabury Press, 1974.
2. Beckford, George L., *Persistent Poverty, Underdevelopment in Plantation Economies of the Third World,* Oxford University Press, 1972.
3. Borgstrom, Georg, *The Food and People Dilemma,* Duxbury Press, N. Scituate, Mass., 1973.
4. ————, *The Hungry Planet,* Collier Books, New York, 1967.
5. ————, *Too Many,* Macmillan, 1969.
6. Brown, Lester, *By Bread Alone,* Praeger, 1974.
7. ————, *In the Human Interest,* W. W. Norton, 1974.
8. ————, *World Without Borders,* Random House, 1972.
9. Cockcroft, James D., Frank, Andre Gunder, and Johnson, Dale L., *Dependence and Underdevelopment,* Doubleday, 1972.
10. Frank, Andre Gunder, *Latin America: Underdevelopment or Revolution?,* The Monthly Review Press, 116 W. 14th St., New York, N.Y. 10011, 1969.
11. Jalée, Pierre, *Imperialism in the Seventies,* The Third Press, Joseph Okpaku Publishing Co., Inc., 444 Central Park West, New York, N.Y. 10025, 1972.
12. Rhodes, Robert I. (ed.), *Imperialism and Underdevelopment: A Reader,* The Monthly Review Press, 116 W. 14th St., New York, N.Y. 10011, 1970.
13. Simon, Arthur and Paul, *The Politics of World Hunger,* Harper's Magazine Press, 1973.

MAGAZINES

See listing at the end of section K, "Meatless, Guiltless?" in Part I of the text.

Recommended Paperback Cookbooks

1. Ewald, Ellen, *Recipes for a Small Planet*, Ballantine, 1973. A wealth of creative complementary protein recipes.
2. Hewitt, Jean, *The New York Times Natural Foods Cookbook*, Avon, 1972. Highly recommended by friends.
3. Hunter, Beatrice Trum, *The Natural Foods Cookbook*, Pyramid, 1961. My early bible. Just reading through all the incredible ideas is mind-expanding!
4. Thomas, Anna, *The Vegetarian Epicure*, Vintage, 1972. Elegant dishes.

Herbs

Index

SIERRA CLUB BOOKS
Eloquent tributes to the irreplaceable natural beauty of this country.

Available at your bookstore or use this coupon.

NOT MAN APART, David Brower, Editor 25539 6.95
Captures the rugged beauty of California's Big Sur coast in image and verse. There are over 90 photos in full color and black-and-white by foremost photographers such as Ansel Adams, Eliot Porter, and Edward Weston, and poetry by Robinson Jeffers.

GENTLE WILDERNESS: The Sierra Nevada,
Photographs by Richard Kauffman,
Text from John Muir 25540 6.95
This exquisite volume captures the breathtaking beauty of the Sierra Nevada mountain range in 80 full-color photographs, plus a condensation of *My First Summer in the Sierra* by John Muir, who founded the Sierra Club in 1892.

SUMMER ISLAND: Penobscot Country,
Eliot Porter 25538 6.95
Here are 90 masterful photographs (48 in full color) that capture the unspoiled beauty of the sea-swept islands off the coast of Maine . . . each one a ruggedly beautiful world rich in wildlife.

 Ballantine Mail Sales
Dept. LE, 201 E. 50th Street
New York, New York 10022

Please send me the books I have checked above. I am enclosing $...................... (please add 50¢ to cover postage and handling). Send check or money order—no cash or C.O.D.'s please.

Name————————————————

Address————————————————

City——————State——————Zip————

Please allow 4 weeks for delivery.

L-45